FANNY BURNEY

Fanny Burney

Sarah Kilpatrick

STEIN AND DAY/*Publishers*/New York

First published in
the United States of America
in 1981

Copyright © 1980 by Sarah Kilpatrick
All rights reserved

Printed in the
United States of America

STEIN AND DAY/Publishers
Scarborough House
Briarcliff Manor, N.Y. 10510

Library of Congress Cataloging in Publication Data
Kilpatrick, Sarah.
  Fanny Burney.

  Bibliography: p.
  Includes index.
  1. Arblay, Frances Burney d`, 1752-1840 —
Biography. 2. Novelists, English — 18th century —
Biography.
PR3316.A4Z664 1981   823′.8 [B] 80-5891
ISBN 0-8128-2761-9

CONTENTS

LIST OF ILLUSTRATIONS

FANNY BURNEY

I
INTRODUCTION TO
MISS BURNEY

The first picture of Fanny Burney that emerges clearly from her unremark-able childhood has for its background Poland Street in the Soho district of London. She stands in the yard of the house, the paved area contained by the outbuildings at the back, the wash-house and the jakes on one side, the store sheds on the other. The air is thick with the smoke of coal fires and the bricks of the house are blackened with it. She is small for her age, which is fifteen, thin and undeveloped, and her long brown hair is free under its cap. She has made a fire of papers on the bricks of the yard and the flames lick agonizingly around sheets of her own handwriting, but her expression is unflinching. Her sister Susanna stands beside her weeping, tears falling fast down cheeks that already show the lovely translucence of hereditary tuberculosis. Susanna, or Susan as she was sometimes called was all her life inclined to take her sister a little too seriously.

The papers Fanny Burney burned there, resolutely and half-heartedly as Emily Brontë beating her dog Keeper, included a childish draft of a story called *The History of Caroline Evelyn*. When the ashes of blackened paper were left to blow about Poland Street the story remained stubbornly in Fanny's mind and developed into her first novel *Evelina,* which was to keep Burke from his meals, please Dr Johnson (largely because it was not by one of the recognized bluestockings) and eventually set her down, un-willing but complacent, in the Court itself, befriended by the sad stupid King and considerately treated by the Queen and closeted young princesses.

Fanny's decision to burn her early writing was her own, just as the secret production of *Evelina* ten years later was her own. Her self-sufficiency was at all times absolute. Family history tells us what prompted the decision, but for the more interesting question of what she meant by it we must go further and examine, not family history merely, but the family character, which had in it a strong element of the theatrical.

Fanny Burney grew up under the influence of two fathers, both writers, but no mother; Esther Sleepe, the first Mrs Burney, had died when Fanny was nine years old. Her true father, Charles Burney, a talented and attractive musician, had governed his life from his earliest years by impulses of affection, his own and other people's. His second marriage, occurring when Fanny was fifteen, was, like the first, a love match, but it could hardly be expected that Fanny would extend her passionate affection for her father to his new wife. It was her father and his friend Samuel Crisp, her 'dear Daddy' by adoption, that she sought to please.

Mrs Stephen Allen, the second Mrs Burney, a beauty, an heiress and a bluestocking, had daughters of her own and a background more worldly than anything the unconventionally-reared children of the first marriage had known. When she discovered, soon after her marriage to Charles Burney, that his daughter Fanny spent her time writing romances she hastened to reprove her, emphasizing the harm it would do her marriage prospects to be known as a scribbler. Fanny certainly must have felt alarm at the warning: Esther Sleepe's girls had no dowries and she, unlike her sisters, had no reputation for beauty. But the influence of her fathers was stronger than any influence the second Mrs Burney was ever to enjoy. Fanny lit her pitiful small bonfire while her parents were away from home, enacted for her own enjoyment the famous scene of tragic renunciation and continued to write, though in a more discreet fashion.

For almost immediately after she had made Susanna weep for her lost romances, Fanny began to keep a journal, a form of writing practised by many young women of her day and marginally more respectable than romances so long as it made no reference to affairs of the heart. Young girls were not to dwell on these in any form it seems. Her father cautioned her about the dangers of keeping a journal and so did Miss Dolly Young. Miss Young was slightly grotesque but kindly and, like Mrs Stephen Allen, had been a friend of Fanny's mother. Esther Burney, dying, had recommended Miss Dolly Young to her husband as an ideal second wife and mother to her orphaned children, but Charles Burney had fallen in love with Mrs Allen. Miss Young, mindful of the responsibilities of bringing up motherless girls and anxious to help, suggested to Fanny that she might be embarrassed if a stranger found and read her diary. Fanny was quite equal to the occasion. Miss Young, challenged pleasantly to open the diary where she chose and see for herself if that was true, was forced to concede that nothing in doubtful taste had met her eye. Fanny felt herself vindicated and continued to write her journal. It developed into a series of considered exercises in recording conversation, delineating character and describing events, became in fact an author's gradus. Parts of it, like the description of her visit to Teignmouth, or Tingmouth as she spelt it, were sent to Samuel Crisp as complete accounts and can be regarded as Fanny's first and privately-circulated literary works. It was broken off to allow time for the writing of *Evelina* and then resumed again, continuing as long as Fanny had eyes for it. Fanny had listened with apparent docility to the advice of others, weighed it against her own considered opinions and decided for herself what she would do. All through her life she was to act with the same stubborn reliance on her own opinion.

Charles Burney's writing of a history of music, with Fanny employed for long hours of the day as amanuensis, must certainly have encouraged his admiring daughter to persevere with her own literary efforts, but of even more influence was her relationship with Samuel Crisp. He was an old family friend of considerable literary taste and some pretensions to writing. He was also possessed of the cool-headed, rational attitude to life characteristic of the early and middle eighteenth century. Fanny Burney was her father's darling and she loved him excessively in return, but she was also from a pre-pubertal age in love with Crisp, both by her father's testimony and her own. The immense disparity in years between them (he was old enough to be her grandfather) as well as his fixed bachelor state, prevented this affection ever being considered as a basis for marriage, but it had two effects on Fanny's life. Because she had to interest Samuel Crisp by letter it encouraged her writing and it also, despite her emotional nature, inhibited her from considering marriage until Crisp died. By that time she was thirty. To make matters more difficult, Crisp still provided, even after his death, an image against which she felt compelled to measure any other suitor. Those less sophisticated, less well-informed, less truly aristocratic were appropriately diminished.

Fanny Burney's great need, like her father's, was to love. When Samuel Crisp's death left her without an object for her affections she had in any case lost the bloom of youth and was not pretty enough or rich enough for anything but a love match. So she was forty before she came quite unexpectedly upon someone like him, someone who deserved loving. By remarkably good fortune she found in her marriage to the French *émigré* Conte Alexandre d'Arblay a complete compatibility of tastes and so was able to love him with that discreet blend of admiration and good sense that Jane Austen's heroines were to display in later years. It was by no means a convenient marriage; indeed it was outrageously romantic. But their loving natures made of it an amorous hard-wearing loyalty that lasted twenty years of their lives.

11

2

MISS BURNEY'S TWO FATHERS

R. Brimley Johnson, in some very shrewd notes on the social position of the Burney family, points out that almost without exception they were entertainers.

> Many Burneys [he said] wrote copiously, with some measure of distinction and abnormal industry; but they were not properly men of letters. As musicians, more or less amateur artists, above all dancing masters, they belong to what is still called 'the profession', that is, a class of old frankly associated with 'rogues and vagabonds' who played a part to amuse the plebs, patronized by the Peers.

As Mr Brimley Johnson points out, their Bohemianism affected the position of the family within the social structure: 'the classes mingled, with intimacy, and friendship indeed, but not fundamentally on equal terms.' It also influenced the kind of entertainment offered by each of the Burneys: Fanny's novels, he suggests, are written 'for the stage or concert-platform; and, for this reason, stand at most outside regular literature, of which she knew neither the vision nor the rules'. Fanny was, in fact, an actress too shy for the stage. 'All the Burneys were given to self-expression – jesters, minstrels and chroniclers to the nobility and at court. She was following the family way.'

Charles Burney, Fanny's father, was the archetype of the successful entertainer. Roger Lonsdale speaks of his neglected childhood and unnatural mother, then draws the conclusion that this resulted in: 'an endless, if harmless desire to compel affection and admiration which would compensate for the inevitable insecurity of his childhood.' Dr Johnson, who felt himself threatened by some men, held in this instance to the opinion of the majority: 'I love Burney,' he declared. 'My heart goes out to meet him . . . Dr Burney is a man for all the world to love . . . It is but natural to love him . . . I much question if there is, in the world, such another man as Burney.' Dr Johnson was not alone in his opinion. Few men can have had more friends than Charles Burney or had a readier attraction at all stages of his long life for distinguished and interesting people. 'A man quite after my own heart,' wrote Mrs Thrale in her diaries. 'If he has a fault, it is too much obsequiousness.'

James Macburney, his father, was, like his son, determinedly agreeable. In addition he had what was perhaps an excess of talents, was witty, an admirable dancer and as good a player on the violin as he was a painter. Fanny said that he possessed 'negligent facility and dissipated ease', by which she meant that things came too easily to him and he wasted his ability. He married twice and reared nine children out of fifteen. In order to bring them up he chose the most profitable of his talents, portrait-painting, and set up at Chester, leaving Charles, his youngest, at nurse in the village of Condover near Shrewsbury. Almost abandoned though he was, he was happy and healthy, very fond of his foster-mother and possessed of the kind of good fortune that was to be with him all his life in the friendship of the rector of the village, the Rev. George Llewellyn, who had been page to Charles I.

Llewellyn was artistic, deeply interested in gardens and, above all, musical. He was a friend of Henry Purcell and had helped Dr Blow with *Orpheus Britannicus*. Charles' eldest half-brother James was already an organist at St Margaret's, Shrewsbury and when Charles was only fourteen the organist at Chester Cathedral, Mr Baker, a friend of Dr Blow, finding himself incapacitated with gout, taught the schoolboy enough to keep the organ going. The connection served Charles in good stead, and when Handel was in Chester in 1741 and asked Baker to help him find sight-readers for the first performance of *Messiah*, Charles Burney was one of those chosen. At sixteen Charles was apprenticed to his exacting half-brother James, but here again his luck or his capacity to attract interesting people saved him. Thomas Arne, on his way to a post at Drury Lane, met young Burney, liked him and carried him off to London as his own apprentice.

Arne was by all accounts negligent in his care of the young man, teaching him little and employing him mainly in copying. Arne's sister, however, the actress Mrs Cibber, made up for this by inviting Charles Burney to her house in Scotland Yard where he met a great many entertaining people, including Garrick, and renewed his acquaintance with Handel.

Then Burney's personal magnetism was able once more to provide a way out of an unpromising situation. Fulke Greville, a young man of considerable wealth and of dilettante tastes, was looking for 'a musician who was also a gentleman' to be his companion. Mrs Raine Ellis, editor of Fanny's early journals, describes Greville as 'coveting all kinds of distinction, from eminence in metaphysics (in which he fancied himself strong) to pre-eminence on the race-course and in the hunting-field, in all the fashionable exercises of riding, fencing, shooting-at-a-mark, dancing and tennis, down, or up, to music and drawing, writing verses and laying out gardens and plantations'. It is also said that Greville invariably travelled with two French-horn players who performed whenever the coach stopped.

Charles Burney, eagerly educating himself in languages and literature as well as musical composition, must have seemed the ideal candidate for the post Greville was trying to fill. Certainly Greville's friends were soon commenting on his desertion of the race-courses for the more spiritual pleasure of watching Charles Burney play on the harpischord. It was not long before Fulke Greville offered Arne £300 to release the young man from his apprenticeship and took him into a life among people of rank and fashion, rather as if he were a beautiful and expensive pet.

It seems probable that Greville's taste for the arts meant less to him than the normal amusements of aristocratic young men, for we hear of Charles Burney at the race-course and at the more exclusive gaming clubs. Fulke Greville was consciously high-born and one of his more undergraduate affectations was to designate as 'fogrum' any attitudes or behaviour that he decided were unsatisfactory: they were 'bourgeois' and the blanket condemnation damned them without discussion. Marriage was, of course, highly bourgeois (Lydia Languish would have agreed with him), and when he married one of 'the greatest beautys in England' (as Fanny was later to describe her godmother Lady Greville) he was able to put a stylish gloss on the matter only by pretending to elope. The girl was of good Irish family and the co-heiress to a large fortune. She was remarkably ·beautiful but her croaking voice and inelegant posture, deliberate affectations perhaps, drew even more attention than her looks. Her father, Mr Macartney, commented that 'Mr Greville had taken a wife out of the window whom he might just as well have taken out of the door', but Charles Burney, who at seventeen gave the bride away, was no doubt impressed by the romance of it all. At the christening of their first baby, who was later to be the well-known beauty Lady Crewe, Burney stood in for a duke. Later, and not until after the birth of his eldest daughter Esther, he told his patron that he too had fallen in love with a beauty. Fulke Greville, busy now with his own affairs, was able to say in a lordly fashion 'Well, why don't you marry her?', conferring the gift on Charles as casually as any other.

'All his life,' Mrs Raine Ellis remarks, 'he [Greville] acted as if he had a lien upon Doctor Burney.' He picked him up and dropped him at his convenience. Fanny in her teens comments admiringly on Mrs Greville's *Ode to Indifference*, which some considered to have been inspired by her husband, and on Fulke Greville's *Characters, Maxims and Reflections – Serious, Moral and Entertaining*. But as the more experienced Madame d'Arblay, sorting her father's letters for publication, she found Greville's 'all clever, but many disputative, quarrelsome and highly disagreeable'. She remarks on his 'highly irritable nerves' and his 'selfish contentiousness', adding 'at war with the world, he lived until over ninety'.

It was at Fulke Greville's house, however, two or three years before his marriage to Esther Sleepe, that Charles Burney met Samuel Crisp who became his lifelong friend and Fanny's adored 'Daddy'. He was twenty years older than Charles and once more Greville's friends were amused by the magnetic power of Charles Burney playing on the harpsichord. Crisp was an only son, brought up by five sisters, and his parents had died quite early in his life leaving him money. He was well-educated and fashionable, interested in music, literature and painting. Fulke Greville describes him as 'a most superior man'. Later he was to write an unsuccessful play, *Virginia*, and this experience was held to qualify him to direct Fanny's reading and writing. Certainly his advice was the best she had and much more to her benefit than some later influences. Crisp never knew Esther Sleepe, but renewed his acquaintance with the family after her death when Fanny was about nine. He was an instant success with the children and as he grew older his affection for them became the most important thing in his life.

Meanwhile in 1749, soon after his marriage to Esther Sleepe, Charles Burney was appointed organist at St Dionis Backchurch, Fenchurch Street. He also took pupils and composed music. Esther, James and Charles, who died at sixteen months, were baptized there. Then he became ill from overwork (though he may have caught tuberculosis from his wife, who died of it). He accepted the post of organist at Lynn Regis for its healthy air and is pleasantly described there as jogging round the country lanes on his mare Peggy, reading Italian poetry with a dictionary of his own compiling in one pocket of his greatcoat and his commonplace book in the other. Fanny, Susan, a second Charles who died in infancy and the Charles who survived to become a classical scholar were

15

born in Lynn. Here also the family came to know Mrs Stephen Allen, who became Charles Burney's second wife, and Miss Dolly Young, who did not. The three were said to be the only women in Lynn who could read. Read to any purpose, that is. They used to hold a kind of literary discussion group while the child Fanny, it is said, listened unobserved.

In 1760 the Burneys returned to London and settled in Poland Street. Charles had recovered his health and begun to worry about his career. Quite soon he had pupils enough to fill his days. Esther Burney, who had been ill for almost a year, produced her last child, Charlotte, and then sickened and died of the consumption that accompanied her beauty. To comfort himself, her husband began a translation of Dante's *Divine Comedy*, chosen because he had not read it with his wife. He also began to make plans to send two of his daughters at a time to school in Paris. Esther Sleepe had come from a Huguenot family and the girls learned French early. Hetty, her eldest girl, was chosen to go, of course, and with her not Fanny but Susanna. Various reasons for this choice have been adduced: Susan was delicate and the air abroad was always considered healthful; Fanny was backward in learning to read. Whatever the reason, nine-year-old Susan now began the first of the Burney journals, an account of her daily life written for the pleasure of other members of the family, particularly Fanny. Another and almost equally significant beginning was made: Charles Burney's interest in French music was stimulated by the contacts he made in Paris, and as a result he began those studies that led to his great *History of Music* and his European reputation.

At about the same time Charles Burney met his old friend Samuel Crisp by chance at the home of a friend. Much had happened to them both in the interval. Samuel Crisp had lived for some years in Rome and, returning, had bought a house at Hampton and filled it with *objets d'art*. He had imported the first piano into England (but Fulke Greville had bought it from him). So hospitable was he, however, that Hampton proved too expensive and he sold up and went to Chessington, then a very rural area, where he shared a house with a friend, Mr Christopher Hamilton. Chessington soon became a country home for all the Burney family. When Mr Hamilton died, Samuel Crisp continued to share the house, but with Miss Sarah Hamilton, his sister. 'He chose a suite of rooms,' Mrs Raine Ellis says, 'with a light and pleasant cabinet at the end of a corridor, which he gave up to Dr Burney as his writing-room when he visited Chessington.'

For young people the house at Chessington had a multitude of attractions. It was roomy, with wide views and extensive gardens. Mrs Raine Ellis summarizes Fanny's description of it by saying:

> It was a house of nooks and corners with 'quarters of staircases' leading to unused rooms; garrets, or rather cells in great number and in all shapes, to fit the capricious forms of the leaded roof; windows in angles nigh the ceiling; carven cupboards and carven chimney-pieces, above blue and white tiles; 'a tall canopied bed, tied up to the ceiling'; japan cabinets with two or three hundred drawers; old pictures and tapestry presenting knights and damosels; before the windows 'straight old garden-paths' and across the leaden ridges of the roof a view of the country for sixteen miles round.

Fresh country food, fresh air and above all the relaxing presence of Daddy Crisp made Chessington a place to take holidays, to recuperate from illnesses, to nurse an anxious heart or to resolve a problem. It was to Chessington that Hetty and Susan took their step-sister, Maria Allen, now Rishton, after her elopement. The situation required *savoir-faire* and who better than Daddy Crisp to provide it. After the publication of *Evelina*, Fanny spent months at Chessington recovering her health and it was there, after M. d'Arblay's proposal of marriage, that she took refuge while she balanced head and heart. From Chessington flowed letters full of worldly advice: 'all men are cats, all young girls mice,' Crisp wrote to Fanny. When the unfortunate Thomas Barlow made Fanny an offer of marriage, sober good sense and the most pressing encouragement came out of Chessington. Hetty, Susan and Fanny all confided their love affairs in Daddy Crisp, even before they mentioned them to their busy father.

Although Samuel Crisp was a friend of the whole Burney family (with the possible exception of the second Mrs Burney and her younger children), steady and dependable in marked contrast to the capricious Greville, it was Fanny who loved him most. The terms in which she speaks of her father are unusually rapturous:

> How strongly, how forcibly do I feel to whom I owe all the earthly happiness I enjoy – it is to my father! to this dearest, most amiable, this best beloved – most worthy of men! – it is his goodness to me which makes all appear so gay, it is his affection which makes my sun shine.

Her love for her father never wavered, not even when he felt himself unable to attend her wedding. But Charles Burney himself discerned clearly that his daughter's feelings for Samuel Crisp, forty-six years older than herself, were indistinguishable from romantic love: 'Fanny's *flame*', her father called him. She wanted no other man while he lived and after his death wanted only to replace him. Nearly twenty years after their first meeting she was to confess to him in a letter: 'For many, many years you have been more dear to me than any other person out of my immediate family in the whole world.' As time went by her feelings generated the like in him, until he was able to match them with the certainty of the phrase, 'Fannikin, the dearest thing to me on earth'.

3

MISS BURNEY'S FAMILY CIRCLE

It was in Poland Street that Esther Burney died and to Poland Street that her widower brought Mrs Stephen Allen as his second wife. This marriage took place in 1767, secretly because Mrs Allen's financial affairs were very firmly in the control of her mother and brothers, and Charles Burney, though he earned a reasonable income, had no capital. The second Mrs Burney owned a house at Lynn and was the beneficiary of a trust, but what money she herself had the handling of, a dowry of £5000, she had already contrived to lose before her marriage by lending it to a Russian timber merchant. The honeymoon was spent, naturally enough, in a farmhouse near Chessington and at first the couple lived separately, but when the news leaked out Mrs Burney, as she now was, came to live in Poland Street together with her first husband's children, Stephen, Maria and Bessie.

The new Mrs Burney was an admirable hostess at Burney's literary and musical parties, and she did much to make the house in St Martin's Street a social rendezvous for all kinds of celebrities. Her husband valued her company and her ability to converse on those subjects – and there were many – that interested him. At first her step-daughters too found her agreeable, but as time went on it was evident that there was discord between them, especially after her own children left home. Fanny writes, 'Her temper alone was in fault, not her heart or intentions', and one or two unhappy pictures stud the family letters of Mrs Burney in hysterics or taking rather too much laudanum. It seems likely that she had a difficult temper since Mrs Arthur Young, her sister, was by all accounts rather a shrew and the children of her first marriage were unpredictable in their behaviour. But she may also have been one of those unfortunate women who suffer from nervous disabilities during the menopause and such problems may have been intensified by the feeling that she was shut out of the intimate family life of the young Burneys. In any case, behaviour that is tolerable in a parent may be totally unforgivable in a step-mother.

The house in Poland Street must have been distinctly crowded even before the children of the second marriage – and there were to be two – were added to the existing total of nine. It was the tall, narrow town house of its time and place, with a wig-maker's next door, but it also had more distinguished neighbours not far away. A closet 'up two pair of stairs' where the children kept their toys was the place where Fanny often did her writing, but she also mentions 'a pretty little neat cabinet that is in the bedchamber, where I keep all my affairs'. This must be the 'closet' into which she ran and locked herself when Arthur Young, an uncle by marriage, was teasing the girls for a sight of their journals. We are told that it was Maria's he wanted to see and that Maria's was on 'her open bureau'. So it seems probable that Fanny's was a room within a room, opening out of Maria's and small, but valued because it was her own and not shared. Maria's room, where the girls could sit by the fire and 'browse' upon dainties brought out of 'Allen's cupboard' was a favourite meeting place for the older girls of the family. It may even have been in this room that the three girls, Maria, Fanny and Susan slept in one bed as Maria so fondly remembered later: 'sitting in Elegant undress over a few dying Embers in my bedchamber relating the disasters of the day and afterwards sleeping three in a bed in a charming warm night in July.'

Poland Street, like all Burney residences, was a house ringing with music, with foreign voices and the voices of children, all contained under the protective roof of Charles Burney's kindliness. Esther Burney's girls, with their strong sense of family loyalty, were concerned for all the children whatever their parentage, but it was inevitable that closeness of age and the common interests of their sex brought together the three sisters, Hetty, Fanny and Susannah, in a very close group. This group did not, however, exclude Maria whom they had known at Lynn for years. Closest of all and for always were Fanny and Susan. Pacchierotti, the singer, remarked of their relationship: 'There seems but one soul – but one mind between you – you are two in one.' This relationship it was that led to Fanny's first attempts at entertaining by writing: the 'journals' each girl wrote were an attempt at sharing experience. Susan contributed more than anybody towards Fanny's development as a writer, but Hetty and Maria, though unconsciously and unintentionally, had each her effect on the material and manner of *Evelina*.

Hetty's influence on Fanny was merely that she lived through her love-story under the eyes of an apprentice novelist. All the children of Esther Burney were talented, all good-looking, musical or literary, and possessed of their father's power to attract. Hetty, who was the eldest, was exceptionally beautiful and sweet-tempered with the delightful sense of fun her letters reveal. When she was eight years old she 'gained great notice among musicians by her astonishing performances on the harpsichord at her father's parties,' says the Gentleman's Magazine. At sixty-eight she was described by Fanny as 'all spirit and vivacity' and 'the spring and spirit of the family'.

Fanny's diary begins when she is fifteen years of age, and it is not long before she begins to hint at the drama that is being played out under her attentive gaze. A widow called Mrs Pringle lived not far away from the Burneys in Poland Street and enjoyed entertaining her pretty neighbours. A most eligible *parti,* a younger son of Sir Henry Seaton (or Seton, the name is spelt variously) attended Mrs Pringle's teas and was apparently attracted to Hetty. Fanny, for all her early reputation as a 'character-monger' was at first favourably impressed. 'A very sensible and clever man,' she called him, and a 'charming man. Mr Seaton was so very clever, droll and entertaining, you can't imagion.' He spared three hours to converse with her and she was flattered, recording the not-very-witty dialogue punctiliously. A number of erasures are to be seen in Fanny's journal at this point, a sure sign that indiscreet or at least personal remarks were originally recorded.

The uncertain courtship continued. At Mrs Pringle's 'the company divided into little partys immediately – Mr Seton and Hetty amused themselves very comfortably together . . . in an uninterrupted tête-à-tête'. Charles Burney took his degree as Doctor of Music. The family went to Lynn where Mrs Allen's house, part of her dowry, had constantly to be lived in. Here Fanny made the interesting remark that Hetty was recovering her spirits which 'sometime before we left town grew melancholy and sad'. However on their return Fanny noticed that 'Hetty was charmed even with the smoak of London'.

The next year, two years after the first mention of Mr Seaton's 'interest' in Hetty, the affair was no further forward. Hetty had dreamed for three months of the masquerade to be held at the house of Mr Laluge, a French dancing master. This was followed by a dance at Mr Pugh's and it becomes evident in the journals that during these social events Fanny's opinion of Mr Seaton has become marred by doubts: 'If the sincerity of this man equalled his sense, wit, polite and insinuating address, I would not wish Hetty a happier lot than to be his,' she remarks. Later she says that she is mistaken in him, that she thought she knew him and now is not sure.

The climax appears to come when Hetty and Fanny are invited to a

21

dance at Mr and Mrs Debieg's, chaperoned by Mrs Pringle. Two of the ladies there are said to be old flames of Mr Seaton, a circumstance which adds to Fanny's belated doubts of that gentleman. She is on edge in his company, fiercely protective of Hetty and intensely critical of Mr Seaton's words and behaviour. She cannot deny his attraction: 'his whole attention was confined to Hetty and his conversation more flattering than ever – equally so at least.' But exasperated by his refusal to commit himself to her universally-admired sister, she concludes her sentence with the words: 'Well might he be proud of engaging her as he did, for she met with the most flattering apparent approbation of every one present.'

Mr Seaton handed Hetty to her carriage and she spent a sleepless night. By the morning she had quite resolved to marry her cousin Charles Rousseau Burney, an admirer of long standing who lived frugally by teaching the harpsichord.

The Burney family was angry with Mr Seaton: its collective pride was wounded. That arbiter of correct behaviour, Mr Crisp, advised Charles Burney to see that his girls had no more to do with Mrs Pringle, who was obviously a careless chaperone, and for this reason and others the decision was taken to move out of Poland Street. Fanny, at the age of eighteen and closely attentive to her sister's romance, must have drawn many long-lasting impressions from Mr Seaton's behaviour and as much later as *Camilla*, when she had experienced the uncomfortable situation herself, she was to refer to 'such love as belongs to admiration and leads to flirtation and ends in nothing at all'. One comment she never makes, romantic that she is, either in her own disappointments or other girls', is that men of that period often found a dowry the greatest of a bride's attractions.

Fanny suffered the embarrassment of cutting Mrs Pringle and the relief of moving to Queen Square. Mrs Burney bought the house while both her husband and Fanny were away, he in Venice collecting information for his 'Present State of Music in France and Italy', she in Drury Lane staying with her newly married sister as was expected of a bridesmaid. It was a handsome house in Bloomsbury, at the upper end of the square looking over the fields to the villages of Highgate and Hampstead on the hills to the north. Alderman Barber, printer to Queen Anne, had lived there and doubtless been visited by his friends Swift, Pope and Bolingbroke. Fanny is enthusiastic about the house: 'We have more than room for our family, large as it is, and all the rooms are well fitted up, convenient and handsome.'

There were serious disadvantages to Queen Square, however. One was the presence of Sir Richard Bettenson, uncle by marriage to Martin Rishton, a young man Maria had already met in Lynn and of whom her mother disapproved. Scarcely was Hetty's 'novel' safely concluded than Maria's began to write itself for her step-sister's delectation. The other disadvantage had something to do with the lease, about which Mrs Burney may have been deceived, for in three years, and again while Charles Burney was away, a hasty move was made to St Martin's Street, a much less salubrious district.

Meanwhile Fanny herself had grown into a young woman of marriageable age. The very balls and masquerades at which Mr Seaton had trifled with Hetty had been the scene of her earliest conquests. At the fancy-dress masquerade, a Mr Tomkin dressed as a Dutchman and at Mr Pugh's dance a Captain Bloomfield were greatly impressed by Fanny. When the Dutchman, as Fanny preferred to call him, for Tomkin was not a romantic name, proceeded to follow up his interest in the formal fashion of the day, Fanny's rejection was prompt and unequivocal. At this period of her life she lacked any interest in possible suitors, though she was insatiably curious about the romances of other girls.

The sister closest to Fanny was Susanna, two and a half years younger but at least as mature. Her talent for writing was the equal of Fanny's and she it was who at the age of nine began the custom of communicating in a journal, a mixture of a diary written to be shared and a detailed letter to someone of similar interests. When the authorship of *Evelina* was speculated upon, Mrs Burney was not the only person to guess at Susan rather than Fanny. She sang exquisitely and her knowledge of music was much praised by the professional musicians who came in and out of the Burney home. Was it that which prevented her from developing her talent for writing? Or was it that she lacked Fanny's detachment, her unwillingness to be involved in living? Susan married comparatively early, had three children and money troubles, was unhappy and succumbed at forty-five to the disease which had killed her mother. Fanny stayed unmarried until she was forty, had one child only, was happy and lived until she was eighty. What was more, Fanny suffered, as we can see from her comments in the early journals, from the need to unburden herself in writing, the compulsive writer's itch. That alone may have made the difference between talent exploited and talent unused.

A portrait of Susanna by her cousin Edward Francesco Burney, shows us a face of much sweetness and no satirical bent. The features are remarkably beautiful, huge eyes under gently rounded eyebrows, a straight delicate nose and a mouth upturned at the corners despite problems enough to turn it down. It was always Susan, described by friends as 'douce', as 'spirituelle', as having a 'peculiar felicity in her manner', who put Fanny's interests before her own. There was no rivalry. Susan's delight in Fanny's success, her total lack of envy and her readiness to pass on all the compliments she hears about *Evelina*, bear out reports of the pleasantness of her nature. Her account of Mr and Mrs Burney reading and enjoying *Evelina* in bed and laughing so loudly that they could be heard in the next room is as dramatically narrated as anything Fanny herself ever wrote, but she it is who passes on the admiration of Mrs Thrale and Doctor Johnson to her sister, she visits Streatham and admires it and its inhabitants, content to play second fiddle, to have Doctor Johnson tell her that he can never love her as much as Fanny.

At twenty-six Susan became engaged to Molesworth Phillips, a close friend of her brother James and a companion to him on Captain Cook's last voyage. Phillips witnessed the killing of Captain Cook and with four of his marines swam for safety. He would have reached it if he had not seen one of his men in danger from the natives. Though he had been stabbed between the shoulders with a long iron spike, Phillips swam to his rescue and in spite of being hit on the head by a stone, managed to drag him off by his hair. Besides his dashing adventures and his friendship with James, Phillips had the advantage of being musical. Charles Lamb liked him and included him with James Burney among his whist players. Sadly enough his promise as a husband was not borne out. He appears to have been unjustifiably callous in his dealings with his wife and children, and his financial affairs are, from the beginning, breathtaking in their complicated inefficiency.

Fanny's two brothers, James and Charles, though their lives and their temperaments were quite different, each displayed Burney characteristics and Burney individuality. James was a little older than Fanny and went to sea at the age of eleven years. By the time Fanny's journal begins, she is alternately worrying about his safety and longing for his letters and his leaves. She gives us, 'character-monger' that she is, an appreciative sketch of James after he has been home a whole three weeks:

> James' character appears the same as ever – honest, generous, sensible, unpolished; always unwilling to take offence, yet always eager to resent it; very careless and possessed of an uncommon share of good nature; full of humour, mirth and jollity; ever delighted at mirth in others and happy in a

peculiar talent of propagating it himself. His heart is full of love and affection for us – I sincerely believe he would perform the most difficult task which could possibly be imposed on him to do us service. In short, he is a most worthy deserving creature and we are extremely happy in his company.

James who became, very briefly, Admiral Burney, went with Captain Cook on his second voyage round the world, an enterprise instigated by the Royal Society. He also went on explorations of the South Pacific Ocean and New Zealand. He helped compile *Cook's Voyages* and kept in true Burney fashion a journal of his own voyages, using the material later for his much-admired books on exploration. He was a friend of Omai the Otaheite who was brought to London from those parts to astonish the natives, and indeed his preference was always for the unconventional in people or behaviour.

In this first family there were also Charles (two sons of that name had died) and the youngest child Charlotte, both too much younger than Fanny to have had a great deal of influence on her, though Charlotte, by then twice widowed, cared for her lovingly in her old age. Charles was both his family's pride and their most painful embarrassment. He was a handsome boy with a pink and white complexion and a disposition that earned him the title of the best-tempered boy in the Charterhouse. Charles Burney had canvassed all his friends for their help in placing him at school, and it was the Earl of Holderness under whose patronage the boy had finally entered, his books and the material for his shirts donated by Mrs Thrale. He had a great love of learning and excelled particularly at classics. He was admitted to Caius College, Cambridge, to the delight of his father, but there was proved guilty of stealing books, particularly Elzevir Editions, from the library. Banished from Cambridge and from home, he took refuge in Shinfield, Berkshire, where he occupied himself with occasional verses expressing remorse and despair.

Dr Burney's old friend, the Reverend Mr Twining, now proved himself to be a source of compassionate encouragement and practical advice. Under his guidance the family rallied in the support of their poor sinner and, when it was ascertained that a degree from Aberdeen University would still enable him to be ordained in the Church of England, he was sent there to redeem his chances. For many years Charles' one instance of weak and foolish behaviour barred his acceptance into the church, though his success when it was at last forgotten proved swift and astonishing.

Charlotte, the youngest of Esther Burney's family, no more than a year old when her mother died, was a surprisingly merry girl. She is said to have spent more time at Lynn than in London during her early years, for Mrs Burney felt that family duty (duty to her own family, that is) demanded frequent visits to her mother and brothers there. Charlotte, who was much the same age as her step-sister Bessie, was taken with her to stay in Mrs Burney's house and, if we are to believe her sisters, fetch and carry for her step-mother. If this was so we hear no complaints of it from Charlotte, who was resilient and totally lacking in self-pity, much given to puns and what she called nannygoats (anecdotes). She was a mimic and more than most Burneys she liked to use the broken English of the foreigners who thronged the house in St Martin's Street. Fanny used it too, notably in her dramatisation of the odious Mrs Schwellenberg when she was resident at the Court, and again in an account quoted by R. Brimley Johnson and oddly similar to some of the Schwellenberg stories, of a French woman being difficult about fresh air in a coach. It is as if Fanny saw the French and Germans as comic types rather than individuals, at least in the early years of her life.

When Clement Francis, surgeon to the East India Company, who had been secretary to Warren Hastings in India, decided to come home and marry the author of that charming book *Evelina,* he married instead her youngest sister. We have no means of knowing whether Fanny, following her usual custom, avoided him after hearing of his intentions or whether Francis was more attracted by Charlotte's gaiety than by Fanny. Charlotte at twenty-five, irrepressible, uninhibited and flirtatious must have been delightful.

Esther Burney's children were all talented and good-looking, and they had, especially the girls, a sensitivity and delicacy of mind quite unlike anything we find in Elizabeth Burney's children. The Allen children especially were eccentric, at times almost grotesquely so. Despite her nickname of La Dama or The Lady, given her we must suppose on account of her elevated social standards, Elizabeth Burney seems to have brought up her younger children as in a free-discipline school and to have allowed the elder ones, for all the talk of whipping, to do more or less what they liked.

Both the girls of Mrs Burney's first family eloped and were subsequently unhappy in their marriages. Maria Allen, wilful and unconventional, an heiress and conscious of it, married in Ypres without her mother's consent. Like the Burneys she had the journalizing habit and her letters are the most amusing of all Fanny's acquaintance, so spontaneous that we laugh aloud in reading them and wish that we had the fifty-year collection that Fanny kept her life long. Her story will be told elsewhere, since her nonchalance and her wild romance were powerful influences on Fanny's writing of *Evelina*, influences her later 'works' were sadly to lack.

Maria's brother, Stephen, who became the Rev. Stephen Allen, had also a far from conventional history. He married at Gretna Green, at the age of seventeen, a girl called Susannah Sharpin and had twelve children. Since he was twelve when his mother remarried, his impact on the Burney household was slight. Elizabeth, always called Bessie and described by Fanny as 'handsome and graceful', was also a disappointment to her mother. Fanny speaks approvingly of her going to school in Paris 'for she was unformed and backward to an uncommon degree'. But here a scandal arose: Bessie eloped with, and then married, Samuel Meeke, described as an adventurer. After his death she married a widower called Bruce, who is said to have kept her locked in the house and short of money. References to Bessie Meeke have probably been excised from Fanny's journal, and we can unfortunately glean no more of her story except that it is horrifying.

The two children born of the marriage between Charles Burney and Mrs Allen could hardly be expected to be dull and indeed they were not. Richard, or Bengal Dick as he was known, went to school at Harrow and at the age of eighteen went out to Calcutta where he became Headmaster of the Orphan School of Kiddepore when he was no more than twenty-seven. Indeed precocity seems to have been a trait of his character, since at nineteen he married in Calcutta a Jane Ross who was then fifteen. They had a numerous family, some of whom returned to England and were known to the Burneys.

The last of Charles Burney's children was Sarah Harriet (or Hariotte). Fanny calls her 'one of the most innocent, artless, queer little things you ever saw and altogether she is a very sweet and very engaging child', while a family friend Mr Twining describes her as 'a little thing buried under a great periwig'. She became, like her half-sister Fanny, a novelist, and it is perhaps a judgment on Mrs Burney who so disapproved of Fanny's scribbling, that she should produce a daughter with that same regrettable habit.

And Fanny herself? She was small, which made her look younger than her real age, dark-skinned, with grey-green eyes and plentiful brown hair. She was short-sighted, which produced in her a habit of stooping and may have been the cause of her reading late. We seldom find visual descriptions in her writing and it is evident that she is the kind of observer who listens, rather than watches. No word is ever lost and Fanny is alert always for the

27

trick of speech, for the word or phrase that characterizes a speaker. She herself picks up affectations of speech quite easily. A tendency to gush overcomes her when she is writing to Susan or to Susan's friend and neighbour Mrs Locke, and she also displays a too-frequent use of foreign words and phrases. The effect Johnson had on her was sad indeed – instead of the spontaneity her writing had when her ear was tuned to Maria's prattle, she now wrote what Macaulay (of all people) called 'a sort of broken Johnsonese'.

It may have been her long love for an elderly man that made her rather sexless. If she was a prude it was because her sexual instincts were in abeyance; her emotions, her moral judgment, were always active however and she had a remarkable capacity for affection, which she exercised all her life in an extraordinary variety of relationships. She could love poor, mad Christopher Smart, who gave her a rose, and the difficult-natured Queen of England. Mrs Thrale and Dr Johnson loved and were loved by her. She was on affectionate terms with the whole vast tribe of Burneys and their intimates, no mean feat in a family. Her husband died with his last thought, if not his last words 'à notre réunion'. 'She possesses,' her unsympathetic step-mother observed, 'perhaps as feeling a heart as ever girl had.'

Fanny's extreme sensitivity, a natural accompaniment, one may think, to feelings so easily aroused, made her notoriously touchy. Mrs Thrale commented on her pride: 'a saucy-spirited little puss', she called her, and there were many instances at Court of Fanny standing on her dignity. The Queen's gift of a lilac tabby silk was unacceptable because it was given through her Mistress of the Robes, Mrs Schwellenberg, and her behaviour on a royal visit to Nuneham while staying with the Harcourts must have been intolerable, simply because she wished to be treated as their guest, not as part of the royal entourage. She wept freely and often, a talent much admired in her period of history, and she could mourn as long and sincerely as she could love.

But perhaps the most admirable quality in Fanny was her courage, and in someone so small and frail it never ceases to surprise us. Her grandmother Sleepe's influence, which was strong in her early youth, gave her a core of rectitude. It remained with her all her life, in whatever other particulars she altered, and she never hesitated to act according to her early teaching. She inherited ill-health from her mother. Over-excitement or over-exertion had always the same enervating effect on her, so that by her later years she was obliged to rest one day in two. The need to 'recruit', as she called it, was always with her to some extent, but since her father wisely allowed her a considerable degree of freedom, providing only that she transcribed his manuscripts for him, she was able to manage her health very well until she entered the Court, where her routine was to a great extent prescribed for her. For most of her life blistering and bleeding were almost regular treatments and her diet was strict:

> Sir Richard Jebb has ordered me to be blooded again [she says], a thing I mortally dislike – asses' milk also he forbids as holding it too nourishing! and even potatoes are too solid food for me! He has ordered me to live wholly on turnips, with a very little dry bread and what fruit I like: but nothing else of any sort – I drink barley-water and rennet-whey.

Cold sponges every day, a daily walk in all weathers and careful attention to diet preserved Fanny's health to a great old age. If we consider the events she lived through and her fortitude in meeting them, we must marvel at how perfectly she overcame the handicap of her frail health: her operation for cancer of the breast without, of course, an anaesthetic, her headlong, non-stop journey to her wounded husband in Trèves would have tried the hardest. And only a brave spirit could have undertaken and made a success of marriage under the conditions Fanny accepted for herself.

But all that lay in the future, in the part of Fanny's life that was still beyond guessing. And who indeed could have guessed how adventurous it was to be, how crammed with the totally unexpected? For Fanny in her early twenties there was the happiness and security of a loving family, and it was this lightheartedness that was such an attractive quality of her early writing. The delight of being young and in London, of visits to the theatre and to Ranelagh, Marylebone Gardens and Vauxhall, was to provide a great part of the attraction of her best-selling first novel *Evelina*.

St Martin's Street was the headquarters of the Burney family at the peak of its social success. Queen Square was a more elegant district but circumstances we know nothing of forced a move and Mrs Burney bought the house that had been Sir Isaac Newton's, in an area no house agent could have described as residential. In the autumn of 1774 the Burneys moved. Charles Burney was pleased with the association with the great astronomer, whose observatory still existed, perched on top of the roof. It had 'four glazed walls . . . contained a fireplace, an ornamental chimney-piece and a cupboard. Its windows commanded wide-spreading views of London and its environs.' Fanny was delighted with this little room, which she was

29

able to appropriate for a study and which was far enough away from the living rooms to be free from interruption.

Constance Hill, who lived when the house was still standing (it was demolished in 1913), comments on the fine old oaken staircase with shallow steps leading up to the drawing-room, with its three lofty recessed windows overlooking St Martin's Street. It had, she says, a carved wooden chimney-piece in the Adam style, a deep cornice and a painted ceiling. Folding doors opened into the library, which led into a small room known as 'Sir Isaak Newton's Study'. The library was used by the Burneys as a music-room, and in it stood the two harpsichords on which Hetty and Susan and then, after her marriage, Hetty and Charles Rousseau Burney, played their famous duets. One can imagine that when the folding doors were opened the drawing-room and library combined to make a concert room in which Dr Burney's famous evening parties could quite comfortably be held.

Mrs Hill suggests that the best bedroom and Dr Burney's powdering-closet were above the drawing-room and the bedroom shared by Fanny and Susan above the library. Maria was now married, and Hetty too; James was at sea on Cook's second expedition and Charles at school, so the number of rooms required for the family was sensibly diminished. The family parlour, or living-room, on the ground floor was a more private part of the house, and here favoured visitors might drink tea at seven o'clock (dinner was usually served at three or four) or, if they were made one of the family, share a frugal supper at eleven. Fanny mentions baked apples, but perhaps other people ate less ascetically.

Visitors came at all hours of the day. Hetty and her husband lived in Covent Garden, Sir Joshua Reynolds in Leicester Square and James Barry near Oxford Market. Dr Johnson and his blind friend Mrs Williams lived at Bolt Court, Dr Burney's mother and sisters in York Street near Covent Garden and David Garrick near enough to drop in at eight o'clock in the morning. Since Garrick was one of Dr Burney's closest friends and a man who was very fond of children, Fanny's interest in the effects of the spoken word must have received a great deal of encouragement in her childhood days and later. He, Mr Crisp and the Rev. Twining became auxiliary fathers to Charles Burney's motherless family and seem never to have lost the habit of concern for them.

But it was by his evening parties that Charles Burney attracted people away from the London clubs and caused an area of narrow streets to be chock-a-block with carriages, sedan-chairs and link boys almost every evening. Continental musicians, who commanded high fees, seemed willing to perform in St Martin's Street out of respect for their host, asking for no other reward than his commendation. Thus Signora Agujari (known as La Bastardini for obvious reasons) who could demand fifty guineas a song, took tea with the Burneys at seven and then sang until twelve. 'A sublime singer', Fanny calls her and she is compared by the whole company with her rival Gabrielli, heard at the opera-house. Prince Orloff, credited or discredited with having strangled the Russian emperor with his diamond-encrusted hands, begged Dr Burney to allow him to hear a performance of what were fast becoming known as 'the matrimonial duets', Hetty and her husband Charles Rousseau on the two harpsichords. Mr Bruce, the so-called Emperor of Abyssinia, attended a concert and James invited to dinner the Otaheitan chief Omai.

So brilliant were the Burney parties that at last Mrs Thrale decided to satisfy her curiosity about them and to bring Dr Johnson along too. It was Fanny's first sight of Mrs Thrale and her eldest daughter and, although she had heard a great deal about the great Lexiphanes, her note on the description in her journal suggests that she had never seen him before. Hetty and Susan played a duet and during their performance Johnson (who regarded music as an irritating noise) arrived in the room.

People who knew Johnson soon ceased to see him objectively, so Fanny's portrait, before her affection for the old man could blur the edges, is particularly valuable:

He is indeed very ill-favoured, is tall and stout but stoops terribly; he is almost bent double. His mouth is almost constantly opening and shutting as if he was chewing. He has a strange method of frequently twirling his fingers and twisting his hands. His body is in continual agitation, see-sawing up and down; his feet are never a moment quiet; and, in short, his whole person is in perpetual motion. His dress, too, considering the times and that he had meant to put on his best becomes, being engaged to dine in a large company, was as much out of the common as his figure; he had a large wig, snuff-colour coat and gold buttons, but no ruffles to his shirt . . . and black worsted stockings.

Fanny talks of his short-sightedness, of his inability to recognize even Mrs Thrale. She adds some comic detail:

He poked his nose over the keys of the harpsichord till poor Hetty and Susan hardly knew how to play on, for fear of touching his phiz . . . He pored over them [the books] shelf by shelf, almost brushing them with his eyelashes . . . At last, fixing upon something that happened to hit his fancy,

31

he took it down, and standing aloof from the company, which he seemed clean and clear to forget, he began without further ceremony and very composedly to read to himself, and as intently as if he had been alone in his own study.

The company was longing to hear Johnson talk and when, chocolate being brought, they returned to the drawing-room, leaving the books, someone cleverly mentioned Garrick, who had been Johnson's pupil and about whom the great man liked to air his opinions. 'Garrick,' remarked the Doctor presently, 'never enters a room but he regards himself as the object of general attention, from whom the entertainment of the company is expected . . .' Johnsonian talk and on a subject peculiarly interesting to the Burneys. Lexiphanes, vocal at last, analysed the actor's temperament and Fanny wrote it all down for Mr Crisp. Upstairs among her private papers lay the rough draft of *Evelina*, which was to bring them all together in totally different roles in a year or two, when Mrs Thrale and Johnson assumed the patronage of the literary talent the whole modish world was talking about, the talent that was Fanny Burney's.

4

MISS BURNEY'S STEP-SISTER

Fanny Burney always referred, even in her private journal, to her elder step-sister as Miss Allen, or even Allen. That is, until the day she wrote: 'Miss Allen – for the last time I shall so call her – came home on Monday last. Her *novel* is not yet over; nevertheless, she – was married last Saturday.'

It is probable that the girls had known one another socially most of their lives. The Allens were an important family in Lynn, and Mrs Stephen Allen, Maria's mother, had married a cousin of the same name. When he died the larger part of her money remained in a family trust administered by her strong-minded mother and her brothers. What money she was able to get her hands on she promptly lost by unwise speculation. Her secret marriage to Charles Burney (who had no capital) reveals that impulsiveness in her character which all her children possessed in some measure, and her habit of going off to Lynn, where she owned a house, and leaving her children and step-children to their own devices cannot have done much to teach them a greater sobriety of conduct. The elder Burney girls, whose formative years had passed before her arrival under the watchful eye of Grandmother Sleepe, were unspoilt by such freedom, but Charlotte, Esther's youngest child, and Sarah Harriet, the youngest child of the second marriage, were spoken of in the family as uncontrolled.

Maria Allen, who had a double inheritance of the wilful, passionate Allen temper, may well have been as beautiful as her mother. No portrait is known. Certainly she behaved like a beauty. She was also indiscreet, very far from being the circumspect young woman admired at the time. But if she was less guarded in her behaviour than Hetty, Fanny or Susan, she was also more practical and down to earth. Maria shows an interest in food such as her step-sisters seem incapable of, and one delightful letter written when she must have been deputizing for her mother begins:

Oh as I come along some house-keeping thoughts entered my noddle as follows – tell Jenny I have altered the dinner on Monday – and intend having at the top fried smelts – at Bottom the Ham – on one side 2 boiled chickens –

on the other a small pigion pie with 3 pigions in it and let the crust be made very rich and eggs in it – in the middle an Orleon plumb pudding – and a Roast Loin of Mutton – after the fish.

She goes on to practical details about window blinds and removing the drugget from the stairs in a brisk fashion that Fanny never echoes, not even when she is living on £120 a year in a cottage. Later, at 'Tingmouth', we hear of Mr Hurrel taking three helpings of Mrs Rishton's hash, proof enough of its excellence.

But it is Maria's love-affair – her *novel* as Fanny calls it – that is her greatest interest. Maria Allen and Martin Folkes Rishton may have met at Lynn. Mrs Allen had some sort of objection to the young man and whatever the objection was, it obviously made the girls of the family feel that Martin was an unsuitable *parti*. He had been a spendthrift at Oxford and had done something 'unworthy of a gentleman'. What it was, we never hear. Rishton's family (he was the adopted nephew of a Sir Richard Bettenson, who had succeeded to a baronetcy and a good income and had then come to live parsimoniously in Queen Square) was also anxious to keep the young people apart. Unfortunately for this sensible plan the Burney family moved into Queen Square in 1770 on Mr Crisp's advice, so that Mrs Pringle, who had so injudiciously introduced the unreliable Mr Seaton to Hetty, should no longer be a neighbour of theirs. From that point a new romantic drama is played out before Fanny's fascinated attention.

The temperature of the love-affair is revealed to us in an account of a Lynn Assembly, to which Maria went entirely against her own inclination, she says, persuaded by a friend called Bet Dickens. Maria had made a half-crown wager that she would not dance. But she broke her ear-ring and her promise, walked home with Martin and was perhaps alone with him for a while. The feverish atmosphere of the assembly, the sense of isolation – 'I was an Alien – quite save that poor bewitched solitary thing' – the broken sentences of reticence and self-consciousness, all these give us Maria's state of mind at the beginning of her infatuation for Martin Rishton. It is plain that Maria's reason, such as it is, is quite overcome.

Out of a wish to separate Rishton and Maria, perhaps even at the Allens' request, Sir Richard Bettenson sent his nephew abroad for two years in January 1771. Five months later Maria, staying in Lynn, hears news that excites her past bearing. Martin Rishton has come back to England. 'When asked what could have brought him over in such a hurry he smiled but said nothing to the question.' Maria has heard that he is in London: his letters are directed to the St James's Coffee-house. She reads into his return such significance that: 'I neither eat, drink nor sleep for thinking of it. Whether I am glad or sorry, I shall leave for another opportunity, or your own clever heads to find out.'

In a characteristic scattering of commissions, Maria teases her step-sisters exuberantly; Susan, who (she knows) is rich, is invited to pay her milliner's bill for her and Fanny, who is in fact indifferent to clothes, is to enquire what is the newest Parisian cut for the sleeve of a riding-habit. The idea of Susan's being able to pay a bill for the extravagant heiress Maria or of Fanny's having any interest at all in fashion was part of the tissue of family jokes that bound these girls together when they were young and light-hearted.

In the late summer of 1771 a letter from Maria to Fanny and Susan begins 'Dear Toads' and goes on to announce her arrival in Queen Square 'next Saturday se'nnight'. She declares: 'I am at present as happy as I can be deprived of Two of the greatest Blessings in Life, your company and the heart of Rishton, tho' I am not quite certain of the latter.' She has seen Rishton 'and danced Next Couple to him a whole Evening'. Maria's letters are seldom very coherent, but it may signify that she moves straight from this thought to the idea of going to Geneva. She intends to winter abroad and has permission to go alone. There is difficulty about the lodgings; she is 'really distressed'. Unusually for her, Maria sounds serious: 'Even setting out at an uncertainty, although very disagreeable, would be better than what my future prospects are in England.' The letter ends with high-spirited jokes that we should recognize as Maria's anywhere: 'You, Mrs Fanny, I desire to dress neatly and properly, without a hole in either apron or ruffles – and go to Madam Giffodières in Wells Street . . .' As is usual with Maria, everyone is given a job to do and the girls are teased for faults that are notoriously her own. Characteristically, too, she goes on to talk about food, making greedy demands for a 'boil'd Orlean plumb pudding all her to herself' at dinner and some toasted cheese for supper.

It is no very great surprise to find that by the beginning of November 1771 Maria is in Geneva. Fanny says she has had 'a charming pacquet' from Miss Allen. It is the Journal she has been keeping 'ever since she has been out'. Maria herself is far less happy. Susan and Fanny have not written to her or acknowledged the Journal. She is being kept short of money and blames her uncles. She threatens to borrow on her expectations (she is nearly twenty-one) or sell her diamonds, which she is glad she took with her. Meanwhile there are a few little jobs Fanny can do for her: expedite the sending of her pianoforte; send her Fordyce's sermons; buy her a tea-caddy in Piccadilly (shop specified); buy and send a little black ebony inkstand with silver plaited tops to the bottles, and a handle like one to a basket of the same metal. Last, and surely most urgent, 'a very pretty naked wax doll with blue eyes, the half-crown sort. Do it up,' Maria commands, 'that it will not be broke with cotton all over it and 100 papers.' All these things, she advises, can be packed in the case of the pianoforte where they will be safe.

A great deal of Fanny's journal for the following year, 1772, has been cut away, presumably in the interests of discretion since we find that Maria is in secret correspondence with Martin Rishton and is keeping Fanny apprised of the course of affairs by sending her copies of his letters and, probably, of her own. She alleges that the reason she wanted to leave England was so that she should not see Martin any more, and she seems to be torn between her doubts of his character and her need to believe in his integrity because she loves him. Susan and Fanny are to corroborate her impression of his letters, which is that they are written by a man of honour. But they are not to tell Hetty, because Hetty is prejudiced, nor Mr Crisp, though he may see the journal as far as the last cahier, where these matters begin to be mentioned. Interestingly enough, there are no jokes in this letter.

That was in April. On 16 May Martin Rishton and Maria Allen met and were married at Ypres. Maria must instantly have left for England, since she reached Fanny and Susan two days later. The girls must have debated how best to break the news, and after about three weeks' discussion, on 7 June, Susan and Maria went to Chessington to invoke the aid of Mr Crisp, leaving Fanny behind, wretchedly conscious of the scenes that would ensue when the news reached Mrs Allen. A joint letter from Maria and Susan tells Fanny how Mr Crisp reacted.

It seems that Maria had begun by hinting that she might marry Rishton and showing Mr Crisp his picture. He responded in his forthright way with a great deal of abuse of the young man – 'If he had been a Mahoon he could not have merited what Crisp said.' Maria followed this up with a message sent by Catherine Cooke, niece of Miss Hamilton who now owned Chessington: 'Mrs Rishton sent compts. and hoped to see him at Stanhoe this summer.' Stanhoe was Mr Rishton's family village, and Mr Crisp was alarmed enough by the message to burst into the girls' bedroom and demand an explanation. Maria fell on her knees and hid her face in the bed. Kate – Catherine Cooke – 'clawed hold of her left hand and showed him the ring'. Mr Crisp then used some very strong expressions, which we are loyally assured were not oaths. When he was finally convinced that the marriage had in fact taken place and had been shown the two letters Rishton had already written to his wife, he questioned Maria closely about the legality of the marriage. Then, satisfied, he declared that he could see that Rishton was 'a man of sence and a gentleman', blithely contradicting his earlier remarks on his character.

After that, Mr Crisp took command. The look of the thing became his chief concern. The marriage was to be made public at once, he directed. Martin was to be summoned to England and Maria was to meet him in London if her mother would not receive them. They were to go to Norfolk and face his family and hers, and Maria was to start using her new name without any further concealment. Mr Crisp wrote to Maria's mother himself, no doubt trying to prepare the way for a reconciliation.

Business over, Maria springs back into her old ebullient self. It is obvious that she is afraid of her mother's reaction and rightly, for Mrs Burney was vehement in her disapproval. But now that she is to rejoin Rishton she is concerned with that alone. Orders fly. Poor Fanny is to speak up for her and encourage Hetty and her maid to do the same. The trousseau is to be ready for trying on. (When did she give the order, we wonder? No particulars of clothes are mentioned in her letter from Geneva.) Fanny is to write by return of post.

The apprentice novelist could hardly fail to be excited by the drama and danger of Maria Allen's story. Mr Crisp's salutary emphasis on the legality of the marriage almost certainly provided Fanny with useful details of the sad fate of Evelina, whose profligate father burned the certificate of his private marriage to her mother and then disowned the child. Fanny is certainly indulging her writing habit with less restraint at this time, and during the next year, 1773, a visit to Maria in Teignmouth gave her the material for a separate journal to Susan, which was passed on to Mr Crisp and his sisters. This was in effect her first literary work and it received much encouragement. Maria, in her usual satirical manner, however, remarked of this or some other writing sent her by the emergent writer: 'And so by way of return to the very curious Manuscript I received, I have named the first cow I ever was mistress of – Fanny.'

Mrs Burney, not content, according to Maria, with giving Martin Rishton an account of 'every vice, fault or foible I had ever been guilty of since my birth,' made it difficult for Fanny to accept invitations from the newly-married pair. A rather farcical visit to Covent Garden Theatre with Sir Richard Bettenson and his sister is described. Mr and Mrs Rishton are in London for a brief visit and have invited Fanny to be of the party, but Mrs Burney's permission seems to have been given very reluctantly. Soon after this Maria writes from Bath where she has gone for her health and mentions her hope of seeing Fanny at Stanhoe House, which they are taking on a seven-year lease but which is not yet ready for them. Her letter suggests some criticism of Rishton's extravagant tastes: he had wanted her to buy 'a suit of mignionet linnen fringed for second mourning' and to wear it at Fischer's concert. She preferred not to go. There is also some suggestion of jealousy, of Rishton's flirting 'with every Miss in his way'. From Bath they move to Teignmouth (always spelt by Maria and Fanny Tingmouth), and Maria writes temptingly to Fanny of the delights of living by the sea.

'Tingmouth', Maria says, 'surpasses everything my imagination had formed of the most beautiful.' She describes the handsome women doing men's work while their husbands are with the Newfoundland fishery for eight or nine months of the year. Then, most tempting of all, she describes their thatched cottage, rented from a Captain Whitbourne almost in its entirety:

> We have it almost all, that is a little parlour not much bigger than the third room in Queen's Square – the furniture is a very elegant set Beaufet painted blue – and Open – filled with Curious odd bits of China, glass *flowers* etc. that the Captain has picked up during his Voyages – a very fine *picture* of our Saviour on the Cross – supposed to be a Raphael – and a Magdalen by Corregio – with a vast many curious prints cut out of Common Prayer-book and I am afraid the old Family Bible is a Loser – the window with very pretty flowers in pots – and a Most delightful Mirtle hedge as thick as any common one in a very little Spot of Garden before the house – we have behind our parlour a Scullery converted into a Kitchen, over this is two very neat Bedchambers with nice Clean Linen Beds.

Maria in fact was the first of the girls to be overwhelmed by the romantic idea of living in a cottage. Fanny was to follow her years later when she married and built Camilla Lacy, but by that part of the century the feeling for romanticism was becoming stronger and more general. 'Mr and Mrs Rishton . . . are turned absolute hermits for this summer,' Fanny comments admiringly. Later she was to describe herself and her husband as living in the cottage at Great Bookham in the same way, and the little house was christened The Hermitage for this reason. The mood of the middle of the eighteenth century had inclined people to gather in cities and organize a social life, but the mood of the end of it was for the pastoral, for simplicity and the company of few, and those uneducated, people.

By May a very pressing invitation to Teignmouth has been sent to Fanny. At first she is obliged to refuse: her father is reluctant to lose his librarian. A letter follows urging her to spend the summer at Teignmouth instead of Lynn, to which her step-mother has already taken herself until the autumn. Teignmouth is not a dressy place and it is not much further away than Lynn. Maria suggests that Martin Rishton would be able to go out fishing and shooting more often if his wife had company, and she adds disarmingly that the rooms are so littered with dogs and poultry that she can ask no one but Fanny.

Further delays produce yet another letter from Maria who was nothing if not tenacious. She scatters her commission as usual – Fanny is to buy Mr Rishton two cricket balls 'made by Pett of 7 Oaks . . . ask for the very best sort, which costs 4s or 4s 6d each – let them weigh 4oz and qu^r or 4 oz and 1/2 each, send them by the Exeter post coach'. Maria goes to work to allay Dr Burney's fears about the danger of travelling by coach. *She* has never been accosted:

> I have been from London to York and from York to London – and am afraid was ever unnoticed by the Vulgar Crew.
>> Full many a flower is born to blush unseen
>> And waste its sweetness on the desert air.
> *Exactly* my case Fanny – Grey [*sic*] certainly thought of me when he composed those lines – I own I am fond of them for that reason.

Maria adds more seriously that Fanny can hardly intend to write Dr Burney's *History of Music* during his absence in Lynn and that he can surely spare her for a month or six weeks 'during the dog days'. There is just one more commission. Fanny is to open an account at Nounes (probably Nourse, the King's bookseller) for Martin Rishton – 'spring a tick' is the expression that young gentleman uses. Fanny is to 'let him know the lad is no sharper' and ask him to send Hawksworth's Journal and Veneroni's Grammar. She must also write a long letter with the books.

By making a very affectionate appeal to Dr Burney, Maria succeeded in obtaining leave for Fanny to visit her. The beginning of the Tingmouth Journal has her arriving there and the Rishtons walking to meet her. At once we are introduced to the exclusive circle of friends approved by

Martin Rishton for his wife's acquaintance. There is a Mr Crispen, 'on the wrong side of an elderly man', travelled and cultivated, fluent in French and Italian. He lives at Bath and is staying in Teignmouth for the summer. Then there are the Phipps, a newly-married couple with a pony-chaise. Then there is Mr Hurrel, a clergyman of £1500 a year, his wife and her sister Miss Davy. Miss Bowdler, a pretty but shockingly emancipated young woman, is *not* approved by Mr Rishton, though she appears not to notice this.

Fanny does not really want any company other than Maria's. Maria's conversation is 'as flighty, as ridiculous, as uncommon, lively, comical and truly entertaining as ever we knew it'. Fanny observes the affection between husband and wife. 'I . . . find it at present difficult to determine which of them is more affectionately, I might say passionately attached to the other.' Her description of Martin Rishton brings into sharp relief the qualities the two of them have in common. He too is whimsical and odd. He has a 'kind of generous impetuosity in his disposition' which it is easy to see in Maria's. And, like her, 'he cannot at all disguise anything that he feels'. Between the two of them they have at least four petted and unmanageable dogs. Vigo and Trump, spaniels, a Newfoundland dog called Tingmouth who always goes swimming with Martin Rishton, and Maria's own Pomeranian, bought for her at great expense in Bath and called Romeo.

The summer entertainments of a seaside town were quite new to Fanny. The Rishtons made up a party to go to the Races, the ladies going in the Phipps' pony-chaise while Rishton and Mr Phipps went in the more dashing whiskey. They joined together also for a variety of walks and rides around Teignmouth. The Hurrels took them sailing, an uncomfortable business as it turned rough. Mrs Hurrel and Fanny were terrified of running foul of the rocks, but Mr Hurrel – fat as Falstaff, Fanny says – was concerned only about his dinner. They put in at Brixham and dined at the best inn in the place, which was just as well, since their plans to leave early the next day and breakfast in the boat were frustrated by the boatswain who managed to destroy all the matches.

Meanwhile Mr Crispen kept up an assiduous flirtation with Fanny. He was, she noticed, attached to the fair sex in the style of the old courtiers. He was a compulsive wooer of women, in fact, and one who would be very disconcerted if his quarry surrendered. Fanny attracted a number of admirers of this kind during her prolonged spinsterhood. No doubt her sedateness and deceptive air of ingenuousness appealed to them. Miss

Bowdler was not pleased to find herself with a rival. Martin Rishton was not pleased with Miss Bowdler's free manners, since he wished to surround his wife with acquaintances of the utmost propriety, and by the end of Fanny's visit neither Mr Crispen nor Miss Bowdler was any longer welcome at the cottage.

An accompaniment to all the outdoor activity was the presence of the dogs. Romeo, who could not be cured of harrying sheep, had his leg broken by Rishton in an attempt to detach him from one of his victims. Rishton was extremely distressed about it and a surgeon was employed to set the leg while Maria and Fanny sauntered out to avoid the disagreeable scene. Fanny's opinion was that the (very expensive) dog would die, but she was made to take it back to Queen Square with her and nurse it, so contributing to its recovery. Romeo lived to a good old age and was taken back to Norfolk by the Rishtons. The spaniel called Vigo, however, tried to swim across the Teign at high tide and drowned.

Probably the major event of the holiday was Teignmouth Races, to which the Rishtons went accompanied by Fanny, with Mr Crispen, Miss Bowdler and a Miss Lockwood, a friend of Miss Bowdler's and a rich old maid, going with them, all self-invited. There was an Ass Race (which sounds stranger than a Donkey Race) and a Pig Race. For this latter the pigs' tails were cut short and soaped. Then they were made to run and became the property of any man who could catch them by the tail and hold them. There was also cricket, with Maria providing a kind of cricket tea, including the hash of which Mr Hurrel ate three helpings. There was wrestling and Mr Rishton intervened with his usual impetuosity to prevent foul play, two brothers called Mills, sons of the Dean of Exeter, who were staying for the cricket, entering the ring intrepidly in his support. A remarkable rowing match between five teams of women concluded the Races, the winners to receive the surprisingly feminine awards of shifts with pink ribbons.

The holiday passed quickly. Mr and Mrs Western arrived in Teignmouth for a week's visit. She was Martin Rishton's cousin and Fanny almost automatically analyses the relationship between husband and wife. Both were rich. Mrs Western had been violently in love with her husband when she married, but he had trifled away her affections with other women and she now regarded him 'with the most perfect, the coldest indifference'. Fanny adds that he has 'the *remains* of an agreeable man' as some women have the remains of beauty.

The Rishtons, Fanny and the Westerns go to see the women of the village draw in the nets. Bare feet and legs, and an outer skirt kilted up to the knee in the shape of a pair of trousers strike them all as barbarous but the women's looks and good health are impressive. Fanny's short-sighted but observant eye notices that they net 'nine large salmon, a john dory and a gurnet' on Monday while on Tuesday the haul is four dozen mackerel.

More cricket is planned. The young Mills have two friends staying especially for the cricket and they bring them along. Fanny is much taken with one of them, a Mr Gibbs who is said to be a very learned young man and has won a Craven Scholarship at Cambridge. A Mr Salter saves her from a cricket ball. Maria, in her new character of married woman and chaperone, affects to be shocked by Fanny's flirtatious behaviour and threatens to tell her father: 'Very well, Miss Fanny Burney, very well! I shall write to Dr Burney tomorrow morning.'

Maria and Fanny study Italian. Martin reads *The Faerie Queene* to them, leaving out 'what is improper for a woman's ear'. They go sightseeing, to Ugbrook, the seat of Lord Clifford, and to the seat of Sir John Davy. Fanny bathes in the sea. They go to church and are convulsed by the anthem which is set by a weaver and quite unaccompanied. Fanny describes it as 'too much to be borne decently . . . so very unlike anything that was ever before imagined, so truly barbarous, that with the addition of the singers trilling and squalling – no comedy could have afforded more diversion'. The men, Martin Rishton and the Mills, go shooting. This impresses Fanny as amazingly arduous.

> They go out before breakfast; after two or three hours' shooting they get what they can at any farm-house, then toil till three or four o'clock, when sometimes they return home; but if they have any prospect of more sport, they take pot-luck at any cottage and stay out till eight or nine o'clock.

Fanny admires Martin's hardiness. 'As to Mr Rishton, he seems bent on being proof against everything; he seeks all kinds of manly exercises and grows sun-burnt, strong and hardy.' In contrast to his toughness, Fanny stresses Martin's consideration for 'female fears'. She tells the story of going with the Rishtons to dine at Starcross, about eight miles from the cottage. It was a stormy evening and Maria was driving Fanny in the whiskey while Martin and the groom went on horseback. The roads were narrow and rough but Martin dismounted, made the groom lead his horse and directed the whiskey on foot over the dangerous terrain.

The end of the holiday comes, half-way through September. Mr Crispen, gallant to the last, returns home and so does Miss Bowdler. The Rishtons take Fanny home and leave Romeo with her in Queen Square, then set out for their return visit to the Westerns at Cokethorpe in Oxfordshire.

Maria, by her own account, was so distressed at the parting with Fanny that her grief made 'the first fifteen miles of the journey very uncomfortable'. Unsettled by his weeping companion Martin Rishton took the Tottenham Court Road instead of Oxford Street on his route to Uxbridge. Next he ran over Tingmouth who was travelling under the body of the whiskey, but the Labrador gave herself two or three hearty shakes and went on with her journey without apparent injury. When they reached Oxford Maria was glad it was raining since Martin Rishton had been known as an undergraduate for his phaeton and four bays, and she knew he would not be particularly anxious to drive her round the colleges in a whiskey. Tactfully she insisted that the weather was unsuitable for sight-seeing and had her hair done instead, but badly, and they set off again.

The next dog to be run over (were they badly trained or was Martin's driving so extraordinarily bad?) was Judge. In this episode they also hurt Tingmouth again, as well as a dog called Swinger. The mud became more impassable. They were compelled to walk the horse at the slowest pace. What was worse was that when they reached Cokethorpe at half-past six the house was totally silent. The shutters were closed. Nobody answered the bell. Presently an old shepherd appeared and explained that the Westerns were on a visit to Buckinghamshire. A letter warning them of this had gone astray. Refusing all offers of hospitality they spent the night at Witney and came back the next day. By this time the casualty roll among the dogs and horses is alarming: 'Whisker [the horse] is knocked up. Swinger is better, Tingmouth has had the distemper, been blooded, and takes regularly the powders of Dr James' (which, Mrs Raine Ellis reminds us, are said to have been fatal to Oliver Goldsmith). He is walked out regularly for exercise, led on a string by Maria, and it is thought that he must *ride* all the way to town. After two encounters with the wheel of a carriage and a bout of distemper it seems the least they can do for him.

The house at Stanhoe is derelict, infested by rats and conspicuously lonely. A ten-year lease is granted them on condition that they share the cost of new window-frames, and although Maria, like anyone else who has ever rented a house, is reluctant to make improvements from which the landlord will benefit, the Rishtons set out to clear the grounds and replant the garden. Maria even begins to find some pleasure in country domesticity: 'Mr R has spared me a very pretty yard and house for my poultry . . . we have got one cow and are to have others and have one of the prettiest, neatest dairies you can imagine. I *potter* after Rishton everywhere.' The servants are 'caballing and insolent' and to have the care of nine of them is intolerable after the man and maid they had at Teignmouth. But Rishton will not let her give herself over to domesticity entirely; he takes her to see how Damon, the new pointer, obeys his master's instructions or to look at a pheasant's nest or to see him shoot rooks.

At this stage of the marriage, the Rishtons' happiness is enviable. We hear that Martin is having a phaeton built in London and that Maria 'woud rather go in a Linnen or Stuff gown' than curtail his expenses. The dashing, extravagant young man she fell in love with is not to be transformed into a prudent husband yet. And Maria, at this period of her life, can talk about the family she will have, joking that she will leave Fanny's manuscript 'as an Inheritance to one of my Sons who shall be instructed Early in All the Hidden misteries of Science that he may understand this great production'. But she had no children and by the time Fanny married, nearly twenty years after Maria, she was ready to confide in her the unsatisfactory nature of life with Rishton.

The years between Maria's marriage and Fanny's had been filled for Maria with the usual occupations of a gentleman farmer's wife. The Rishtons were living at Thornham now. Her kitchen and her dairy had for twenty years been her chief concern. There was quite enough money, and many wives of the period, expecting no more from their husbands than she had, would have been content. She summarizes her advantages rather bitterly:

> If I could be contented with being mistress of a house of my own I mean as far as domestic regulation, allowed to have full power to hire or discharge the Female Servant, cloathed and taken care of when I am ill – to amuse myself with my fancy work, Drawing, Music (when alone) to read what Books I like, to have a Maid kept to wait upon me, to walk out when I like, to keep as much poultry as amuses, to order any new houses or other whims to accommodate my feathered friends, to pay Bills and order any thing into the House and to be Allow'd any Sum I chuse to expend on Cloathes or to relieve any distressed Object in the Kitchen, or other, the Physic while ill. I have the means of Happiness to my Heart.

Maria is trying to say that materially she lacks nothing. Her unhappiness springs from the emotional rift between herself and her husband. 'I go to sleep,' she says, 'without saying goodnight.'

Fanny's advice, when Maria seeks it, is always that marriage vows are binding. She advises patience and a determination to make the best of the situation. And indeed Maria had no legal redress. If she left her husband he was not bound to keep her, even though her own fortune had become his on marriage. Her social position would be very difficult without a man's protection and she would have no opportunity of remarriage. It was true that he could divorce her if she were proved to have committed adultery, but then, who would marry her, penniless and disgraced? As to Rishton, who was known to have had at least one mistress, he had by no means given grounds for divorce, since he had never been actively cruel to his wife.

In 1793 Maria writes that she has raised the subject of a separation with Rishton and received an emphatic refusal. He loves her still, he says, and is unwilling to live without her. He sees no point in a separation after so many years. Since it would be almost impossible for her to leave her husband without his consent, Maria allows the matter to lapse for a while and contents herself with her friendships. 'I love Mrs Coke every day more and more,' she mentions. We are reminded of Mrs Thrale's love for Fanny and Susan's for Mrs Locke.

Then, in 1796, Mrs Burney died and Maria was free of an important constraint. To grieve an ailing mother by leaving her husband would have been uncomfortable, and just as uncomfortable would have been that ailing mother's satirical comments on daughters who marry against their family's wishes and rue the day. Maria's sympathies are all with Dr Burney: 'I believe latterly extreme sufferings added to the quantity of laudanum that she constantly took at times caused a temporary derangement from the extreme irritability of her nerves. God bless your dear Father for his goodness to her . . . I always loved him as a parent.' Dr Burney's kindness to Maria and his willingness to offer her his protection now solved one of her problems, as her mother's death had solved another. Maria began again to petition Rishton for a separation.

Maria's letters to Fanny now begin to be much more explicit about her objections to life with Rishton. He neglects her, it seems, and at the same time expects to choose her company. His dislike of her mother has resulted in his forbidding meetings between mother and daughter. His dislike of the Rev. Stephen Allen, Maria's brother, is even more vehement and leads to the final critical scenes. She is not free to go where she likes and he is very unpleasant in company to those of her friends he does not care for. To reinforce this criticism of her husband, Maria also begins hinting at his *affaire* with a Mrs Hogg of Holkham, an *affaire* perhaps twenty years old but still, she believes, smouldering between them. It is of the utmost secrecy, since Rishton will punish her financially if she is known to mention it.

It is at Holkham that the next discussion takes place between the Rishtons on their future plans. Martin Rishton is very emotional at the thought of a separation. He protests he still loves his wife and that if she goes he will be 'left to misery and self reproach, an object for the finger of scorn to point at'. He weeps and begs. He offers to amend his ways. The terms of the separation are discussed. He offers her £300 a year (she will take no more) and a share of the furniture, plate and linen. He speaks of leaving her all he had ever intended to leave. He wants to have Stancliff (an upper servant and a protégée of Maria's) as a housekeeper. Maria's arrangements are made. She will live at Chelsea, help Sarah and provide a home for her when Dr Burney is dead. She will visit her brother for two or three months of every year. She advises Rishton not to try to keep a dairy. This last may be a reminder of the twenty years she has served Rishton as dairy-keeper at Stanhoe and Thornham, but the reference to her brother is certainly a taunt. Few people in the family liked the Rev. Stephen Allen but Maria was not going to be forbidden his company.

After this dramatic scene, matters drift indecisively. It is tacitly assumed that Rishton will take warning and behave less like a tyrant. Since he makes no move to draw up a deed of separation, Maria is left to wonder whether this is his intention or whether she should assert herself in some way that will force the issue. It is a distressing time for her. She writes to Fanny that she is 'shattered and low from the quantity of opium I had been obliged to take to still the violence of my headache and the irritation of my nerves'. Inaction would be weakness, Maria decides: 'I shall rivet my chains only the faster if I pursue such a pusillanimous conduct after having gone to such lengths and make him despise me. After having seen him *tremble* at the Voice of truth from an injured woman.' She plans to visit Chelsea in the spring and there to come to a clear decision about her marriage. Meanwhile, on Fanny's suggestion, she invites her niece Mary, daughter of the Rev. Stephen Allen, for a long stay.

No doubt Mary Allen was invited for her company and because a visitor in a house tends to produce more civilized behaviour in its inmates, but it was her projected visit that took all indecisiveness out of the situation. Perhaps Fanny guessed as much. Martin Rishton was to fetch her. Weeks went by and Mary, whose clothes were ready and whose box was packed, remained at Lynn. When Maria was forced to ask Rishton which day he was fetching her he calmly replied: 'I don't intend she shall come at all. I will not submit to have that family forced upon me, they are quite disagreeable to me and nothing shall alter my determination.'

Maria points out that this is a 'breach of contract', though nothing like a contract can be said to exist between them. He says he would rather have a separation than endure her relations. He offers her the use of the coach to make visits, or the liberty to invite other visitors, or a six-week visit to Cromer. She decides however to leave Thornham and packs in the early hours of the morning to keep her decision from Stancliff. Now that he sees her determination, Rishton becomes alarmed. He offers his wife *everything* – except Mary. However, if she must go he will drive her in the whiskey to save appearances, together with her maid and her luggage. So, with the horse at walking pace, Rishton took five hours driving Maria to Mrs Coke's house, arguing and pleading all the way. She had always been his 'pride and his delight' he said. The next day she left the Cokes for Chelsea.

At Chelsea, sharing a room with Sarah Harriet, Maria's health and spirits are low. She occupies herself with disparagement of her husband and anxiety over her allowance. The taxes have caused Rishton, she says, to lay down both the carriages. She seems to think this is no more than an excuse to circumscribe her movements, if she should ever return. He has not parted with a single dog, nor any of his shooting equipage. She will accept any allowance he gives, 'it will be only the difference of keeping a maid or waiting on myself, of travelling in a Post Chaise or a Stage Coach and using a printed Callico round drop instead of a Chintz one'. Rishton protests even more passionately that she must not leave him and insists she keep a manservant, as a condition of her allowance, to which he adds fifty guineas a year for his keep. Unfortunately he wants her to promise never to go to Lynn. This she refuses to do, not even if her allowance depends on it. But what will she do about money? She has been paying ready money for everything – 'I wanted a new hat but I have done without'. All she can do is give the footman his liveries and greatcoat and six months wages for removing to Chelsea, go with her maid to her brother's at Lynn, dismiss her maid there and become a governess to her brother's children.

Fortunately, she is not driven to these extremes. Rishton gives her the allowance, less £22 7s. She sees this as part of a plot, but it turns out to be no more than a miscalculation, which, Rishton writes, James will arbitrate upon. Later we hear of another 'ruse' of Rishton's. If we are to believe

Maria, 'he chuses to bring Lady Day twice into the same year, by which means he makes out five quarters'. The thought of paying income tax sends her into a very flurried state, and it is finally agreed that Rishton will pay her tax (which was ten per cent) and she is to dismiss the man-servant he so insisted on. He will then pay her £300 a year and, she notes resentfully, save £20. But still, she has not been made to promise to stay away from Lynn.

Maria had not long arrived at Dr Burney's lodgings in Chelsea when the scandal of James and Sarah Harriet arose and she has the bad luck to be suspected of complicity in the matter. Dr Burney gives her a letter for James refusing his proposal to take lodgings close at hand and board at Chelsea. Since Maria does not see James she gives the letter to Sarah Harriet, mentioning the proposal and the Doctor's objections to it. Sarah Harriet accuses her of interference and the two elope. Maria's hopeful view that the relationship is brotherly only is countered by the Doctor with a story 'he has heard from her mother' and his horror at his own suspicions prevents him putting about with any confidence the story concocted by the family that Sarah has gone to keep house for her brother since Susan is coming from Ireland to look after Dr Burney. Major Phillips' refusal to allow Susan to make the journey casts further doubts on the plausibility of this explanation.

Quite soon after the elopement, Molly, the maidservant at Chelsea, received a letter from Sarah asking for her clothes and went to Fetter Lane with them. She related that 'the woman of the house emptied their slops for them once or twice a day when Sally had deposited them in a tin pail she had bought, that they cooked their own dinner and went to market and the woman washed for them'. It was also reported that Sarah had never looked so well – 'her face so clear from Humour'. Later Maria reports that the two are living 'in the most grovelling mean style . . . Taken a dirty lodging in a suspicious house in the Tottenham Court Road where they have found out that the Woman's daughter is a Common Prostitute who brings home a different Visitor every night'. Maria finds life at Chelsea very uncomfortable during this period. Dr Burney is bitterly unhappy, and the family are disinclined to believe what they are told about Sarah and James. Maria, for no very good reason, is suspected of encouraging Sarah in her imprudent behaviour.

Tragically Susan never did reach Chelsea, but her daughter Fanny took Sarah's place in her grandfather's home. By that time Maria had become more settled in her mind than she had been for years and had decided to rent a house in Bury St Edmunds where many of her mother's family lived. She wrote to Fanny from her aunt Mrs Allen's, where she was paying a visit, saying that she would go down to Bury at the end of the month, visiting London on the way 'to buy a few necessaries'. She was working, she said, a deep border for a carpet for Mrs Allen's dressing-room, painting a flower-stand and making card-boxes, 'up to my knuckles in paint and size'.

In Bury, Maria finds such happiness as is possible in her situation. She has a bedchamber to herself, after sharing a bed with her maid for two years, 'a very good drawing-room – a small room for poor Stancliff – a very pretty Bedchamber and Dressing Room where my niece and Godman sleep – and a very airy Garret – for a Nice little Maiden whom I have hired as a Female Scrub and give her Four Pounds a year, tea included'. It will be seen that Stancliff has left Rishton and that Maria's niece Mary is with her at last. Maria becomes very friendly with a Lady Peyton and her relatives. Together they do fancy-work and make artificial flowers. She asks for, and is promised, the old spaniel Grog who is past being a sporting dog. 'I have every reason,' she writes to Fanny, 'to be satisfied with my choice of Bury to set up my staff in – I have met with great Civility and a most flattering Reception from all the Family.'

The rest of Maria's life passed uneventfully but she wrote to Fanny until she died in 1821. 'I hear very often,' Fanny commented soon after Maria's marriage, 'from Mrs Rishton whose friendship, affection and confidence will, I believe, end only with our lives.'

5

MARRIAGE AND MISS BURNEY

Fanny Burney had, in the Tingmouth Journal, found a means of enchant-ing her friends. Her second journal, intended for Susan alone, was forwarded by her to an importunate Mr Crisp who kept and enjoyed it as he had Maria's Geneva letters. Susan, in return, sent Fanny a journal of life in Dr Burney's household so unrestrained that she later felt the need to destroy most of it. One wonders what it could possibly have contained: references to Mrs Burney's unreasonable temper, perhaps. Mr Crisp, who had become increasingly disabled by the diseases of old age and was in any case cut off from society at Chessington, began to depend on Fanny's letters for entertainment. She wrote set pieces on Omai, the Otaheitan, and his reactions to sophisticated London society; she wrote on concerts by Signora Agujari, Caterina Gabrielli and the concert at Dr Burney's house for Prince Orloff. She was in the intoxicating situation of an author who has found an appreciative audience, as well as that of a lover who knows how to please his 'flame'. Mr Crisp even went so far – much to Fanny's horror – as to circulate these pieces to his sister Mrs Gast, who passed them on to friends. Fanny must have begun to see herself as a writer. Then all at once an undistinguished young man appeared and offered her marriage.

For a girl without a dowry and with no very dazzling good looks Fanny had had her share of offers. On the occasion when Hetty and Susan were ·taken to school in Paris, Susan's journal mentions a young man in the coach, a lieutenant called Williams, 'who entertained me very much by his ridiculous account of a passion he had conceived for my sister Fanny, whom he saw at the inn'. Was it a joke? It would have been a joke in very doubtful taste if the girl had been totally unattractive.

In her eighteenth year we find Fanny admired at dances by Captain Bloomfield and proposed for by Mr Tomkin whom she had met at a fancy-dress dance disguised as a Dutchman. A Mr Macintosh, a rich young man with a habit of addressing Fanny in indifferent verse, is mentioned at much the same time as the Dutchman and there is talk of a Russian, a M.

Pogenpohl, a 'fine gentleman without any foppery or pretension', who was gallant to Fanny.

All this was before she reached the interesting age of twenty-three, once considered a kind of watershed for young ladies, an age when they must slide unobtrusively into spinsterhood or begin to take their young men seriously. At twenty-three Fanny met Mr Barlow and something crystallized in her mind, if only the certainty that an arranged marriage, a career marriage one might almost call it, was not for her. She had other career interests. The young man was inescapably 'fogrum', as Fulke Greville had taught Charles Burney to call it – well meaning, not interesting enough for Fanny. He had no style. Later, when Crisp was dead and she allowed herself to consider marriages where her heart was not seriously committed, it was only where the men concerned had style, as well as ability and money. But what she really wanted was to love her husband.

On 1 May 1775, a date that would have been appropriate for the beginning of a romance, Fanny went by invitation to Hetty's house to drink tea and meet a family Hetty believed she ought to be kind to. They were a Mrs O'Connor and her daughter by a first marriage, a Miss Dickinson who was deaf and dumb. This family were old acquaintances of Fanny's grandmother Burney, so she was of the party, as well as two aunts. Much more interesting, however, and perhaps a little unexpected, was the presence of a Mr Barlow, a young man who had lodged with Mrs O'Connor for two years. We question whether this was coincidental. Had the family decided it was time Fanny was married or had Barlow asked for help in finding a wife?

There was nothing at all wrong with Mr Barlow. He was short, but even Fanny describes him as handsome. He was well-bred. He was good tempered and sensible and had read quite widely. Just the husband for Fanny, one can imagine them all deciding, and the young man settled in to be what Fanny calls 'prodigiously civil' at once, almost as if he had made his mind up in advance. It was this, in fact, that so alarmed Fanny: 'I could not but observe a *seriousness* of attention much more expressive than complimenting.' She could have tolerated a cat-like aloofness but not this direct approach. Perhaps, too, the situation alarmed her. It had its dangers. Here were the senior women of the family presenting her with a young man who wore an air of unmistakable self-confidence. She scented, doubtless, a trap.

The tea-party developed along far from comfortable lines. When a game of questions was proposed, Mr Barlow asked Fanny 'what she thought was necessary in Love'. She answered, 'Constancy', which cannot really have been much use as a key to how to please her. When the party broke up and another visit was proposed for the following week, he was extremely pressing and hoped to see her there. Worse still, when the older ladies were kissing Fanny goodbye, Barlow with a mumbled apology gave her 'a most ardent salute' and then, standing at the door, watched the coach out of sight. Four days later Fanny received a written declaration, couched in language so studied and elaborate that we realize it must have occupied the whole interval.

Had Mr Barlow been given assurances by Fanny's female relatives that encouraged him to take the situation so much for granted? When one considers the rest of the story it does not seem unlikely. When Fanny complained to her family, it was only to discover that they were on his side. Dr Burney asked 'a great many questions' and then suggested she should write back saying it was too soon to know her own mind. When she objected to this he advised her not to reply at all.

Hetty, the next day, was anxious to persuade Fanny to be more open-minded and, above all, to make one of the return party at Mrs O'Connor's. Her grandmother and her spinster aunts, to her consternation, all spoke up for Mr Barlow and warned her of the fate of spinsterhood. Fanny wrote a formal note discouraging her admirer, only to incur her father's disapproval. By now it was very clear that this was either a deliberate piece of family matchmaking or a chance opportunity they were determined Fanny should snatch at. 'Poor Fanny is such a prude,' Dr Burney had observed of his much-loved daughter. He would not have been surprised then that she had to be coaxed and persuaded before she would listen to an honourable proposal of marriage.

Hetty, to her sister's chagrin, next wrote about the affair to Mr Crisp, 'representing in the strongest light the utility of my listening to Mr Barlow'. His reply gave her the impression that everyone was against her except her father. If he were to join in the chorus of persuasion she would be hard put to it to resist, but she thanked God most gratefully he had not interfered.

Nothing is more startling than the instantaneous fashion in which Fanny rejected her suitors in those early days. 'I took not a moment to deliberate – I felt that my heart was totally insensible' she says. Did she really believe in love at first sight? Or is her reaction that of a girl whose affection lies irretrievably elsewhere? It seems that her writing, and Mr Crisp's approval of it, left no room for any other man.

Samuel Crisp's letter of advice to Fanny was, as always, a model of sound sense and that which he most prided himself upon, worldly wisdom. The young man's character is good (he has heard). His precipitancy is evidence only of a strong passion. He will improve on acquaintance. The family ought to go carefully into details of his income, but if that stands up to scrutiny she should seize her opportunity, since such a chance may not come again. In any case she is to go on seeing him and especially is she to accompany Hetty on the next visit to the O'Connors.

It is not pleasant, in the twentieth century, to watch Fanny's realization of what might happen. The idea that she, the very special Fanny Burney, might be required to make a workaday marriage with a rather undistinguished young man dawns on her gradually and she is afraid. She will not move one inch towards the trap she believes she can see set for her:

> They tell me they do not desire me to marry, but not to give up the power of it without seeing more of the proposer; but this reasoning I cannot give in to – it is foreign to all my notions. How can I see more of Mr Barlow without encouraging him to believe I am willing to think of him? I detest all trifling. If ever I marry, my consent shall be prompt and unaffected.

Mr Barlow was not her style, that much she could tell from the first encounter and from the self-conscious, elaborate letter, so unlike Mr Crisp's aristocratic nonchalance. And to be married for life to someone worthy and dull and – fogrum. She would rather stay unmarried, live with her easy-going father and love Mr Crisp. Accordingly, when the rest of the family paid their return visit to Mrs O'Connor, Fanny defied Mr Crisp's expressed wishes and sent word that she had a cold. Soon after breakfast on the following day a caller arrived at the Burney house and turned out to be Mr Barlow. He was elegantly dressed and stiff with embarrassment. Mr Barlow purported to be paying a formal call to enquire about Miss Burney's cold, but she suspected him of either wishing to 'speak to' her or of trying to find out whether her cold was genuine. After half an hour – the proper duration of a social call – he got up to go, scarcely having exchanged a word with Fanny who had left the conversation to Susan and her mother.

Mr Barlow was nothing if not persevering and the serried ranks of female relatives knew their duty when they saw it. Fanny, conscience-stricken at her own deceit, enquired of them whether her excuse had been accepted by Mr Barlow without question and they instantly saw this as a sign of weakening. A 'chance' meeting was arranged at the grandmother's house, a meeting in which Barlow proceeded along the lines he obviously considered orthodox while Fanny tried in vain to make it clear to him that she was not merely feigning reluctance. Barlow followed this up with yet another letter, hinting terrifyingly that the next step would be a declaration in form and daring to use Fanny's Christian name. (She corrected his lapse by substituting 'Madam' when she copied the letter into her journal.)

It may have been this rash familiarity which convinced Fanny that the situation was getting out of hand. She decided to put an end to the whole business. Naturally she must ask her father's permission before writing to Mr Barlow. Equally naturally, she thought, he would give it. So before she went to the opera that evening with her mother and Susan, she told her father that she intended, with his permission, to write to Mr Barlow in the morning. Interestingly enough her father said little, but asked for the letter and put it in his pocket unread. He had not, in fact, given the permission she required and now she was 'half afraid to ask'. More interestingly still there followed in the early afternoon of the next day another call by Barlow and this time he did ask to 'speak to her'. Dr Burney advised her not to be too hasty. Mrs Burney left the front parlour for the back. Mr Barlow was waiting for her alone.

'He came up to me,' Fanny says, 'with an air of tenderness and satisfaction.' We hold our breath and wait miserably for the situation to crumble. There is some talk of an answer to his first letter, an answer which, Fanny remembers uncomfortably, has not in fact been sent. She tells him that she has no intention of ever marrying but he finds that impossible to believe. He scarcely knows her, she says. He has known her quite long enough, he declares – fifty years could not have more convinced him. Perhaps she has some insuperable objection, he enquires: his situation in life, his character? When she hastens to reassure him on that count, he asks whether he may not speak to her family of 'the state of his ·affairs', that is, his income, and so confirm his total acceptability.

The scene continues and we sympathize with Fanny's admirer. Nothing in his script has prepared him for a girl who has no objections to him but simply will not consider marrying. Mrs Burney and Susan drift in and out on various pretexts, but there is no glad announcement to be made. There is a protracted ritual of farewells. 'He then took his leave – returned back – took leave – and returned again.' He tries to kiss her and she prevents it 'with surprise and displeasure'. She allows him her hand, then withdraws it and rings the bell decisively.

Fanny's relief overcomes her sensitivity. 'I could almost have jumped for joy when he was gone, to think that the affair was thus finally over.' It would be a brutal statement, if we did not know how much she was afraid.

But Fanny's joy is premature. Hetty and her husband call in the evening. When Mr Barlow had taken the precaution of asking Mrs O'Connor whether Fanny had any pre-engagement or whether she had ever expressed any antipathy to him, she had reassured him on both counts and promised to ask Hetty to be his advocate. So after Fanny's refusal Barlow had rather naturally called on Hetty, anxious to know where he had gone wrong. He was disconsolate, feverishly analysing his behaviour and inclined to attribute his failure to his early declaration. Certainly that was not in his favour, but the truth is that nothing could have made him acceptable to Fanny at that point in her life. She was in love with another man.

Hetty had been asked to be Thomas Barlow's advocate and Dr Burney appeared to know this, since he now sent for her upstairs (in his study) and 'made a thousand enquiries'. The next day came the situation Fanny had been dreading. In fear and incredulity she heard her father speak in favour of Mr Barlow and urge her not to be peremptory in the answer she was going to write. Never had she been so distressed. There was no real objection she could make to Mr Barlow. If her father 'advised' her to marry him, she could offer no valid reason why she should not.

Then, at the height of her despair, comes a scene with Dr Burney in which little is said and everything is understood. Fanny goes into the study to say goodnight to her father, hoping, no doubt, for a chance to put her point of view. There is some conversation about a new Court mourning gown for her and for Susan. Dr Burney offers to help the two girls with the expense and hands over the money, after the fashion of fathers who have been a shade too strict with their children. Fanny begs to be allowed to live with him and they embrace fondly while he assures her that she may live with him for ever. Only she is not to be too hasty. Fanny had already written her rejection of Mr Barlow; since she had told him that the letter was written and that it contained a rejection, she saw no sense in writing anything else. 'I rather determined,' she says, 'if my father had persisted in desiring it, to *unsay* a rejection than not to write it after having declared I already had.' But her father never mentioned Mr Barlow again.

Mr Barlow, however, continues to importune Hetty and to ask her to arrange an 'accidental' meeting. When this is denied him he turns up at the Burney house. The visit is shortened by the arrival of other company, but it is evident that Fanny is beginning to feel friendlier to the young man, if only she were not so terrified of being forced into marriage. Mrs Burney makes teasing remarks about 'a gentleman whose visits are admitted'. Mrs O'Connor, in front of Fanny's grandmother and aunts, accuses her of cruelty and of breaking Mr Barlow's heart. James Burney and Maria 'tee-hee'd and made some apt and witty remarks' when they caught sight of the seal on Fanny's letters, a classical female head, which they nicknamed her 'Madonna seal'. They pretended to believe that she had vowed herself to celibacy for ever. But Fanny's is the last word: 'My father and Mr Crisp,' she writes, 'spoil me for every other male creature.'

6

MISS BURNEY'S NOVEL

Mrs Raine Ellis who edited the Early Diary writes of Fanny Burney's journal for 1778 as 'giving a happy ending (befitting a novelist above all others) to all that has gone before in these volumes. It is,' she says, 'the *third volume* of a fresh and lively story which widens and deepens towards its joyous close. A lover made happy, it is true, is not to be found therein, but the pride and happiness of a father and the rapture of the most amiable and affectionate of clever families make the wedding little missed.'

At an age when most girls are concerned only with the business of settling themselves in life by marrying, Fanny was acting as her father's secretary during the time he was writing on his Italian Tour, his German Tour and then his *History of Music*. In the intervals of this work she began drafting her novel, first in rough and then in a handwriting carefully designed to be unlike that in which she copied her father's work, to avoid any possibility of recognition by the publishers who saw it.

The year 1775 was the one in which Fanny made her successful protest against marrying Thomas Barlow. In 1776 the first volume of Charles Burney's *History of Music* was published. He and Mrs Burney then set off for Bristol with Charlotte, leaving Fanny and little Sarah alone in the house since the other young people were on holiday. Singularly little correspondence is preserved from 1776. Madame d'Arblay, writing in her old age, says it was destroyed because it was 'on family subjects'. In early 1777, however, the copying of the rough draft of *Evelina* is under way. It is hinted at first in a letter to Susan: staying with her beloved Mr Crisp at Chessington Fanny writes: '. . . we pass our time here very serenely and, distant as you may think us from the great world, I sometimes find myself in the midst of it, though nobody suspects the brilliancy of the company I occasionally keep.' She is referring, of course, to the titled characters in *Evelina*. We are reminded of Jane Austen's secret writing by Fanny's. 'Do you know,' she says to Susan, 'I write to you every evening while the family play at cards? The folk here often marvel at your ingratitude in sending me so few returns in kind.'

Although there is no journal in the ordinary sense for 1777, there is an account of a visit to Fanny's Uncle Richard at Barborne. After her visit to Chessington, during which she had been free to write undisturbed for many hours of the day, Fanny returned, as she had promised her father, for the party at which she met Mrs Thrale and Dr Johnson for the first time. Before she could well record her impressions for Mr Crisp, Uncle Richard was snatching her off for a visit, the events of which she described in what we now know as the Worcester Journal. The character studies in this journal are rounder and fuller than those in her earlier work, while the lively fun of the amateur performance of *The Way To Keep Him* is quite as amusing as anything in *Evelina*. Fanny has become a novelist.

Uncle Richard arrived, Fanny says, with his son James and his daughter Becky, and these three accompanied her to Barborne Lodge. Here Fanny made the acquaintance of 'Little Nancy', Anna Maria Burney, later called Marianne, the child of Esther and Charles Rousseau Burney and not yet seven years old. Fanny and her husband, General d'Arblay, were later to effect the introduction of Marianne to M. Bourdois which resulted in their marriage.

At Barborne Lodge the excitement of amateur theatricals was under way. Meals were neglected in favour of costume and scenery making or time spent with the hairdresser. The play was *The Way To Keep Him* and Fanny took the part of Mrs Lovemore to the satisfaction of some of the audience, though her uncle reminded her that she did not speak loudly enough: 'Only speak out, Miss Fanny,' said he 'and you leave nothing to wish.' The play was followed by *Tom Thumb* with little Nancy in the hero's part and a great deal of applause.

Fanny's delight in the performance and her terror and self-consciousness at performing in front of even a family audience are characteristic of her. Her usual contempt of clothes is forgotten in her enjoyment of the stage costumes.

James was dressed in a strait body with long sleeves, made of striped lute-string, lapelled with fur and ornamented with small bows of green, blue, garnet and yellow. The back was shaped with red. His coat was pompadour, trimmed with white Persian; his shoes were ornamented with tinsel; he had a fan in his hand, a large hoop on and a cap made of everything that could be devised that was gaudy and extravagant, feathers of an immense height, cut in paper, streamers of ribbons of all colours and old earrings and stone buckles put in his hair for jewels . . . He had the full covering of a modern barber's block, toupée, chignon and curls all put on at once. The height of his head, cap and feathers was prodigious; and, to make him still more

58

violent he had high-heeled shoes on. His face was very delicately rouged and his eyebrows very finely arched . . .

Then Fanny says something about the appearance of the giantess Glumdalca that gives us an insight into her nature in that year of *Evelina*: 'You cannot imagine how impossible it was to look at him, thus transformed, without laughing . . .' If she had kept that innocent sense of the ridiculous, the product of the happy nonsense of a warm-hearted family, and avoided the temptation to be moral or philosophical, what might she not have written after *Evelina* to enhance her reputation.

When Fanny was snatched away by her Uncle Richard to Barborne, she and some of the younger members of her family shared a secret important enough to excite her even without the additional stimulus of theatricals. Her 'Prelude to the Worcester Journal', explaining her neglect of her usual journal during the previous summer, shares the secret with us:

> When with infinite toil and labour [during the last year] I had transcribed [in a feigned hand] the second Volume (of my new Essay) I sent it by my brother [Charles] to Mr Lowndes. The fear of discovery, or of suspicion in the house, made the copying extremely laborious to me; for in the day time I could only take odd moments, so that I was obliged to sit up the greatest part of many nights in order to get it ready. And after all this fagging, Mr Lowndes sent me word that he approved of the book; but could not think of printing it till it was finished; that it would be a great disadvantage to it, and that he would wait my time and hoped to see it again as soon as it was completed.

Madame d'Arblay, as Fanny was to become on marriage, never forgot the warning she had been given by her step-mother years before that a young woman's reputation could not easily survive her being known as a writer. Consequently she was desperate to preserve her anonymity if and when she published her book. The well-known publisher Dodsley refused to consider an anonymous work, and so a lengthy and evasive missive was sent to Mr Lowndes in December asking him to reply to a Mr King at the Orange Coffee House in the Haymarket.

When Mr Lowndes expressed himself willing to read the manuscript, the young people of the family who were in the secret dressed Charles up in 'an old greatcoat and a large old hat, to give him a somewhat antique as well as vulgar disguise'. He was sent out in the dark of the evening with the two volumes that were finished (though the second one may still have been in draft) and in a few days the admirable Mr Lowndes replied briefly: 'I've read and like the manuscript and if you send the rest I'll soon run it over.' His answer is still to be seen in the Barrett Collection in the British Museum, handwritten with a pen dipped in the brown-black oxgall ink of the time, a quick scrawl dashed off with a pen in need of mending. All the amazing events of Fanny's long life were to follow from this brisk acceptance of her first novel.

Fanny was dismayed by the impossiblity of finishing her book now that the family had returned from their summer visits. Only at Chessington did she have all her time to herself. She makes her comment on Lowndes' letter in her journal:

> Now this man, knowing nothing of my situation, supposed, in all probability, that I could seat myself quietly at my bureau and write on with all expedition and ease till the work was finished. But so different was the case that I had hardly time to write half a page in a day; and neither my health nor inclination would allow me to continue my nocturnal scribbling for so long a time as to write first and then copy a whole volume. I was therefore obliged to give the attempt and the affair entirely over for the present.

That was in mid-January and the next months must have been very frustrating for her. Fortunately however she was allowed to visit Chessington in March where she had the opportunity to write her 'journals', as Mr Crisp supposed them to be, during most of the day and evening. It must have been a trial to keep her promise to her father and return in time for Uncle Richard's visit but she was a dutiful daughter. Dutifully she confided in her father before she set out for Worcester that she had plans to publish a novel. He scarcely took her seriously but she felt the better for her confession. By the time she returned from her visit in July the holiday season had begun again, the family dispersed and she was able to work undisturbed until, at the end of August, Mr Crisp and his sister Mrs Gast carried her off to Chessington where, during September and quite unknown to them, she finished the book.

Meanwhile two events, each in its own way devastating, were in preparation for the Burney family. Elizabeth Burney had been in Paris during the summer to collect her favourite daughter Bessie from finishing-school. While her mother was enjoying the girl's obvious social superiority and expensively-developed talents, Bessie eloped with an adventurer called Meeke. Mrs Burney hastened to England and to Streatham where she expected to find her husband, who had recently been engaged at £100 a year to dine with the Thrales once a week and give their eldest daughter a music lesson. Charles Burney was not there but Mrs Thrale, who sounds remarkably smug about the whole business, offered her sympathy and sent her on her way. Later she wrote to Johnson, who was away on a visit:

> Mrs Burney . . . is the Doctor's second wife, you know and had a fine daughter – a great Fortune – by her former husband; whom she has kept some years in France and about two or three Months ago she went over to fetch the Girl home, and I have seen some of her Letters to her Husband expressing the happiness she was enjoying at Paris in Company of this fine Daughter; how she delayed her Return because this Daughter so introduced her into high Company . . . but he writes me word that Mrs Burney was coming over . . . all alone in great Distress, her fine Daughter having eloped from her at Paris.

Charles Burney was soon to have a catastrophe in his own family too serious for smugness on anybody's part and his pity for his wife, his awareness of her enemies' triumph, only foreshadow the other cruel blow he was soon to suffer.

The conduct of young Charles Burney, at Caius College, Cambridge, must, like Bessie's, have seemed to cast a slur on the parents who reared them. It is easy enough for parents to be made to feel a sense of guilt. A daughter who elopes with an adventurer makes a social error of a fatal kind. But a son who steals from his university . . . ? Fanny, many years later, examining Dr Charles Burney's magnificent and scholarly library, thought she saw the impulse that had motivated him – 'a mad rage for possessing a library,' she said. But his career appeared to be destroyed and to the brothers and sisters staunchly supporting him, the older members of the family consulting where they might to give him an alternative career, Charles seemed less than penitent. 'Facile, good-humoured and open to conviction,' was Susan's scathing comment on her brother. Fanny used him as a model for Lionel Tyrold in *Camilla* and it is possible that some of her profits from *Evelina* were diverted towards helping him. His help with the publication of that book had, alas, to be discontinued since he was, the family told everybody, 'in the country'. Edward Francesco Burney, the artist and another of the Worcester cousins, took the completed manuscript to Mr Lowndes in Fleet Street when it was quite finished.

Events moved quickly in the publishing world in those days. By the middle of January Fanny received a private message from her aunts who were in the secret and had already enjoyed the book, saying that a parcel had come for her under the name of Grafton. The parcel was, of course, her novel, accompanied by Mr Lowndes' laconic suggestion that she should correct it for the press. She read it to her aunts as a means of correcting it and persuaded Edward Francesco to act as Charles would have done and return it to the publishers. It was published at the end of January.

Success grew, slowly at first and then wildly. When Dr and Mrs Burney were staying at Streatham the girls seized the opportunity to invite Edward to tea. Then, for a joke, they all went to Bell's Circulating Library to enquire for *Evelina*. It was in all the circulating libraries, Edward was told. Charlotte reported Aunt Anne, who was Charles Burney's sister, and Edward to be reading it aloud (though without revealing the name of the author) to poor cousin Richard the family dandy who had been seriously ill and, what was almost worse, lost the two curls that were obligatory for a fashionable young man.

The ripples spread. Aunt Anne reported 'a thousand things that had been said in its praise', but assured the ever-anxious Fanny that nobody had guessed her authorship and that the book was generally supposed to be a man's. Cousin Becky of Barborne suspects, as her brother Richard has not, that Fanny is the author and writes to Susan saying so. Dr Charles Burney gets hold of it and reads it to his wife in bed while Susan listens to their laughter through the wall. Lady Hales, Mrs Thrale and, unbelievably, Dr Johnson read it and are all delighted. Mrs Williams, Dr Johnson's friend and a minor poetess, begs to borrow it. A charming scene related by Mrs Raine Ellis tells how Richard, restored to health and just about to go home to Worcester, expresses his longing to know the name of the author of his favourite book. Aunt Anne threatens to reveal it if Fanny will not. When Richard is particularly lavish in his praise of Lord Orville, the hero of the book, Fanny lets fall that she does know the name of the writer. He continues to praise the book, saying that no man living, except perhaps Dr Charles Burney, was capable of such insight into character. He continues to beg that Fanny will tell him or that she will write the name if she will not speak it. She writes 'no man', folds the paper, swears him to secrecy and leaves him to open it. After a moment enlightenment dawns and, according to Susan, who is in the room, he colours violently. Then, forgetting the foppish affectations he so loves to assume, he offers to go down on his knees in earnest to the author he has so much admired and who turns out to be none other than his cousin Fanny.

Four months after the publication of *Evelina* Fanny was taken ill and, as a matter of course, sent off to Chessington to recover. She had been under considerable strain and her health was always delicate. Besides, like a great many first novels, *Evelina* had a good deal of its author in it.

Was Evelina Fanny? Fanny's heroine was described as 'the offspring of Nature and of Nature in her simplest attire'. She was a girl then with whom Fanny might well have identified, especially looking back over a gulf of nearly ten years to contemplate herself at seventeen. Evelina was under the care of a Mr Villars who in many ways bore a resemblance to Samuel Crisp. He had been tutor to Evelina's grandfather who had married unwisely. He had brought up the baby girl resulting from this marriage, a Miss Evelyn. She grew up and returned to France to visit her mother, now Mme Duval, a comic Frenchwoman. An attempt was made to force her into marriage (shades of Mr Barlow!) but she preferred to elope with a Sir John Belmont whom she married without a witness. Here we are bound to remember Maria Allen's escapade and Mr Crisp's warnings. Baulked of her fortune, Belmont tore up the marriage certificate and when, cast off by Mme Duval, she had a daughter and died, it was poor Mr Villars who again had the task of bringing up the baby, giving her the euphonious name of Evelina Anville.

Evelina has a dear friend called Maria. She visits London and the play-houses including Drury Lane where Garrick is acting. The Park, the Mall, Kensington Gardens, a private ball and the dress shops are all mentioned. Fashionable linen costumes and hair dressed high over a cushion, both mentioned in Maria's letters to Fanny, are brought into the story. Evelina is accused of a breach of etiquette at a ball and we can find a very close equivalent in Fanny's early journal when she was dancing with Captain Bloomfield. She is taken to Ranelagh, where Hetty went with her cautious Mr Seaton and where Mrs and Miss Allen took Fanny more than once. She is critical of her grandmother Mme Duval in a way that reminds us how little the Burney girls liked their step-mother. A young man boarding with the Brangtons may have owed a little to Mr Barlow. Mrs Selwyn's satirical remarks are like Maria's, while Mr Macartney is said by some to be a portrait of Fanny's brother Charles when he was sent down from Cambridge. All these and other resemblances must certainly have made Fanny somewhat self-conscious when she was identified as author.

But nothing, we surmise, was likely to embarrass Fanny quite so much as the thought that in Lord Orville she had portrayed her ideal lover. He met Evelina at a private ball and was at once impressed by her beauty. He was aristocratic and gentle, almost indifferent to considerations of class or fortune, deferential, flatteringly jealous but well-mannered with it, and so on. Many girls have imagined such a man as a foil to their narcissistic young beauty, Fitzwilliam Darcy cured of his uppishness. The difference between Fanny and most other girls is that in the end Fanny met him and married him, title and all. When she married at forty-two her husband was Lieutenant-General le Comte d'Arblay, an officer of the (Noble) *La Garde du Corps de son Roi* and sometime commandant of Longwy; a knight of the Order of St Louis, the Legion of Honour and the *Lys,* and his character resembled Lord Orville's as closely as mortal man may hope to come.

(*above*) The Burney family.
From left to right: Charles,
Dr Burney, Fanny, the first
Mrs Burney and Susan (*from
The History of Silhouettes
by E. Nevill Jackson,
published by Methuen. Artist
and location unknown*)

(*left*) Dr Charles Burney
by Joshua Reynolds
(*National Portrait Gallery*)

The house in St Martin's Street (*from* The House in St Martin's Street *by Constance Hill, published by John Lane*)

The library or music-room in St Martin's Street (*from* The House is St Martin's Street *by Constance Hill, published by John Lane*)

7

MISS BURNEY AT STREATHAM

'But Mrs Thrale – she – she is the goddess of my idolatry. What an *éloge* is hers!' So Fanny wrote when the first praise of *Evelina* was beginning to come in. The aunts and sisters and cousins all said they had enjoyed the book. Her father had dazzled her with his critical approval. But Mrs Thrale was a different matter. She was the friend and rival of Mrs Cholmondely, one of London's social dictators. She was Dr Burney's patron in the sense that she paid him to dine at Streatham once a week and give her daughter Queeney a music lesson before dinner. And more than that, much more, she was the friend and dear hostess of Samuel Johnson. Scarcely a month after Mrs Thrale's ecstatic praise of *Evelina,* occurred the scene Fanny was to describe in her old age to Sir Walter Scott. Hearing, through Susan, of Johnson's admiration of her book, she danced an impromptu jig round the mulberry tree in the garden at Chessington, to the bewilderment of Mr Crisp who was not yet in the secret.

Mr Arthur Tourtellot, in his book on Fanny Burney, tells a wicked story about Mrs Thrale's first interest in *Evelina*. It seems that Mrs Cholmondely, quite by chance, read and liked the new anonymous novel. Mrs Cholmondely was connected to both the aristocracy and the stage, for her husband was the son of the Earl of Cholmondely and nephew of Horace Walpole, while her sister was the popular Peg Woffington, an actress famed for her breeches parts. As a hostess Mrs Cholmondely was anxious to keep up her reputation for literary taste, so she quickly arranged a tea-party for about forty or fifty of her closest friends, including Dr Burney and Dr Johnson, and left the book conspicuously on a centre table for her guests to pick up. As might have been predicted, Dr Johnson pored over the book and then announced his approval to his hostess very loudly indeed for all to hear. The ruse worked, it seems, and such guests as Burke and Sir Joshua Reynolds went away to read the book and to report back enthusiastically their appreciation of Mrs Cholmondely's discernment. Delighted by her success, she promised to discover the name of the writer.

Mrs Thrale, piqued by her rival's triumph, if we are to believe Mr Tourtellot, determined that she would be the first to discover who, in fact, wrote *Evelina* and might well have been unsuccessful had it not been for Dr Burney. Somewhere in his busy life someone had mentioned writing a book and had told him the name of it. He asked for *The Monthly Review*, read the account of the novel carefully and then sent the servant out to buy Fanny's book. When Mrs Thrale asked his opinion of *Evelina* he was able to tell her what all London wanted to know. Mrs Thrale could scarcely recall the quiet girl she had met at Dr Burney's musical evening, but she saw a way to score over Mrs Cholmondely. Fanny was invited to Streatham.

Fanny's agonized concealment of authorship, disregarded by her father as soon as he saw that the novel was creditable, was far more important to her than her family were able to realize. An observer does not benefit from being observed. In spite of her admiration for Mrs Thrale and, of course, for Dr Johnson she could hardly be persuaded to accept the invitation, but Dr Burney insisted. Nowhere in England would she meet such distinguished writers, such influential people. And Mrs Thrale could be very disarming: 'We all long to know her,' she told Dr Burney. 'I am now at the summit of a high hill,' Fanny wrote to her sister Susan that summer. Fearfully she spoke of the caverns, gulfs, pits and precipices below. Of the great heights visible to her now she said simply, 'I have not the strength to attempt climbing them.' But her father's ambition and the enthusiasm of Mrs Thrale and Dr Johnson was to encourage her in a more persevering frame of mind.

It is not at first sight easy for us to see how Mrs Thrale could offer social advancement to a Burney who had been accustomed from her earliest years to the company of such family visitors as Garrick and Nollekens, of Dr Hawkesworth, the editor of Byron's and Cook's Voyages, as well as Mason the poet and Barry the painter. But the Burneys and Mr Crisp, for all their studied unconventionality, were well able to appreciate the usefulness of the connection. Mrs Thrale had been born a Salusbury and boasted that this powerful Welsh family traced its descent from an illegitimate son of Henry VII through Katherine of Beraine. But none of this mattered beside the fact that Hester Salusbury, later Thrale, had used her natural intelligence and literary taste, together with the lure of Johnson's presence and the generously-spent money of her rich brewer husband, to set up a very distinguished social circle indeed. The playwright Arthur Murphy was constantly in the house and he had introduced into it Samuel Johnson who made Streatham his base for many years. The wit Lord Mulgrave, Sir Philips Jennings Clerke, Edmund Burke, Windham, Boswell, Sir Joshua Reynolds, Garrick (who had been Johnson's pupil when he ran a school), Sir William Weller Pepys, Mrs Montagu, Mrs Boscawen and other Blues such as Mrs Vesey and Mrs Chapone all visited Streatham, ate Henry Thrale's impressive dinners and joined in the conversation on books. There was nobody one might not meet at Mrs Thrale's, and she was extending her circle of acquaintances all the time. By Fanny's first visit (exploratory on both sides), Hester Thrale had been presented at Court and had even visited the more interesting and influential Devonshire House, the centre of the Whig party.

The Thrale marriage had been arranged when all other means of obtaining a comfortable settlement for Hester Salusbury had failed. Her parents had been Hester Maria Cotton, sister of Sir Robert Cotton, owner of the estate of Lleweney, and John Salusbury of Bach-y-Craig, with whom she had fallen irremediably in love. John, though educated at Cambridge and commissioned in the militia, had no money. He had been expensively reared on loans and mortgages and was also seriously in debt. Hester Maria, refusing all other offers of marriage, paid his debts, rented a house, Bodvel Hall in Caenarvonshire, and married him. Here Hester was born to be the only living child of parents who were soon chafing against the poverty and domesticity of a lot their own romanticism had brought upon them.

Six or seven years of this were more than enough for young Mrs Salusbury. Her husband's mother died at Bach-y-Craig, but the estate was too heavily indebted to be of use. There was nothing for it, she decided (for she had from the first taken all the decisions) but to go back to her brother Sir Robert Cotton, using little Hester as a means of reconciliation. The plan succeeded admirably. Hester, a pretty, precocious child, educated by her parents in French until she was almost bilingual, pleased the childless widower. The Salusbury's were set up in London, first in King Street, Soho and later in Albemarle Street. John Salusbury, never a favourite of Sir Robert's and now regarded as distinctly superfluous by his family, was sent back to Flintshire to attempt to straighten out his business affairs. Here he inevitably fell into the hands of swindlers, while little Hester was openly named Sir Robert's heir.

Then calamity struck. Sir Robert died suddenly and intestate. The John Salusburys were poorer than before. But it was not long before Hester was once again admired for her precocity and again by somebody with money. Thomas, John's younger brother had achieved riches by marrying a cultivated but unattractive heiress. Since his wife's frail health resulted in childlessness, she took great delight in the company of her niece, who studied Italian and Spanish to please her. By the time Hester was seventeen her abilities were such that Lady Salusbury (for Thomas had succeeded to his father-in-law's position in the Admiralty and with it a knighthood) decided to engage a tutor for her. Arthur Collier came into her life, destined to have almost as powerful an influence on the young girl as Daddy Crisp had had on Fanny Burney. It was too late (fortunately, perhaps) to impose strict academic discipline on Hester's learning. Collier and his friends wisely concentrated on stimulating her developing mind and encouraging her to write, especially verses.

When Hester reached the age of nineteen in 1761, her future seemed assured. Sir Thomas, now a widower, was keeping her parents and she was acquiring a reputation as a writer of promise. Then two newcomers appeared in the neighbourhood of Offley Park. The first and perhaps the more disastrous was the honourable Mrs King, a widow. She promptly began a successful wooing of Sir Thomas, so causing Hester to be disinherited once again. The other was that quite extraordinary Prince Charming, Henry Thrale, a young man described by Sir Thomas, who had met him several times in London, as 'excellent . . . incomparable . . . a Model of Perfection'.

At this stage of his life, despite his lack of aristocratic family connections, Henry Thrale was in fact a very presentable *parti*. Sir Thomas had obviously brought him back from London to his favourite niece in much the same spirit as that in which a mother cat brings a particularly fat mouse home to her kitchen. 'A tall and good-looking man in an ordinary sort of way', is the most usual description of him; presentable, without being handsome, seems to be the general opinion. He was trade indeed, but second generation trade. He was inclined to insist that his family had risen from poverty by means of the brewing trade, but he had been educated at Oxford and possibly Eton, sent on the Grand Tour with William Henry Lyttelton, later Lord Westcote (his father paying the expenses for both) and allowed £1000 a year to become a fashionable young man about town, drinking, gambling and acquiring quite a reputation with the girls.

As soon as Henry Thrale's father died, however, he settled down to run the family business and even attempted a parliamentary career. Boswell describes him only two or three years later as 'one of the most eminent brewers in England and Member of Parliament for the Borough of

Southwark. Foreigners,' he goes on to remark, 'are not a little amazed when they hear of brewers, distillers and men in similar departments of trade, held forth as persons of considerable consequence. In this great commercial country it is natural that a situation which produces much wealth should be consideed very respectable; and, no doubt,' he adds without marked enthusiasm, 'honest industry is entitled to esteem.' Dr Johnson, who had every reason to feel warmly towards Thrale, observed more absolutely: 'An English Merchant is a new species of Gentleman.'

The courtship that followed Henry Thrale's arrival at Offley was remarkable even at a time of arranged marriages. Secure in the admiration of Sir Thomas, who had promised his niece as much as £30,000 when she married with his approval, Thrale set himself to capture the next most important fortress, Mrs Salusbury's heart. The picture we have of her by Zoffany shows a forbidding countenance and severe widow's weeds, but she was much loved by her daughter and by the man who soon became her son-in-law. Henry Thrale saw no great need to break down the opposition of Hester herself and did not attempt it. John Salusbury's dislike of Thrale, Dr Collier's possibly jealous opposition and the malign mischief-making of Thelwall Salusbury, Hester's cousin and rejected suitor, were all check-mated by the irrefutable fact that Sir Thomas looked like marrying again, that he would part with large sums of money only as a settlement on Hester's marriage to an acceptable suitor and that if she delayed she might easily lose everything. Thrale's proposal – written to Mr and Mrs Salusbury – was duly accepted by the latter. John Salusbury, who was by no means willing to accept the proposal but from whose hands all vestige of family authority had long since been relinquished, had a stroke brought on by fury at the marriage arrangements and died.

Henry Thrale took his young, spoilt, poetry-writing wife to the house his father had built in Streatham, a country house in what is now an inner suburb. Professor James Clifford describes this house as facing directly on to Tooting Upper Common. 'A sweeping drive of a hundred yards led from the lodge gates to a compact, three-storey brick house, surrounded by a park of about a hundred acres. At the back of the house were farm buildings, domestic offices, green-houses, stables and an ice-house. Behind these and to the west was the kitchen garden, with forcing-frames for grapes, melons, peaches and nectarines.' By the time Fanny Burney joined the Thrales at Streatham various additions had been made, including a fine library and a summer-house for Johnson to work in.

The family business in Southwark was a great deal less comfortably housed and in winter when, because the six-mile drive to and from Southwark was endangered by highwaymen, Henry Thrale insisted upon his family living there, few people were inclined to visit: 'The house at Southwark was appalling,' C. E. Vulliamy tells us in his book, *Mrs Thrale of Streatham*. 'It stood in Deadman's Place [now Park Street] near Bandyleg Walk, Dirty Lane, the Naked Boy, the Clink, Frying Pan Alley and St Mary Overy's Dock. It was in the neighbourhood of prisons, meeting-houses, burial-places, timber-yards, bleaching-grounds and hospitals. Near the brewery were a few forlorn trees.' Streatham, with its host of servants and the pleasures of its table, was always the social centre for the Thrales.

As was the custom for a newly-married couple, Henry and Hester Thrale took guests with them to Streatham to relieve the tensions of their newly-formed relationship. Mrs Salusbury and a cousin, Hester Cotton, stayed for a time and Arthur Murphy, the playwright, Henry Thrale's inseparable university friend, was constantly in the house, even when the Thrales were at Southwark. Arthur Murphy's interest in Hester's writing, a matter her husband cared little about, went far towards relieving her loneliness. A very little later, some two years after the marriage, he introduced Johnson to the Thrales. This unlikely house-guest was to provide Hester Thrale's greatest comfort during a life in which twelve confinements were to follow each other with scarcely an interval, most of them resulting, disappointingly, in the birth of yet another girl and all too many of them producing those sad children who were to die in infancy.

Dr Johnson began by dining with the Thrales on Thursdays, increasing his visits when he grew more fond, as he undoubtedly did, of his host and hostess. His manner and appearance repelled many women less discerning than Mrs Thrale. Even his biographer, Sir John Hawkins, who admired him, speaks plainly in the matter:

> The great bushy wig, which throughout his life he affected to wear, by that closeness of texture which it had contracted and been suffered to retain, was ever nearly as impenetrable by a comb as a quickset hedge; and little of the dust that had once settled on his outer garments was ever known to have been disturbed by the brush.

The lack of sight in his left eye, the result of scrofula, the twist in his shoulders that made his wig sit awry, the nervous twitching and the shambling gait alarmed those who were making his first acquaintance. Fanny Burney describes him later at St Martin's Street when the Thrales had done their best to make him presentable. On his first introduction to them he was still in that stage of slovenliness of which Hawkins notes:

'At meals, he made a book serve him for a plate . . . he very seldom changed his linen or washed himself.'

We may speculate on whether the chief attraction of the Thrales for Johnson did not at first consist in their magnificent dinners. Hester Thrale never went into the kitchen. Food was her husband's hobby and, ultimately, a contributory cause of his death. Mr Crisp wrote to his sister Mrs Gast after he had been entertained by the Thrales:

> I met a vast deal of Company at Streatham, where everything was most splendid and magnificent – two courses of 21 dishes each, besides Removes; and after that a dessert of a piece with the Dinner – Pines and Fruits of all Sorts, Ices, Creams etc. etc. etc. without end – everything in plate, of which such a profusion, and such a Side Board: I never saw so much at any Nobleman's.

Johnson was always a voracious eater, with a particular passion for fresh fruit which it cannot easily have been possible to gratify in Fleet Street during the eighteenth century. While the Thrales were revelling in his literary conversation at those Thursday dinners, his own thoughts may have been on a lower plane.

A genuine friendship grew up between Henry Thrale and Samuel Johnson, based perhaps on common hypochondria and compensatory eating but certainly also on mutual respect. Finding Johnson ill at his home in Johnson's Court, a prey to the melancholy that so haunted him, Thrale abruptly arranged for his removal to Streatham where for the next sixteen years he would be cared for and have six or seven peaches before breakfast if he wanted them. Hester Thrale was ordered to arrange the details of this beneficial plan and in doing so she provided herself with the most extraordinary solution she could have imagined to her neglected state.

From his first acquaintance with her, Johnson treated Hester Thrale's writing with respect. She had his encouragement and his talk about the new writers at a time when maternity might otherwise have engrossed her whole mind. Johnson enjoyed her children and came to be very fond of her. He it was who suggested she keep a journal, a record of her daily life which might indulge her pleasure in writing and at the same time focus her interest on her daily life. The Family Book, as it was called, was meant to be a record of the lives of the twelve Thrale children, their growth and their health and their interests, almost a joint and minutely particularized biography. Mrs Thrale's self-centredness was such that it turned into a more personal diary, known now as Thraliana, fascinating for the comments she makes on people and events. Henry Thrale played his part;

73

he saw to it that Johnson's clothes were clean and of sober good quality with silver buttons, that he wore silver buckles in his shoes (though Boswell says he refused to give more than a guinea a pair for them) and changed his shirt at seemly intervals. When there were visitors to dinner it was the task of a servant to stand outside the dining-room door ready to provide Johnson with a company wig instead of the everyday one his poor sight had caused him to frizzle in the candle. Perhaps this company wig was the one Boswell describes as bought during their travels in France, 'A Paris-made wig of handsome construction'.

Meanwhile Johnson went back to Fleet Street every Saturday to provide three good dinners for his strange collection of lodgers before returning to the Thrales on Monday. 'The lame, the blind, the sick and the sorrowful,' Mrs Piozzi (as Mrs Thrale later became) observes in her Anecdotes, 'found a sure retreat from all the evils whence his little income could secure them.' Mrs Anna Williams, the blind writer of verses, Francis Barber, the negro servant to whom Johnson attempted to teach Latin and Greek, Mr Robert Levet, a general practitioner among the very poor, paid, as often as not, in gin, were among those who depended on his generosity. Since he knew from experience how unpleasant it was to be poor and proud, Johnson took great care to see that in all his giving he gave in friendship and preserved the dignity of the unfortunate.

For the Thrales the care of Johnson, like his care of his lodgers, was a duty undertaken out of respect and affection. But their reward was considerable and immediate. The constraint between an ill-assorted husband and wife was replaced by conversation so lively that men of some distinction began to make their way to the Thrales' dinner-table. Mrs Thrale achieved a reputation, not quite as a Blue, but certainly as a woman before whom the Blues might display their plumage. Johnson was given the agreeable task of overseeing the extension of the Streatham Place Library. As well as 'the delights of a villa and the convenience of an equipage' he now had as many books as he needed conveniently at hand. Later the learned ladies came to Streatham, Mrs Montagu and Sophie Streatfeild, who also had been tutored by Dr Collier, and then Miss Burney. By the time of her arrival, Mrs Thrale had, with Dr Johnson's help, emerged from her twelve confinements and the loss of eight children, including her favourite son Henry, as vivid a personality as ever she was and with her zest for living quite undiminished.

Into this situation came Fanny Burney, fresh from her unexpected and delightful triumph with her first novel *Evelina*. Mrs Thrale, who had known and loved Dr Burney for a great many years without ever taking notice of his shy daughter, believed by some to be retarded, had coaxed her to make the visit and flattered her into repeating it. Fanny believed that her reason was compounded of admiration and affection, and offered, at first, much the same in return. But Mrs Thrale, who was a very feminine woman, offered little sincere admiration to any of the female race. Fanny, comparatively sexless, had affection to offer everywhere, to sisters, old gentlemen, relatives, so long as she could respect the morals of the objects of her idolatry. So in August 1778 we find Mrs Thrale observing of Fanny: 'Her grace is the grace of an actress, not a woman of fashion – how should it? The Burneys are, I believe, a very low race of mortals. Her conversation would be more pleasing if she thought less of herself.' At the same time Fanny is describing Mrs Thrale as 'a goddess' and allowing herself an unbridled enthusiasm for her kind hostess. Yet the friendship between the two women is conducted on so rapturous a plane that it is easy to lose sight of the ambition that inspired them both.

Hester Thrale was in this summer about thirty-eight or -nine. In June she had given birth to little Henrietta, the last of her children by Thrale and one who was not to die for nearly five years. Her husband was at the peak of his prosperity, building the new library at Streatham and commissioning eleven portraits by Reynolds of famous friends of the Thrales, including Dr Burney, to hang round it. His health was already failing. She was short and thickset, with large 'Salusbury hands' capable of dealing out the brisk blows her children complained of. She had fine grey eyes and chestnut hair. Charlotte Burney writes in 1778 when Hester Thrale was thirty-seven: 'I fancy she is about thirty tho' she hardly looks twenty-eight, for she is blooming and pretty enough to prove that nature has not been a little partial to her in any respect.'

Fanny's first visit to Streatham was managed so tactfully by her hostess that she was willing to go again, and not only to go but to stay. The first and most important difficulty was the question of how Miss Burney was to be flattered without any mention being made of her book, since she would retreat into agonies of shyness if any reference was made to it. She combined a retiring temperament with a keen sense of her own value and importance, and it is amusing to note Mrs Thrale's ability to adjust to both these characteristics. 'Though she was so very civil,' Fanny writes of her, 'she did not even *hint* at my book, and I love her much more than ever for her delicacy in avoiding a subject which she could not but see would have greatly embarrassed me.' She also records carefully all the eulogies in Mrs Thrale's letters and also her remark that 'she should always think herself much obliged to Dr Burney for his goodness in bringing me, which she looked upon as a very great favour'.

Before the month was out Fanny was back at Streatham for a longer visit. This time there were no complaints of dusty roads, no anxieties. Her rapturous appreciation, as evidenced in her journal, was all-inclusive. Even the journey was 'charming'. Queeney, Mrs Thrale's eldest daughter, has never in her life been described as charming, but Fanny concedes, 'I begin to like her'. Henry Thrale, whose indifferent health made him a lethargic host, is moralized upon forgivingly. But Dr Johnson was at his best, gaily sociable and good-humoured, insisting that Fanny required a bacon and egg supper (after a Streatham Place dinner!) and seizing her hand at breakfast and kissing it. He also, to her delighted horror, teased her about her book, while Mrs Thrale tried in vain to change the topic of conversation. Johnson loved children and the rather immature Miss Burney alarmed him much less than more worldly ladies often did.

But Mrs Thrale! Fanny declared herself so much in love with Mrs Thrale that she had better say no more. Very little later in the journal, however, she is irresistibly drawn back to the subject:

> But I fear to say all I think at present of Mrs Thrale, lest some flaws should appear by and by that may make me think differently. And yet, why should I not indulge the *now* as well as the *then,* since it will be with so much more pleasure? In short, I do think her delightful; she has talents to create admiration, good humour to excite love, understanding to give entertainment and a heart which, like my dear father's, seems already fitted for another world.

Fanny was wiser than she knew in expressing some reservations about a woman as vital and changeable as Hester Thrale. The fashion of the day was for emotional attachments between women. No doubt some escape was needed from the brutal coarseness of a woman's lot. Romanticism about eighteenth-century marriage would have been ludicrous, but romanticism about friendship was harmless enough. Hester Thrale, if Fanny had known it, was far too robust a character to be pinned down in lapidary phrases. She it was who began to learn Hebrew at sixty-four, who gave a ball for six hundred people on her eightieth birthday and danced until the small hours of the morning. She it was who, as she lay dying, too weak for witticisms, sketched the outline of a coffin in the air to amuse her friend Dr Gibbes. So the ecstatic letters exchanged between the two women and the hour-long conversations in adjacent bedrooms seemed the very extreme of intimacy, but in the end, Hester Thrale's greed for living and

Fanny's closeness and propriety showed themselves to be incompatible.

Among the topics of the long private conversations was surely the provision of a husband for Fanny, which Mrs Thrale seemed to regard as her first consideration. Next she would set about establishing Fanny as a writer, but first, a husband: time was running out and Fanny was in her late twenties now.

The candidates put forward (but never by themselves) as possible husbands for Fanny are a disturbing selection. By holding firmly in mind that Fanny, dowerless and of less than aristocratic family, could expect money in a husband only if she was willing to forgo almost everything else, we can just, but only just, avoid the suspicion of contempt on Mrs Thrale's part for Fanny or for the institution of marriage. There was Sir John Lade, seven years Fanny's junior and nephew of Mr Thrale. It was considered that with his money to support her Fanny would be free to write, but his weak character is evidenced by the speed with which he frittered away his estates. Jeremiah Crutchley, possibly an illegitimate son of Mr Thrale, but for some reason wealthy, was strongly fancied but he developed an interest in Queeny, possibly his half-sister. A Mr Smith, second cousin to Mr Thrale, was poor, so marriage to him would have defeated its purpose. Mr Rose Fuller, a neighbour, appears to have been a pleasant bore and Captain Fuller, a military man might have done very well, but nothing came of it.

Scarcely more successful was Mrs Thrale in her attempts to forward Fanny's literary career. Arthur Murphy, a successful playwright even if we no longer interest ourselves in his plays, was egged on to give her advice. 'If I,' said Mr Murphy, looking very archly, 'had written a certain book – a book I won't name, but a book I have lately read – I would next write a comedy.' Mrs Thrale spent three hours alone with Fanny, putting the advantages of the idea to her, telling her of the large sums Hannah More had obtained by *her* play and suggesting that both Murphy and Dr Johnson would help her with the publicity. Later she went a little further: 'My ambition is that Johnson should write your prologue and Murphy your epilogue; then I shall be quite happy.' Dr Johnson, when consulted, encouraged her in the idea but advised her to keep the project a secret. Daddy Crisp at Chessington, who, despite his eagerness to see Fanny among the wits must have looked back with regret to the time when he was her chief adviser, gave a grudging assent to the proposal. His own play, *Virginia*, which had been entirely unsuccessful, had proved to him the difficulties of dramatic composition.

So *The Witlings* was written and the secret kept by a silent young woman who knew how to listen and give nothing away. 'Mrs Montagu, Mrs Greville, Mrs Crewe, Sir Joshua Reynolds, Mrs Cholmondeley and many inferior etceteras, think they have an equal claim, one with the other, to my confidence,' Fanny remarks about this time, with her characteristic air of enjoying a secret. The difference between her own demure appearance and the shrewd thoughts that occupied her mind always delighted Fanny. She was at this time almost constantly at Streatham where the house rule was that each occupant should have the morning to himself. Mrs Thrale and she were both hard at work. Presently we find her noting: 'The long and the short of it is, I have devoted them [her private hours] to writing and I have finished a play.' Not entirely irrelevantly, she adds: '*Evelina* continues to sell in a most wonderful manner.'

On 21 May the Thrales left Streatham for Brighton where they took their usual lodgings in West Street (the court end of the town). Fanny was delighted with the journey, the scenery and, of course, her hostess. Mr Thrale and Queeney were becoming more congenial to her every day. To add to everyone's enjoyment Arthur Murphy drew up in a chaise at the door soon after they arrived. He made a great many coquettish references to *The Witlings,* which he was reading. Dr Delap, Bishop of Peterborough, also turned up with *his* play, which Mr Thrale was trying to recommend to Dr Johnson. Quite soon this was presented to Fanny for criticism and the Brighton lodgings were soon farcically astir with veiled references to both plays and the alarm of their bashful writers at any hint of their anonymous authorship. 'During dinner,' Fanny notes, 'I observed that Mr Murphy watched me almost incessantly, with such archness of countenance that I could hardly look at him; and Dr Delap did the same, with an earnestness of gravity that was truly solemn.'

After their return to Streatham at the end of May, Mrs Thrale and indeed the whole family were horrified by Henry Thrale's first stroke. It was not his first serious illness: nearly three years before an infection described as either cancerous or venereal had been happily resolved as the latter. But it was the beginning of the period of ill-health that resulted in his death and it was directly caused by anxiety over business affairs. On 8 June, soon after the return from Brighton, Thrale had visited his sister Mrs Nesbitt to hear the reading of her husband's will. The two men had been speculating jointly in business affairs, Thrale standing security for his brother-in-law for a very considerable amount. When the terms of the will revealed that the estate was in alarming difficulties, the effect on

Thrale was profound. He collapsed at dinner and was brought back unconscious to Streatham by his sister. Mrs Thrale rushed to his side and Dr Burney (for Johnson was in Lichfield) hastened to fetch a physician from London.

The attack, though it was soon over, left Thrale more lethargic than ever and in an almost permanent state of depression. His sole pleasure now lay in voracious eating, which he could not control, even on doctors' orders. The food at Streatham had always been a speciality of the house and a macabre effect must have been created when the Master sat at his dinner table gorging himself, as all the guests were aware, into an imminent grave.

Hester Thrale was now responsible for two men, Johnson and her husband, both prone to the 'black melancholy' of which the late eighteenth century complains so often and so pitiably. One marvels at the indomitable nature of this woman who endured one catastrophe after another and remained unbreakable. The time was to come when even her cold Thrale daughters pitied her state and decided on the advice of the doctors that she must not be racked further. Now she confided her misery and irritation to her journal only and set about filling the Streatham house with friends to keep Thrale's spirits at their precariously maintained and only moderately equable level.

These friends in their turn posed problems. Dr Delap, who was usually a considerable comfort to Hester Thrale, was at this time trying to persuade Johnson to write a prologue for his play, *The Royal Suppliants,* which was to be put on at Drury Lane chiefly because of Mrs Thrale's intervention with Sheridan. She finally wrote the prologue herself, in a coach, driving about London, trying to find an absconding brewery clerk. Sophie Streatfeild, the beautiful Greek scholar with whom Henry Thrale was probably having an *affaire,* must also have been a very demanding guest, and the gentlemen – perhaps out of kindness to their hostess – talked of her continually with a gently disparaging mockery. As for Miss Burney, she little knew at the time (Queeney was to enlighten her later) how her touchiness and fear of patronage annoyed her hostess. Mr Thrale had insisted on paying for 'a suit of gauze lino' (i.e. linen) for Fanny and probably for the remarkable hats in which she and Queeney are usually depicted, since it is likely that they came from Mrs Thrale's milliner. But in spite of her being supplied, Mrs Thrale says, with 'every wearable, indeed, every wishable', the ungrateful young woman liked to go home at intervals, if only to write *Cecilia.* Her knack of falling ill when Mrs Thrale was ill herself or had quite enough nursing on her hands must have been equally hard to bear:

> Fanny Burney [Mrs Thrale writes] has kept her room here in my house with a Fever, or something she called a Fever: I gave her every Medcine and every slop with my own hand; took away her dirty Cups, Spoons etc., moved her Tables, in short was Doctor and Nurse and Maid – for I did not like the Servants should have additional Trouble lest they should hate her for't – and now – with the true Gratitude of a Wit, She tells me that the World thinks the better of me for my Civilities to her. It does! does it?

Yet the virtue of cheerfulness, so much prized in women when houses and nurseries were full, never deserted Mrs Thrale and whatever she wrote in her journal she behaved with unfailing sweetness to all the strange characters who ate at her table and shared the dazzling conversation.

By the end of 1778 Mrs Thrale suspected that she was pregnant again, but, not surprisingly, she miscarried. Trouble with the clerks at the brewery seemed to necessitate the Master's presence. He insisted on Hester's accompanying him to Southwark. The unsprung coach of the day was a cruel conveyance for a woman whose child was already due. But Hester Thrale endured the journey stoically and on her return was carried to her room where she fainted five times and then 'miscarried in the utmost Agony before they could get me into bed'. The child was a boy, full term and without blemish. Thrale would never come so close to fathering a male heir in his life again.

Henry Thrale was in no state to comfort his wife. His mood was now so depressive that he was unable to grieve with her or help her recover her spirits. She wrote *Three Dialogues by Hester Lynch Thrale* and in these allowed herself to speculate on the reactions of her friends to news of her death, an idea combining melancholy and a kind of sardonic humour in a manner characteristic of Mrs Thrale. Her friends appear and speak, each of them with his individual and maddening foible brought into the open, Thrale boorish, Johnson belligerent, Seward hypochondriac. It is the work of a woman surrounded by friends and yet pathetically alone.

It was at this time the opinion of the doctors that both husband and wife needed a holiday. Henry Thrale, a combination now of lethargy and restlessness, decided on Brighton but the journey was first made through Sevenoaks to Tunbridge Wells where the Streatfeilds lived. Fanny Burney went with them. Mrs Thrale had hoped that a meeting with Sophia Streatfeild would reanimate her husband, but the two 'met with but little

80

eagerness on either side'. In Brighton little more excitement was to be found. Queeney and Fanny longed for London. The Thrales spent some of their time discussing Henry Thrale's will and choosing executors, but hunting and eating were the invalid's chief occupations. The weather was chilly and when November came and Mr Thrale developed a cold, it seemed wise to return to Streatham. At Reigate he collapsed in a terrifying manner. Mrs Thrale's strength of character asserted itself. She sent two servants ahead to remind them at the inn that dinner had been booked, but still there was no warm room for the patient, no fire and no dinner. She 'worked like a servant: she lighted the fire with her own hands – took the bellows and made such a one as might have roasted an ox in ten minutes'. Fanny Burney had no help to offer in the situation, but Mrs Thrale had always been equally 'at home in the salon, library, sickroom or nursery'.

When Henry Thrale was sufficiently recovered, they continued their journey to Streatham where Fanny almost immediately became ill and took to her bed. 'Sweet Mrs Thrale,' she records, 'nursed me most tenderly.' She does not seem to have been totally incapacitated. She pops downstairs for a hand of bridge with Mr Thrale and is soon out of bed and installed in Mrs Thrale's dressing-room, wrapped up in a bundle of cloaks to have dinner. Dr Johnson and Arthur Murphy insist on visiting her, Murphy witty and flattering about her play, *The Witlings,* which her father and Mr Crisp had now finally decided would not do. Satire of the great ladies of the literary scene was hardly likely to forward Miss Burney's career they said. They advised against production and the play was reluctantly abandoned by its author who began, instead, on *Cecilia.* But a harassed Mrs Thrale could hardly persuade Murphy out of her dressing-room so anxious was he to tell Fanny how much he liked *The Witlings.*

In March William Weller Pepys, brother of Sir Lucas Pepys the distinguished physician and 'prime minister' of Mrs Montagu, the 'Queen of the Blues', wrote to Mrs Thrale giving her advice on the management of Thrale during the forthcoming elections. He had had a second stroke in late February and it was important to conceal his state of health from the voters. Accordingly the Thrales and Fanny Burney went on a prolonged visit to Bath so that the candidate for election could be kept well away from Southwark and other areas of political activity. Here, as her Bath Journal shows, Fanny Burney was regarded as a celebrity, Mrs Thrale as a friend and rival wit of Mrs Montagu and the new acquaintances they both made included wits and Blues of some distinction.

Mrs Thrale and Fanny, at Johnson's request, now began a series of visits to London, chiefly for electioneering purposes. Queeney was left in charge of the household, including her father, and her mother rejoined her in Bath after a week of strenuous activity. The Gordon Riots, anti-Catholic demonstrations led by Sir George Gordon, broke out in London and spread to some provincial towns including Bath. Here the rumour started that Thrale was a Roman Catholic. It even appeared in the Bath and Bristol newspaper and Mrs Thrale felt constrained to remove the family to Brighton for safety at dead of night. When she visited Southwark to see how the brewery had fared – for breweries as well as Roman Catholic chapels were among the targets of the mob – she discovered that the cool-headed Perkins had calmed the rioters with food and free beer, and so prevented otherwise almost inevitable damage. The Burney family were anxious for Hetty, pregnant and living in a very vulnerable part of the town, and we hear of Susan watching the fires in Leicester Square from the observatory with 'her knees all knicky-knocky' because the Orange Street chapel next door to the Burneys had for a time been mistaken for a Catholic church. Fanny's friendship for the Thrales must have been very seriously tested at this time, for her family were in considerable danger and she was not with them.

Mrs Thrale spent the summer at Brighton with her husband, Queeney and her younger daughters Susan and Sophy. She wrote extravagantly affectionate letters to Fanny, complaining of the dullness of the company:

> And so my letters please you, do they, my sweet Burney? I know yours are the most entertaining things that cross me in the course of the whole week; and a miserable praise too, if you could figure to yourself my most dull companions.

Mr Thrale worked very determinedly at enjoying himself; as his wife wrote in her journal, 'he walks now with the ax's edge turned inwards, like Ld Ferrers after sentence'. The Burneys visited Chessington and, in August, the Thrales also paid Mr Crisp and Fanny a visit. Mrs Thrale would have liked to take Fanny with them to Brighton but Fanny knew her duty. For the early part of the winter she was at home writing and in December, January and February she was working on the first volume of *Cecilia* at Chessington with scarcely a break, though she managed to be at Streatham for part of December.

The long months of loneliness at Brighton had a very far-reaching result in the life of Mrs Thrale. She watched her husband dining and play-

Thomas Lowndes agrees to read *Evelina* (Egerton M.S. 3695 f5. Reproduced by permission of the British Library)

Thomas Lowndes offers twenty guineas for *Evelina* (Egerton M.S. 3695 f9. Reproduced by permission of the British Library)

Fanny Burney by her cousin Edward Francesco Burney (*from the Collection at Parham Park, West Sussex*)

ing at cards. She wrote her letters to Fanny: 'Adieu, dearest, loveliest Burney! Write to me kindly, think of me partially, come to me willingly and dream of me if you will, for I am, as you well know, ever yours . . .' And then, who should she see standing in the doorway of a circulating library but Gabriel Piozzi whom she had met at one of Dr Burney's evening parties. He was an attractive man of about her own age and already quite a celebrity in Brighton where he was playing and singing at public concerts. Mrs Thrale arranged for him to give her daughter Queeney lessons. 'He is amazingly like my father,' she said. She began for the first time to take an interest in music.

The dissolution of Parliament, on 1 September, tore Mrs Thrale away from this pleasant social scene. Thrale insisted on returning to Southwark, though all summer he had endured a series of minor attacks of ill-health and the threat of another stroke was always imminent. Johnson acted enthusiastically as his public relations man, but Thrale's unfitness was evident. He was taken very conspicuously ill in church, of all public places, the day before the polls and when the results were known it was clear that his political career was over.

In October the Thrales returned to Brighton. Since Fanny Burney could not be persuaded to join them, Dr Johnson, though he had never cared for Brighton and was in any case correcting proofs of his *Lives of the Poets,* overcame his reluctance and kept Mrs Thrale company. When Dr Pepys, Thrale's physician, returned to London in November the Thrales felt compelled to follow him and they remained in Streatham throughout December, entertaining a horde of young people to dances for which the distinguished Piozzi played. Indeed, he did more. He taught Queeney 'the vocal part of music', raised Henry Thrale's spirits by playing to him on the harpsichord and taught Italian, particularly Italian poetry, to Mrs Thrale.

In January 1781, the problem of the brewery became acute. Perkins had carried the burden of running the business for some time, since we can hardly suppose Dr Johnson or Mrs Thrale to have been very much help. He spoke now of a partnership, of studying 'the operative part of the business' and taking over the organization completely. It was convenient for Perkins to take over the Southwark house in Deadman's Place as well, a house Hester Thrale had never liked . . . 'yet I hate to be edged out of it by Perkins'. Mr Thrale rented a furnished house in Grosvenor Square for the rest of the winter. With the axe blade turned towards him, Southwark had ceased to exist.

Mrs Thrale, excited beyond words at her new social milieu, set about a season of entertaining. Not only was it what she had always dreamed of, but the Master wanted it, the Master needed it. She changed her dinner-hour from a provincial four o'clock to a more fashionable eight o'clock. She ordered a dress that particularly interested the Burneys, since it was inspired by Captain James Burney's Otaheite souvenirs. The trimming alone, it seems, comprised glebe skins and gold to the tune of £65 and, judging by the account in the Morning Herald, all this was applied to striped satin in a native design and supplemented with artificial jewels. Though Mrs Thrale was never a social climber, she must have felt very successful at the beginning of this year. And yet, as so often happens, the life that seemed now to be reaching its culminating point of success had already begun, under the surface, to alter its character irremediably and for the worse.

Johnson had been allocated a room at Grosvenor Square, as at Streatham, to the amusement of some of his friends, such as Boswell and Hannah More. The publication of *Lives of the Poets,* however, intensified his feud with the Blues, already operating to his disadvantage in Bath. He was invited only to large parties where his adversaries could ignore him, never to the smaller more intimate gatherings. Now he had published unfavourable criticism of the poet Gray, close friend of Horace Walpole. He had moreover written slightingly of Lord Lyttelton, friend of the Blues. Mrs Montagu accordingly, though she remained amiable to Mrs Thrale, barred Johnson from Blues parties altogether and the old man, who had been Streatham's main attraction to visitors, became a social disadvantage to his friends. Fanny Burney had been invited to Streatham after the success of *Evelina*. Before she published *Cecilia,* Streatham as a social and intellectual centre had virtually ceased to exist.

In February 1781, distracted by Mrs Thrale at Grosvenor Square and by her approaching separation from Susan, whose engagement to Molesworth Phillips was soon to be announced, Fanny found the drudgery of writing more than she could bear and succumbed to a fever. Daddy Crisp felt the need to bring her home himself in a chaise and there Mrs Thrale had a physician ready and waiting. Her ambitious father was anxious for her to follow up her success with *Evelina* and the friends she had made at Streatham expected great things of her. The strain on a sensitive mind and a frail physique was intolerable. 'I am afraid of seeing my father,' Fanny confesses, knowing that she has not so much as planned the last volume. But the writing had to be laid aside while Fanny slowly overcame all fears of a relapse.

While Fanny was recuperating, the last strange events of Henry Thrale's life were taking place at Grosvenor Square. In a mood of extreme restlessness, the mood that alternated with one of complete torpor at that stage of his illness, Thrale ordered plans made for a trip to Italy. Five years before such a trip had been planned and the same group of people were to go now. Thrale and his wife, Johnson, who was far from well, Queeney and Baretti, the children's language tutor, an irascible man whose dislike of Mrs Thrale was mutual, were the chosen travellers. Fanny Burney to her infinite chagrin was not invited.

On 4 April, before plans for the Italian trip were complete but not before he had signed his new will, Thrale planned a sensational music party. The evening before he had eaten as voraciously as usual or perhaps more so: 'eight things, with Strong Beer in *such* Quantities the very Servants were frighted'. He retired to his room to rest. The ensuing story is well known and characteristic of both father and daughter as Mrs Thrale tells it. It seems that Queeney, going into the room, found him lying on floor. 'What's the meaning of this?' says she in an Agony. 'I chuse it,' replied Mr Thrale firmly. 'I lie so o'purpose.' Despite the best efforts of Dr Pepys he died within a few hours, Johnson beside him to the last. Curiously enough the death of Thrale, who had never seemed to be an integral part of his wife's literary coterie, caused it to burst apart and scatter. More curiously still, each component part seemed to suffer from the disintegration. We observe in them personality changes of a disquieting kind and realize to what extent their volatile natures had depended on the leaden stability of Henry Thrale. He was genuinely 'the Master'.

Mrs Thrale's first resource was flight. Taking only Queeney she made for Brighton via Streatham to receive the consolation of the old gouty solicitor Mr Scrase, her current 'Daddy Crisp' as Fanny calls him. It is true that women did not attend funerals in those days, but to leave before the event argues an emotional indulgence of a notably uncontrolled kind. And she was used to death. There are stories of her writing 'jocular French verses' for Queeney at this time, stories on which Fanny Burney comments that 'her mind was cruelly disordered'. Fanny herself would have loved to be the person to whom Mrs Thrale turned in her misery and stresses accordingly the irrational element in Mrs Thrale's reaction, the 'flashes of spirit [presumably tempers] that are part of her character and do her nothing but good'. Fanny writes to Daddy Crisp from Streatham and mentions the adverse effect upon her own health of Thrale's death. This fragility – an inheritance from a consumptive mother – must always have discouraged Mrs Thrale from too heavy a dependence on her, and tended perhaps to produce in Fanny herself a certain self-centredness, such as we do not all look for in a confidante, especially if our lives have demanded as much self-abnegation as Mrs Thrale's. Piozzi, 'amazingly like' her indulgent father, promised more comfort for the future. The rift had begun.

8

MISS BURNEY SUPPLANTED

'The power of one sex over the other does certainly begin sooner and end later than one should think for,' Mrs Thrale remarks in her journal. She might well have added that it persists in the most unlikely circumstances. The month of May, immediately after the death of the Master, found a curiously house-party atmosphere prevailing at Streatham. It is true that Mrs Thrale is apt to frighten them all by fainting away. 'Dear creature,' Fanny remarks perfunctorily, 'she is all agitation of mind and body.' But Fanny herself is obviously making up her mind to have Jeremiah Crutchley: 'his whole conduct manifests so much goodness of heart and excellence of principle that he is fairly un homme comme il y en a peu.' Mrs Thrale persists in her eternal badinage about how well the two names Mr Crutchley and Miss Burney go together and Fanny in analysing the relationship between the two of them in terms always to her own personal credit. Dr Johnson, now the man of the house, is 'charming, both in spirits and humour. I really think,' Fanny says, 'he grows gayer and gayer daily, and more ductile and pleasant.'

Johnson had respected Henry Thrale increasingly as the years in his company passed and he was more than a little disappointed to find that the widow did not quite install him as head of affairs in Thrale's place. One very obvious reason was the newspaper campaign to link Johnson and Mrs Thrale as lovers and, when the period of mourning was over, future marriage partners. Boswell, whose lack of delicacy was characteristic of his time and class, composed verses called 'Ode by Samuel Johnson to Mrs Thrale in their supposed approaching nuptials'. Fanny reported this to Mrs Thrale, who must have entertained quite a different image of a second husband. Johnson was over seventy and eccentric. No woman could possibly have cast him in a romantic role. L. B. Seeley observes:

> When seated he constantly moved his body backwards and forwards on the chair, rubbing his left knee in the same direction with the palm of his hand . . . When not speaking he would give vent to various inarticulate sounds. Boswell, who observed him with the minute attention of a naturalist studying

some new species of animal, has distinguished several varieties of these. Sometimes the philosopher clucked like a hen; when pleased he emitted a half-whistle; when annoyed or embarrassed . . . he would mutter 'too, too, too' under his breath. At the close of a violent dispute 'he used to blow out his breath like a whale'.

If we are to believe Mrs Thrale, she received a great many proposals at this time: the brewery was worth a great deal of money. But it is likely that the picture of Gabriel Piozzi in her mind, so gentle, so very like her ineffectual father, drove out all others.

The relicts of Henry Thrale gathered themselves together and arranged to run the brewery in committee. Dr Johnson was enchanted by the image of himself as a business man. Mr Crutchley, John Cator, a retired timber merchant, Henry Smith, a relative of Thrale's, and Hester Thrale herself were to help him. But Henry Smith, a barrister, aged twenty-five and the only family connection available, had no desire to run a brewery. Mrs Thrale had experienced the pleasures of social life and had no wish to continue to be 'Lady Mashtubs'. There was no male heir and every possibility of the girls losing their inheritance if the business was run by amateurs. It was decided to sell.

The price for the brewery was £135,000 to be paid over four years. Perkins had married prosperously seven years before Thrale's death and he managed to bring in his brother-in-law and two rich Quakers, David and Robert Barclay. Mrs Thrale, anxious to be rid of the responsibility and perhaps conscious of Perkins' worth, lent him money to help buy his quarter and the sale was completed. Mrs Thrale was free now to take her place as a rich lady of fashion and when the period of mourning should be over to take up the kind of entertaining her husband's death had interrupted.

In June, just as Mrs Thrale was beginning to realize that her feelings were increasingly disturbed by Piozzi, he departed for Italy and a visit to his parents, leaving her waiting for the post like a girl and desperately anxious about his safety. During that summer she not surprisingly fell ill. Fanny, worried about Charles, who had been refused ordination, about James, who had not had the promotion he deserved, and about Hetty, who had had yet another baby, fell ill in September. Perkins at the brewery fell ill and Johnson was a prey to low spirits and poor health. In November Mr Crisp managed to persuade both Streatham and St Martin's Street that Fanny must finish her book. Susan's marriage was planned for early January and by dint of slaving in the peace of Chessington at a manuscript she was almost coming to dislike, Fanny was able to be home for Christmas Day, to attend the wedding at St Martins in the Fields and to go with the wedding-party to Chessington as was the custom.

While Fanny was away her father had made all the arrangements for the publication of her book, choosing the bookseller Payne, whose daughter James was courting, to bring it out. The copyright was sold for £250 and the men of business, Dr Burney and Mr Crisp congratulated one another on her good fortune in making money so easily and 'sitting by a warm fire'. Fanny was still copying the later volumes when the first was printed but the book was an instant success and sold so well that the booksellers must have made a huge profit.

After the sale of the brewery Mrs Thrale hoped that she would be able to live peacefully at Streatham, educating her children and entertaining her friends. Dr Johnson was teaching Queeney Latin, Dr Burney was teaching Queeney, Susan and Sophy the harpsichord, and Piozzi, who had returned to England at the end of November, was responsible for singing lessons. Thus Mrs Thrale combined the care of her daughters with her own best interests. Piozzi was becoming accepted into the family and his frequent presence at Streatham was accounted for. But the cost of maintaining Streatham was high and Mrs Thrale had never been used to frugality. It was a final blow when, on the failure of a lawsuit, she was called upon to pay Lady Salusbury an old family debt, £8,000 compounded at £7,500.

It was the end of the old Streatham life made plain and visible. Mrs Thrale was forced to borrow from her daughters, to let Streatham for three years, to winter in Bath and then, with Piozzi as a guide, to travel in Italy with her three elder daughters. Dr Johnson was becoming a gloomy companion. 'Years of drudgery, privation, neglect, a slovenly contempt for the rules of health and cleanliness, had injured irreparably a constitution which must have been originally tough and resistant,' C. E. Vulliamy justly observes. Queeney, at seventeen, may have been too closely involved with Crutchley, whom Mrs Thrale believed to be her father's natural son. Fanny Burney – Mrs Thrale was not yet ready to separate herself from Fanny Burney. But Piozzi was a stronger lure.

When the house was let, the Thrales went to Brighton. Johnson was with them, but although he had encouraged Mrs Thrale in her Italian trip, he had been ill-tempered and low in health ever since. He had no idea of the seriousness of Mrs Thrale's feelings for Piozzi, though Queeney and Fanny Burney had been told the secret recently at Streatham. Fanny joined the party at Brighton and was fêted everywhere as the author of

Cecilia, but so strongly did she disapprove of Mrs Thrale's behaviour that there was no pleasure in her company either. The crisis came when Mrs Thrale, true to her nature, set out the whole emotional position in her diary and showed it to Fanny and Queeney. Fanny wept, Hester Thrale wept, Queeney remained dry-eyed and contemptuous. The party returned to London where Mrs Thrale took a house in Argyll Street.

In London Mrs Thrale soon discovered that the gossip in the press, which had linked her name with all sorts of unlikely candidates for marriage, now named Piozzi openly and with outrage. From the viewpoint of the twentieth century it is not easy to see what were the objections to the marriage, but at that time they certainly existed. He was of good family, but to match Mrs Thrale he should have been of aristocratic birth or possessed of a fortune. A musician was, by definition, a performer. He was Italian and, worse, a Roman Catholic. It was incumbent on any sincere Christian to despise him for this: Dr Johnson and Fanny Burney could neither of them be reconciled to Piozzi's lack of the true faith. To us the worst result of such a marriage would be that, since the Thrale daughters were all young – Harriet was only three – the trustees would certainly not allow the heiresses to be brought up by their mother if she behaved so injudiciously. Hester Thrale, when she married Piozzi, was to be robbed of her children and then accused of abandoning them.

These were, at that date, reasonable objections. But for Queeney, Fanny Burney and Dr Johnson the chief objection was that they wanted their lives to go on as before. Queeney accused her mother of turning out her children 'like puppies in a Pond to swim or drown'. Johnson, who had become accustomed to living like a rich man, protested that she cared for no one. 'You she still loves,' he conceded to Fanny, 'as she loves her little finger.' Fanny advised her that 'The mother of 5 children, 3 of them as tall as herself, will never be forgiven for showing so great an ascendance of passion over Reason'. Mrs Thrale in an interview with Piozzi, told him that all thought of marriage between them must be over. Queeney demanded – and got – the return of her mother's love-letters. Piozzi left England intending never to see Hester Thrale again.

Mrs Thrale now departed to live economically at Bath with her three eldest daughters, leaving the two youngest, who had just recovered from illness, to attend a school in Streatham under the care of their old nurse and two distinguished physicians, both friends of the family. So it was oddly unjust that in a few days she was to have news that Harriet was dead and Cecilia dying. Cecilia recovered and Mrs Thrale returned to the cold hate engendered by Queeney in her elder children. She countered by refusing to take part in the social life of the town and kept them hard at their books. It was a dull life for them all.

Fanny Burney had been able to endure living at home much more easily while Mrs Thrale was in Argyll Street. She could not afford an establishment of her own and it did not please her to be an expense to her father and an irritation to her step-mother. Later in her life, when she wrote *The Wanderer,* she was to draw a character called Mrs Ireton, who was like Mrs Schwellenberg of the Court, or like Mrs Burney.

> You may think it sufficient honour for me [Mrs Ireton rages] that I may be at the expence of your board and find you in lodging and furniture and fire and candles and servants? You may hold this ample recompense for such an insignificant person as I am? . . . and I was stupid enough to suppose, that that meant a person who could be of some use and some agreeability; a person who could read to me when I was tired and who, when I had nobody else, could talk to me.

If the Lynn heiress talked to her step-children in these terms, and there is evidence left after much has been suppressed to suggest that she habitually did, their eagerness to live elsewhere is understandable. But while Fanny could run in and out of Mrs Thrale's houses, attend parties and go with her to assemblies at other fashionable houses, St Martin's Street was endurable.

So many were the invitations for the distinguished authoress of *Cecilia* that Fanny was compelled to keep days free of engagements for the sake of her own nervous health; 'quiet days at home' she called them. So she describes dinner at Lady Gideon's, where 'everything in the house both of decorations and refreshments and accommodation was in greater magnificence than I have yet seen'. She describes Blues parties and bishops, an opera rehearsal, meetings with her favourite singer, and Susan's, Pacchierotti, and Mrs Thrale's parties. Miss Monckton's assembly is faithfully described. Miss Monckton was a short, fat woman between thirty and forty, afterwards Countess of Cork, 'splendidly and fantastically dressed, rouged not unbecomingly'. She followed the social rules prevailing among the Blues, 'the rank and the literature', meaning that they would admit only the aristocracy and writers to their parties. Miss Monckton adopted the new casual approach to entertaining: guests were not announced by servants and the hostess merely nodded to them as they arrived. She disapproved of any formal arrangement of the guests and preferred them scattered. We are made aware by Fanny's description of the slowness of movement entailed in wearing long trains such as the Thrale party wore and the uncomfortable weight of sacque-back dresses. Dr Johnson was at the party and Sir Joshua Reynolds and Edmund Burke who so admired Fanny's novels. But Fanny hated to go alone to parties and after Mrs Thrale's departure for Bath she declared herself 'heartily sick and fatigued of this continual round of visiting and these eternal new acquaintances'. She was ready for a new way of life and she thought she saw what it might be.

At one of Mrs Thrale's assemblies Fanny had met 'the two Mr Cambridges, father and son' and she had begun to find the latter very much to her taste. Richard Owen Cambridge, the father, possessed 'a beautiful villa on the banks of the Thames at Twickenham', as Boswell tells us, and a notable collection of books. He was a wit, and, in a small way, a writer, having written a burlesque poem called 'The Scribbleriad' and contributed to a periodical called 'The World'. His son, George Owen Cambridge, was a clergyman and became known for the memoir he published of his father. George Owen appeared to follow Fanny from one party to another, flourishing compliments and writing flattering verses. Instead of praising her books, as did almost everybody else, he praised her favourite relatives, like Captain Phillips, Susan and Mr Crisp. Richard Owen, the father, also made much of her, in a way that must have suggested he was getting to know a future daughter-in-law. The daughters of the family were friendly. And yet no proposal ensued. It must have been infuriating for Fanny to watch Mrs Thrale, who had had one marriage, slip so easily into another.

Not only had Fanny's hopes of marriage been raised by the attentions of George Cambridge, but she had recently been introduced by Mrs Chapone to one of the most distinguished of the Old Wits, Mrs Delany, friend of the Duchess of Portland and loved by the King and Queen. She could afford no breath of scandal now. Scarcely a week after her first meeting with the Cambridges, Fanny told Hester Thrale that she must come to a decision if she wanted to preserve her reputation. The confrontation followed between Queeney and Gabriel Piozzi and Mrs Thrale's half-hearted but effective dismissal of her lover. It was later that Mrs Thrale wrote of 'Dear Burney, who loves me *kindly*, but the world reverentially . . .' and she forgot, perhaps, that it is easier to despise convention if you have a private income. Fanny had social disadvantages enough without being associated with newspaper gossip.

Soon after Mrs Thrale's departure for Bath Fanny suffered one of the most serious losses of her life in the death of Mr Crisp at Chessington. One by one her refuges, Streatham, Chessington, were being stopped. Mrs Thrale continued to lead the life of a recluse at Bath, sinking ever more deeply into a state of hopeless despair. Johnson was writing regularly with news that he was not well, but she made no attempt to see him or care for him. Even when he had a paralytic stroke in June, she was indifferent. She writes – but eight months later – 'Johnson is in a sad way doubtless; yet he may still with care last another twelvemonth'. Fanny continued with painful loyalty to keep Mrs Thrale's counsel. Only to Susan does she mention 'the difficulties under which I labour not to offend or afflict that beloved friend, and yet to do nothing wrong'. She herself had nobody left. In Mrs Thrale's place she visited the desolate Johnson, watching him sicken and die while Mrs Thrale's drama reached its climax and her own was indefinitely postponed.

Mrs Thrale's nervous breakdown, imminent for some months, followed immediately on her nursing of Sophy, who was suffering from a kind of brain fever. She had always taken the somewhat dramatic view that her parting from Piozzi must kill her. She speaks in a letter of

the dreadful anniversary of a day which, instead of killing me, as it ought to have done, gave to two innocent, unfortunate people a cruel and lingering death – like the arrows tipped with African poison, which, slowly and gradually retarding the vital powers, at length (in about three years, I think) wholly put a stop to their exertion!

Queeney, who had stoically watched her sister through her agonizing illness, now attended her mother while hysterical laughter and tears alternated. The doctors, since they had no other treatment to suggest, advised the recall of Piozzi. The daughters, no doubt exhausted beyond endurance, consented to this course. Mrs Thrale began at once to take a turn for the better.

It was six months before Piozzi began his journey. It is true that Mrs Thrale's letter would take time to reach him in Italy and that the winter weather would make the journey over the Alps almost impossible. He had in his time suffered intolerable humiliations from rich employers in England and if he had been encouraged by Hester Thrale it was only to be repudiated by her family. But his manifest reluctance brought Mrs Thrale into renewed contempt. She was forty. She had had twelve pregnancies. She burned for an Italian music master and he – lacked interest. Queeney and Fanny Burney, cold young women, writing their secret letters to each other, were scornful. Their scorn was to be echoed through the fashionable drawing-rooms of London as soon as the news got about.

Mrs Thrale, and Sophy whom she had nursed, wrote further letters to Piozzi. Mrs Thrale promised him that she would live in Italy and that he would matter more than her children. Indeed her children, organized by Queeney, now told her that they refused to live in Italy and insisted upon taking over the house that had been left them in Brighton. With some difficulty Mrs Thrale found a suitable chaperone and in June, when Piozzi at last arrived in London, the parting took place without marked reluctance on either side.

All this while the letters – almost love-letters – continue to be exchanged between Hester Thrale and Fanny Burney. Mrs Thrale speaks of 'remembering last winter', and remembering it 'with tenderness'. She knows – or guesses – that Dr Burney will not allow his daughter to visit her in Bath, though she keeps a room ready and aired. She longs to see Fanny, though she must know that their friendship is running out. All her life it is said, Hester Thrale put one person on a pedestal at a time. There would be no room for Fanny beside Piozzi. In May, at a time when Piozzi had finally capitulated, Mrs Thrale made a brief excited visit to London and lodged in Mortimer Street seeing no one except the Burneys. 'Dear Burney . . . I believe equally pained as delighted with my visit, ashamed to be seen in my company, much of her fondness for it must of course be diminished,' Mrs Thrale records with malicious insight, adding, 'Yet she had not chatted freely so long with anybody but Mrs Phillips, that my coming was a comfort to her.'

On 1 July Piozzi arrived in Bath in such a weak state of health that Mrs Thrale's physician, Dr Dobson, was contemptuous. 'This fellow will never serve the purpose of Mrs Thrale, whose health requires a *Man*,' he is said to have declared. As C. E. Vulliamy remarks in his book *Mrs Thrale of Streatham*: 'An ironical or retributive providence decreed the sudden death of Dr Dobson on the morning of Mrs Thrale's wedding at Bath.'

Mrs Thrale was married to Piozzi with two ceremonies, Catholic and Protestant. Mrs Piozzi's careless, happy letter asking Fanny to 'wish her joy' was answered with a formal note that appeared to exclude Gabriel Piozzi from her felicitations. A phrase to the effect that Mrs Piozzi had 'deserved her husband's affection', that is, had worked hard for it, was also tactless. Poor Fanny, after she had made so many criticisms of the marriage privately, was too much of a Cordelia to reverse her attitude in public. Mrs Piozzi's reply made it clear that loyalty to her husband demanded her friends' acceptance of him too. Fanny wrote back 'a letter of ice', and Mrs Piozzi's nonchalant reply, 'Give yourself no serious concern, sweetest Burney', was her last communication with her former friend until they were old ladies together in Bath.

Fanny took refuge with the Lockes, Susan's neighbours in Surrey and her own new friends, and when she returned to London it was to find great excitement among the Blues. They and the Press had sat in judgment on Mrs Piozzi and brought in a verdict of insanity. What was the use of a woman cultivating her mind if she was to succumb in middle age to the frenzies of romantic love? Fanny reports in a letter: 'The outcry of surprise and censure raised throughout the metropolis by these unexpected nuptials was almost stunning in its jarring noise of general reprobation, resounding through madrigals, parodies, declamation, epigrams and irony.' The cartoons were also fairly obscene. But the Piozzis made their slow preparations for travelling abroad, building a special carriage with a portable harpsichord fitted under the seat. In September they set out with a little dog, which spent the journey on their laps alternately. 'It hurts me,' Mrs Piozzi observed, 'to leave London without seeing Miss Burney, tho' she had played a false and cruel part towards me I find.' It was to be thirty-six years before she and her sweetest Burney met again.

9

MISS BURNEY AND MRS DELANY

'Young Mr Cambridge,' Fanny writes, 'need not complain of my taciturnity, whatever his father may do. Who, indeed, of my new acquaintances has so well understood me? The rest all talk of *Evelina* and *Cecilia* and turn every other word into some compliment; while he talks of Chessington or Captain Phillips and pays me, not even by implication, any compliments at all.'

Mr George Cambridge had an instinctive knowledge of how to please Fanny. The problem that exercises us, as it certainly did her, is why he cared to employ it. If he had been desperately anxious to marry her he could not have pursued her around London more ardently. He had a habit of hovering near her chair, waiting for the adjacent one to empty so that he could sit in it. Knowing, we must suppose, how dear Chessington was to her he rode there to pay Mr Crisp a visit. We catch the tone of his humour in an exchange made on the subject. 'How did you find the roads?' he was asked, for Chessington was notoriously difficult of access. 'Pretty well. Never above the horses' legs,' was his cool reply. Marianne Francis was later to comment on 'his natural stock of dry-humour and love of a joke' and if we read Fanny's journals during the period when she and Mr George Cambridge meet so constantly at parties it is easy to see that they share not only love of the same people but the sense of the ridiculous all the Burneys so valued.

It would be possible to dismiss Fanny's expectations of marriage as simply a misreading of the young man's friendliness. But other people formed the same impression as Fanny did of his intentions. Mrs Thrale, at about the time of her departure for Bath, writes:

My dearest Miss Burney has apparently got an Admirer in Mr George Cambridge; if they marry, I shall have perhaps more of her company than now, for her Mother-in-law [step-mother] is a greater Tyrant than any Husband would be, especially a Man whose heart is apparently engaged.

It was Mrs Thrale too who blamed the elder Cambridge for interfering between his son and Fanny: 'One wd wonder what Fathers are *for* but to keep their sons away from amiable women that they are not (God knows why) to marry.' And the very last thing Mr Cambridge did was to keep his son away from Fanny. Indeed some of Fanny's friends formed the impression that this elderly, married man was courting her himself. Fanny writes:

> He listens to every syllable I utter with so grave a deference that it intimidates and silences me. When he was about taking leave, he said, –
> 'Shall you go to Mrs Ord's tomorrow?'
> 'Yes, sir.'
> 'I thought so,' said he, smiling, 'and hoped it. Where shall you go tonight?'
> 'Nowhere; I shall be at home.'
> 'At home? Are you sure?'
> 'Yes.'
> 'Why, then, Miss Burney, my son and I dine today in your neighbourhood at the Archbishop of York's and, if you please, we will come here in the evening.'

Family visits to Twickenham – and there are a number of them in the eight years of Fanny's friendship with George Cambridge – are frequently the occasion for Mr Cambridge senior to monopolize Fanny and walk ahead of the others talking to her. On one such occasion he lets fall the observation that 'almost all the felicity of his life both had consisted and did still consist in female society'. In a tête-à-tête at Fanny's home he makes what some would consider a curiously ambiguous remark:

> Gay as you may think me, I am always upon the watch for evil: only I do not look for it, like the croakers, to be miserable, but to prevent it. And, for this purpose, I am constantly turning about in my own mind every possible evil that can happen, and then I make it my whole business to guard against it.

In Mr Cambridge's confidence to Fanny about the seriousness of his daughter's illness and the impossibility of her recovery he employs a grotesque phraseology: 'I have something very interesting to say to you . . .' he begins, and one wonders at the note of family intimacy in the words. Can he have assumed that Fanny, at thirty-one, would be happy to cultivate the chance of being his adopted daughter and a sister to the man who, like Hetty's Mr Seaton, did everything but declare himself? Was Fanny, whose preference for older men was so marked, lacking in the kind of attraction that would make a young man think of marriage?

Did Mr Cambridge, whose son 'adored him', overrule his son's wishes in the matter? We shall never know. Most of the passages referring to Fanny's love for George Cambridge have been cut from the published journals and exist only in manuscript. Even if we had them they would be one-sided. Professor Hemlow quotes a particularly bitter comment from the suppressed excerpts:

> Who . . . could pardon except on a death bed – could or can pardon such wanton, such accumulating – such endless deceit and treachery? I can use no other words; his conduct has long past all mere impeachment of trifling – it has seemed irrepressibly attached to me – it has been deemed honourably serious by all our mutual acquaintances.

George Cambridge, who became Prebendary of Ely and Archdeacon of Middlesex, was a very valuable help to Fanny in later days when, married to a young and beautiful wife, but childless, he helped her try to establish that difficult young man Alexander d'Arblay, her only son, in the Church of England. When Fanny lay on her deathbed he did indeed come, to read the prayers for the sick, but she was past forgiving anyone by then and he was not admitted.

Fanny's first acquaintance with the Cambridges developed at a time when almost every other of her close personal relationships was giving her anxiety. January 1783 had witnessed the dramatic scene in which Mrs Thrale had given Piozzi his *congé* (not forgetting to borrow £1000 from him before he went). In March she had retired to Bath where Dr Burney forbade Fanny to follow her. In April Samuel Crisp had died. In June Johnson had had a stroke and in July Mrs Thrale had become Mrs Piozzi. For the rest of the year Fanny was to watch over Samuel Johnson as he lay dying, no word reaching him from his dear hostess Mrs Thrale. The inexplicable behaviour of the Cambridges was to continue for many years yet, but in that hard year Fanny must have longed for the comfort George Cambridge's declared affection might have offered.

What did, in fact, take the place of her still-ardent love for Mrs Thrale was a considerably more temperate friendship with a much older woman and one of unexceptionable social status and moral reputation. If Fanny's family or the Cambridges had worried about the damage to her reputation caused by her association with Mrs Thrale, Mrs Chapone's invitation to her to meet Mrs Delany must have gone far to reassure them. And to Fanny, as she lived through that difficult year, Mrs Delany provided a haven that not Streatham, nor Chessington provided any more.

Nothing has so truly calmed my mind since its late many disturbances as her society: the religious turn which kindness and wisdom from old age gives to all commerce with it, brings us out of anxiety and misery a thousand times more successfully than gaiety and dissipation have power to do.

It was at a Blues party at Mrs Ord's that Mrs Chapone first mentioned to Fanny that 'Swift's Mrs Delany' was among her unknown friends. She had gone to the party with Queeney Thrale, leaving Mrs Thrale to keep Dr Johnson company, and had found there her sister Charlotte 'looking pretty and innocent', as well as a number of her acquaintances, including young Mr Cambridge whom she had only recently met. Mrs Chapone offered to show Fanny a letter she had received from Mrs Delany. It reported that she and her friend the Duchess of Portland were reading *Cecilia* for the third time 'and they desire nothing so much as an acquaintance with the amiable writer'. A few days later Fanny visited Mrs Chapone by appointment and was shown 'a head of Mrs Delany; I admired it much; there looks much benevolence and sense in it'.

'I am glad,' said I, 'to see even thus much of her.'
'I hope then,' said Mrs Chapone, 'you will give me the pleasure of introducing you to know more of her.'

Three weeks later the meeting with Mrs Delany took place, with Mrs Chapone to make the presentation. An introduction to Mrs Delany was honour indeed. The Old Wits, the older generation of cultivated women, regarded only rank and literature as criteria of respectability. And the Duchess of Portland, Mrs Delany's friend, had little use for novels. A long letter of praise from Mrs Montagu on the newly-published *Cecilia* was thought to account for her permitting Mrs Delany to receive Fanny Burney. The Duchess, of course, had rank so elevated that her friend never referred to her except by her title. Mrs Delany was connected by her second marriage to Swift and was still in possession of letters from the great names of the middle of the eighteenth century.

When Mrs Delany was the seventeen-year-old Mary Granville, she went to stay with friends, Lord and Lady Landsdowne. Ronald Fletcher in *The Parkers at Saltram* tells the story: she was amused 'to great mirth' by a 'fat, snuffy, dirty, gouty and sulky' old Cornishman of sixty, of enormous 'unwieldy bulk and crimson countenance'. Then, to her horror, she discovered that this was the man it had been arranged she should marry. She did marry him out of a sense of duty and lived with him in a remote old castle with broken-down ceilings, weeping every night of the seven years before he died. During the greater part of that seven years he was brought home drunk at six o'clock in the morning. He left her disappointingly little money. After twenty years of widowhood she had made a love match with Dr Delany, intimate friend of Dean Swift. Her family considered him to be inferior socially, but she was happy.

Mrs Delany now lived in St James's Place. Mrs Chapone, Fanny's escort, could stay no longer than half-past seven, but since the Duchess of Portland, whose views on Fanny were, of course, all-important to Mrs Delany, had promised to arrive by seven the situation was quite manageable.

Mrs Delany's drawing-room bore witness to her hobbies of copying pictures and creating flower pictures. This she did by cutting out shapes of tinted paper and arranging them in almost a three-dimensional effect on a background. The British Museum still has a volume of these flower pictures, and they were much admired by her friends. She had been sent specimens to copy from many of the great gardens of England and had intended to make a thousand pictures, but her failing eyesight had caused her to stop short of the mark. The uselessness of the occupation, the ladylike unassertiveness of simply reproducing flowers in coloured paper must have satisfied many of her friends that Mrs Delany was free from dangerous ideas. It was an art the Duchess of Portland and the Royal Family could admire without anxiety.

Although age had made her a little bent, Mrs Delany was still tall and her face was disarmingly benign, grandmotherly, like Mrs Sleepe's as Fanny was quick to point out: 'Benevolence, softness, piety and gentleness are all resident in her face.' The qualities that had troubled her in Mrs Thrale, a rather flashy attractiveness and a defiance of convention, were quite alien to Mrs Delany. She greeted Fanny with a reassuring, though quite sincere confession that she was behind the times: 'You must pardon me if I give you an old fashioned reception, for I know nothing new.' And she kissed her, a greeting Fanny bore without reluctance.

There were arch references to the characters from Fanny's books and she in her turn was called upon to admire Mrs Delany's paintings. Then they went in to dinner, which was 'plain' and 'neat' – quite unlike the Streatham meals no doubt. Fanny introduced the name of Crisp into the conversation and Mrs Delany was glad to remember her former friendship with his sister, Mrs Gast. When the guests were taken upstairs to the drawing-room, the unstimulating details of the flower pictures became the topic of conversation: 'The effect is extremely beautiful. She invented it at seventy-five! She told me she did four flowers the first year; sixteen the second; and the third 160; and after that many more . . . but alas! her eyes now fail her, though she has only twenty undone of her task.'

The Duchess of Portland duly arrived at seven and was received by her friend with the curious formality that had survived the years. Mr Crisp was mentioned at once. Then the two older ladies began to speak of *Cecilia* with such warm-hearted appreciation, such sensitive praise that surely not even Fanny's delicate susceptibilities were really alarmed. The final strophe and anti-strophe of Mrs Chapone and Mrs Delany nearly brought tears to her eyes, she says, but they were tears of gratification:

> 'We must all join in saying [Mrs Chapone declared] she has bettered us by every line.'
> 'No book [said Mrs Delany] ever was so useful as this, because none other that is so good was ever so much read.'

This commendation from the two awesomely élite old ladies must have pushed Fanny yet a little further from the mood in which she wrote *Evelina* and added to the damage done to her style by her efforts to give her writing moral significance. The good days were gone for Fanny and were not to return for a decade. Happiness lost, she clung nervously to an ideal of unimpeachable worthiness such as Mr Cambridge, or his father, such as Mrs Delany and then Queen Charlotte could not help but approve.

It was not very many months after the beginning of her friendship with Mrs Delany that the great sorrow of Mr Crisp's death struck at Fanny and for a while drove out of her mind all thoughts of Mr Cambridge and his intentions, all thoughts of the scandal surrounding Mrs Thrale. Samuel Crisp, ill in Chessington, was being nursed by Susan without any real improvement becoming apparent. The situation became more alarming and Fanny hastened to his bedside only to find him dying. Dr Burney tried to comfort her but in vain. When the death had taken place he reminded her – but gently – that she had other duties and that excessive grief is an indulgence.

She returned to St Martin's Street bereft of her second home and her second father, more lonely than she had ever been. The house in St Martin's Street was empty now of those brothers and sisters who had been most dear to her and it was also being made increasingly intolerable by her step-mother's domineering moods. Her spirits must have been low indeed.

That was in April. Dr Johnson's last illness began in June. While the Thrales were in Bath, early in the year, Johnson wrote to Queeney telling her that he was not well. He mentioned the poplars in the little Bolt Court garden, which he cherished because they came from Streatham. His attempt to regain Mrs Thrale's interest by his frequent letters was hopeless, however, because she was totally obsessed by her passion for Piozzi. In June he had a stroke. It had come upon him in the early hours of the morning while he was asleep and it deprived him – ironically enough, since he had been such a magnificent talker – of his powers of speech. Hawkins has it that he tried to repeat the Lord's prayer, first in English, then in Latin, then in Greek, succeeding only in the last. Fanny Burney, however, repeats Mrs Williams' more elaborate story of his composing a Latin prayer begging to retain the use of his intellect and finding, when he tried to speak it, that his voice was gone. The doctors, Mrs Williams said, pronounced him to be in no danger and expected a speedy recovery.

Fanny was obliged to go straight from Bolt Court to Mrs Vesey's house to meet Mrs Garrick. Horace Walpole was there, but she was in no spirits to talk to that formidable conversationalist. The next day a visit to Dr Johnson gave her encouraging news and soon he was dining with Sir Joshua Reynolds at the Club. 'I called the next morning to congratulate him,' Fanny says, 'and found him very gay and very good-humoured.' There followed a whole day spent at Twickenham with the Cambridges who had invited Dr Burney and his wife as well as Fanny. By the rules of the world the Cambridges and the Burneys lived in this was indeed a very odd gesture if George Cambridge did not intend to marry Fanny, and Mr Cambridge senior's tendency to monopolize her and write her verses does not make matters any easier to understand.

Fanny was to need Mrs Delany's soothing qualities during the latter part of this year more than ever before. Johnson was better, it is true, but his eagerness for her visits spoke of his extreme loneliness now that Mrs Williams was dead. Fanny called on him, made his breakfast, stayed two hours and 'could hardly get away'. Six weeks later – but six weeks is a long time to someone in Johnson's situation – he writes an angry, formal note complaining that she does not visit him. He had once drawn the distinguished guests to Streatham and now he would not beg for company. But he longed for it unbearably and responded to it as he had not always done when it was freely available: 'Dr Johnson was, if possible, more instructive, entertaining, good humoured and exquisitely fertile than ever. He thanked me repeatedly for coming and was so kind I could hardly ever leave him.' Mrs Thrale was giving Fanny more and more cause for anxiety. 'Sat Nov. 22nd I passed in nothing but sorrow – exquisite sorrow for my dear unhappy friend who sent me one letter that came early by the Bath Diligence and another by the post. But of these things no more.' At a Blues party Dr Pepys held a long private conversation with Fanny upon the state of Mrs Thrale's health, which approached complete breakdown. There is no mention of the details of this even in the privacy of Fanny's diary, but in Bath the physicians had reached the conclusion that, if Mrs Thrale did not marry Piozzi, madness or suicide might well ensue. Even the Thrale daughters had been persuaded of the. necessity.

These months of 1783 must have provided some perplexing contrasts for Fanny. She had only to pay a visit to Mrs Vesey's to have the Cambridges, first father and then son, arrive, uninvited and unexpected, anxious only to seek Fanny out and talk to her. The Streatham days had been happy ones but it was a long time since Fanny had been heard to giggle as she does at some of these parties. And what is so pleasant is that we know that George Cambridge too is amused and in the same irreverent fashion, even if good manners demand that they do not laugh outright:

Lady Spencer brought with her a collection of silver ears, to serve instead of trumpets, to help deafness. They had belonged to the late Lord and she presented them to Mrs Vesey who, with great naïveté, began trying them on before us all; and a more ludicrous sight you cannot imagine . . . During this came Mr George Cambridge. The sight of Mrs Vesey rising to receive him with one of her silver ears on, and the recollection of several accounts given me of her wearing them, made me unable to keep my countenance.

Mrs Vesey moves about the room, dropping silver ears as she goes and just when young Mr Cambridge is going to speak she interrupts with a question:

'Do you know Mr Wallace, Mr Cambridge?'
'No, ma'am.'
'It's a very disagreeable thing, I think,' said she, 'when one has just made acquaintance with anybody, and likes them, to have them die.'
This speech set me grinning so irresistibly that I was forced to begin fillipping off the crumbs of the macaroon cake from my muff, for an excuse for looking down.

And yet this gaiety, which was perhaps not troubled yet by doubts of Mr Cambridge, had to be set against the anxious secrets she carried for Mrs Thrale and which her loyalty would not let her so much as hint at, not even to Susan or Charlotte. Rumours circulated, but Fanny stubbornly refused to confirm or deny what was said:

> It is too true that many know all – but none from me. I am bound, and should be miserable not to say, if called upon, and not to know, if not called upon, that no creature, not even you to whom I communicate everything else, nor the trusty Charlotte with whom I live and who sees my frequent distress upon the subject, has tempted me to an explanation. General rumour I have no means to prevent spreading.

Early in December, adding to the burden under which Fanny laboured, came the news that Johnson was 'in a most alarming way'. This time Fanny realized that he was dying – 'what a cruel heavy loss he will be' – and until his death her journal records a most incongruous alternation of parties, conversations with the Cambridges and visiting at Johnson's sickbed, the only woman, it seems, that made her way there. Mrs Thrale, who might have come, is at Bath waiting for her lover Piozzi, who had been summoned with her daughters' permission but who made no haste to come.

So 1783 draws to an end, bringing with it as a farewell gift Mr Burke's kind appointment of Dr Burney to the post as organist at Chelsea College, with residential apartments included in the perquisites. 'This is my last act in office,' Burke is said to have declared and there must have been very real advantages to Dr Burney in so steady, so settled an establishment for his later years, especially since his family was now so diminished. But the year can only have finished on an unhappy note for Fanny when she spent its last evening by Dr Johnson's bed, promising at his request to pray for him, aware as never before of his fear of the death now approaching.

The Old Wits, all friends of Mrs Delany's, must have speculated, in their reticent way, on Fanny's plans for the future. In early 1784 we can see clues that suggest the way they think she ought to go. In January 1784 Fanny dined with Mrs Delany:

> The venerable and excellent old lady received me with open arms and we kissed one another as if she had been my sweet grandmother, whom she always reminds me of. She looks as well as ever, only rather thinner; but she is as lively, gay, pleasant, good-humoured and animated as at eighteen. She

sees, she says, much worse; 'but I am thankful,' she added cheerfully, 'I can see at all at my age. My greatest loss is the countenance of my friends; however, to see even the light is a great blessing.'

The company was all women and all *bas bleu*. Mrs Carter and Miss Hamilton came, Lady Dartmouth and Mrs Levison and Miss G., a maid of honour of whom Fanny records, 'she has had, it seems, a man's education; yet she is young, pretty and at times very engaging'. Most impressive of all, the Duchess of Portland came in the evening. Fanny cannot have failed to recognize the learning, moral worth and high social rank of those by whom she was now accepted.

Interestingly – and perhaps ominously – a new note was introduced into Fanny's conversation with Mrs Delany. 'She showed me a most elegant and ingenious loom, which the Queen made her a present of last summer at Windsor, for making fringe; and a gold knitting needle given her by the King.' There is reference also to 'a beautiful case of instruments for her curious works', that the Queen had presented her with. She had signed the accompanying letter 'your affectionate Queen', Fanny says. The kindness of the royal couple, their capacity for giving carefully chosen and generous presents is certainly being emphasized. But nothing explicit has yet been revealed to Fanny of the purpose behind this campaign.

At Bath, Mrs Thrale, recovered from the worst effects of her illness now that Piozzi had been sent for, continues to write lovingly to Fanny. 'Thanks, thanks a thousand, my prettiest, dearest Burney! This charming letter makes amends for all. And you remember last winter, do you? and remember it with tenderness?' She ends, 'Adieu! I am really almost drawn together from emptiness and sinking. Love me, however, while I am your L.T.' In March she is busily educating her daughters and a very exacting regime of history and literature seems to be filling the time between one husband and another. 'Ah Burney,' she ends, 'you little know the suffering and, I will add, the patient suffering of your L.T.' After this letter, Fanny tells us, most of Mrs Thrale's letters had to be destroyed, 'for conscientious reasons'. Of her own life we hear that she is to dine with Dr Johnson on a salmon sent by Mrs Thrale, that Susan's first child, a girl, is walking now and that her father is allowing her to refuse more invitations. She is not at all happy in the London social scene, brilliant as it is, and declares: 'I can go nowhere with pleasure or spirit if I meet not with somebody who interests my heart as well as my head, and I miss Mrs Thrale most woefully in both particulars.' The friends who meet her requirements are diminishing round her and soon after the year is out she will have lost another of their number.

In the spring of 1794 Susan and Molesworth Phillips settled in a cottage at Mickleham in Surrey and in doing so introduced first to Susan and then to Fanny a new friend who they agreed from their first acquaintance could certainly interest both heart and head. This was Mrs Locke who, with her husband, lived in Norbury Park just up a path leading from the bridge near the Phillips' house. William Locke was Dr Burney's idea of a really cultivated man. His mother had been the mistress of a William Locke, M.P. for Grimsby. The boy was given a good education, culminating in the Grand Tour. He was a close friend of Richard Wilson the landscape painter. Six years before his death William Locke M.P. made a will leaving almost all his considerable wealth to the boy who had until that time been known by his mother's name.

The younger William Locke married a beautiful seventeen-year-old, Frederica Schaub, daughter of a Swiss diplomat, and in 1774 began to build Norbury Park, which is still in occupation, a house commanding some of the most magnificent views in Surrey. The drawing-room at Norbury was painted from floor to ceiling with landscapes and the ceiling was painted to represent the sky. With a green carpet stretching from wall to wall the room 'resembled a trellised pergola opening on all sides to ideal English scenery, with the perfect views from the windows completing the circle'. The positioning of the house reflects the more natural and romantic trends that had gradually been emerging throughout the latter part of the eighteenth century and foreshadowed the mood of the Romantic Revival. It is precisely this mood that we can see reflected in Fanny's sensitive emotionalism, in her preference for simplicity and in her determination to live in a cottage if that was necessary to be with the man she loved. Mrs Locke, at first meeting, had pleased Fanny by her affectionate nature. 'I love her already. And she was so kind, so caressing, so soft; pressed me so much to fix a time to visit Norbury; said such sweet things of Mrs Phillips and kissed me so affectionately in quitting me that I was quite melted by her.' Dr Burney might – and did – use the word 'viscosity' in referring to his daughters' Norbury friendship, but Fredy was admitted to the select ranks of those who interested both heart and head.

So, too, was Mrs Delany, though she was eighty-three. With the help of a magnifying glass she sorted old letters, letters from Swift and Young and other names that inspired reverence in Fanny. She told her anecdotes about these writers. Her friends, such as Lady Mansfield who has recently died, mean a great deal to her but she feels there is little she can give them now; she can only take. She speaks openly of how much she values Fanny's company, but with a restraint and sincerity that contrasts with Mrs Thrale's excess. The hours must have seemed long to Fanny, reading old letters and listening to reminiscences but perhaps it was a small price to pay for absolute respectability, which she might need vouched for at any moment. And a plan was forming in her head that resembled uncannily the plan in Mrs Delany's. Only their reasons differed.

At Mrs Ord's Fanny meets, among others, Mr Smelt, who speaks in a complimentary fashion of *Cecilia* and finds a common acquaintance in the Lockes. It was Mr Smelt who was to be charged with the delicate task of offering Fanny a position at Court. That was still in the future, and meanwhile Fanny had problems enough to occupy her mind. The impending death of Kitty Cambridge, which kept her father and brother in Twickenham and away from town, must have saddened her, as did Susan's failing health, which was soon to take her to Boulogne in the hope of improvement. The separation grieved Fanny unbearably, especially since to visit France seemed to her a near-impossibility, though she was forced to accept the plan as necessary for her sister's welfare. But the situation nearest her and most demanding was the quarrel of Dr Johnson with Mrs Thrale and the consequent acceleration of his decline towards old age and death.

At the time of her mother's re-marriage Queeney, installed at her own demand with her sisters and chaperone in the house their father had left them in Brighton, wrote to tell Dr Johnson of their unhappy plight. He wrote back indignantly and sympathetically, promising his support. Queeny's letter was followed by Mrs Thrale's. In reply to this Johnson wrote the well-known and angry letter: '. . . you are ignominiously married . . . God forgive your wickedness . . . may your folly do no further mischief.' He was ill, nearly seventy-five and a little jealous. He had loved Mrs Thrale for a great many years and her dead husband had been good to him. She replied, perhaps glad of the opportunity, that she would not see him while he spoke so disrespectfully of her new husband.

While she was home from a month-long stay with the Lockes at Norbury, which had turned itself into almost another Streatham, Fanny had her father set her down at Bolt Court so that she could visit Dr Johnson. He was alone and ill, but in very good spirits. Fanny was impressed by the brightness of his mental faculties 'though the poor and infirm machine that contains them seems alarmingly giving way'. She promises to return soon and the old man calls after her, 'Remember me in your prayers'. She longs to ask him to pray for her, but it seems, she says, presumptuous. She can no longer disguise from herself the fact that his condition is worsening fast. That Sunday of witty conversation and affectionate farewells was the last she was able to see of her old friend.

Less than two weeks later, after a further pleasant stay at Norbury, where Captain Cook and Madame de Sévigné were the daily reading, Fanny called on Dr Johnson but was told he was too ill to see her. He had been given permission to take as much opium as he pleased, and he had thanked and taken leave of all his physicians. He was said to have reconciled himself to death. The next day Dr Burney was able to spend half an hour with him and he apologised then for not admitting Fanny, saying he had been very ill. He sent her the message that he hoped he would throw the ball at her yet. When Fanny, desperate to make her own farewells, attempted once again to call at Bolt Court, she found the bedroom crowded with people she did not know and received from a wretchedly hesitant doctor the news that Johnson was too weak to see her. 'Going on to death very fast,' was the bulletin issued to the household at large. On 20 December Fanny wrote in her journal: 'This day was the ever-honoured, ever-lamented Dr Johnson committed to the earth.'

Sir John Hawkins, Johnson's biographer, who saw him regularly in the days before his death, gives us a little more detail. On 30 November he had 'eaten heartily of a French duck pie and a pheasant'. The dropsy increased and made it almost impossible for him to kneel and pray, and it grieved him to pray sitting. He busied himself with destroying papers and dictated a codicil to his will, leaving an annuity of £70 to Francis his negro servant, an injudicious legacy in Hawkins' opinion. By 13 December his appetite was totally gone and, uttering the words 'Jam moriturus', he had 'at a quarter past seven, without a groan or the least sign of pain or uneasiness, yielded his last breath'.

A circumstance that troubled his friends after his death were the deep wounds in several parts of his body. What had happened was that, to relieve the dropsy that bloated his limbs, Johnson had dug deep, first with a lancet and then with scissors, into his legs and thighs. He had believed that if he could drain the water in his limbs he would live, but the report of the doctors after his death was that he was suffering from: 'Two of the valves of the aorta ossified. The aircells of the lungs unusually distended. One of the kidneys destroyed by the pressure of the water. The liver schirrous. A stone in the gall-bladder of the size of a gooseberry.'

On 30 December in this eventful year Fanny was committed to a Blues party at Mrs Chapone's. No mention is made of the presence of the Cambridges who are presumably still in mourning. Sir Lucas Pepys reads her a letter from Mrs Piozzi which suggests that she is happy. The furore has calmed down. Nobody else mentions Mrs Piozzi, though there is much talk of Johnson. The next day she tried to visit Mrs Delany but found she was not up yet. There was nobody else she could turn to in her unhappiness. Susan was in Boulogne and Mrs Piozzi on her wedding trip. Mr Crisp and Dr Johnson were dead. Then she remembered the dear Lockes and went to await their arrival in Upper Brook Street. 'Dear, charming people! How did they soothe my troubled mind!'

10

MISS BURNEY AT THE COURT

When Mrs Thrale left Streatham and Samuel Crisp died, only one home remained to Fanny and that was, properly enough, her father's. Charles Burney earned by unremitting hard work a good income, but he was not a rich man. His wife, as she constantly reminded the family, helped with the expenses of the house and if he kept a carriage it was to enable him to give more lessons in the course of a day. He had dependants still at home and was pledged for some of Molesworth Phillips' debts. Moreover, he had been ill. Daughters were expected by Fanny's age, which was more than thirty, to have acquired husbands to keep them. Besides that, it would have been difficult for Fanny to adjust to living at home, enduring her stepmother's difficult temper and paying the regular round of visits by which a spinster daughter varied her life. She was used by now to a very comfortable standard of living and to intelligent companionship. What was more, she had to find a way to move on from the fame of being a bestselling novelist, since she strongly suspected she was written out.

Much the pleasantest solution to Fanny's problems at this juncture would undoubtedly have been marriage to George Cambridge. But over the years his lack of enthusiasm had become more than just perceptible. She continued to hope, could not in fact believe that his obvious devotion meant nothing of any importance in his life and in making any plans for the future took care to keep his sister informed, in case other, pleasanter plans might be hinted to her. But a new possibility was now suggested and one that would certainly add distinction to her career. Her friendship with Mrs Delany had brought her to the notice of the King and Queen. Dr Burney's musical career was already well known to them and he shared with the King a passion for Handel. His *History of Music* was dedicated to the Queen. Vistas opened up. Behind the solid worth of the elderly learned ladies lay another even solider El Dorado, pious, respectable and yet socially impeccable. Fanny Burney was offered service at Court. It was a pity that she would so much have preferred to marry Mr Cambridge.

In July 1785, not much more than six months after the death of Johnson and when Fanny's friendship with Mrs Delany was quite comfortably established, the Duchess of Portland died. The Duchess, among other kindnesses, had always invited Mrs Delany to her country house at Bulstrode for the summer so that she would not have to stay in her airless apartment at St James's. Now the new Duke of Portland had other uses for the house. News of this reached the Royal Family. Anxious for Mrs Delany's health, the King gave evidence of the very real kindness of which he was capable. He offered her a house at Windsor and an annuity of £300 to run it. She was to bring nothing but her clothes. The house was to be fully furnished and provided with plate and china, glass and linen, even stores of food in the cupboards, wines, sweetmeats, pickles and so on. George III's passion for minutiae was to have full fling.

Although she was reluctant to move house at such an advanced age there was no refusing the royal gift; by the autumn Mrs Delany was living at the Castle Gate in Windsor and in November Fanny joined her. The King and Queen were said to be enthusiastic about Mrs Delany's new friendship. Novels were considered a doubtful form of reading at court, but *Cecilia* carried the seal of Mrs Delany's approval and was to be admired, they were happy to discover, for its moral worth.

The Court of George III was remarkable for its concern with morality. The King was a slow and stubborn man. He had conceived a passion for Lady Sarah Lennox when he was first of an age to marry, but Lord Bute, whose influence over the Princess Dowager, George's mother, was notorious, did not wish for a royal alliance with the Hollands who were his rivals. Instead of the pretty girl he fancied, George was married to Charlotte of Mecklenburg-Strelitz who was seventeen years of age but remarkably plain. He transferred his affections to his unalluring bride so whole-heartedly that in twenty-one years they had fifteen children, but one effect was that he became rather obsessed with the idea of duty and the sacrifice of personal preferences. He tried to convey these ideas to his sons, but in vain. His daughters he sequestered, as hot-blooded men are inclined to do.

When an idea was safely lodged in George's mind it was impossible to dislodge or even moderate it. He was economical to the point of meanness, examined the household bills, demanded fruit and vegetables from his own gardens and laid it down that only the Royal Family, the Maids of Honour and the chaplains were to eat in the Palace. He visited the nurseries at six in the morning, a particularly trying time in nurseries, and supervised a strict regime for the education of his sons. But his children grew up healthy and beautiful, and the Prince of Wales was able to converse intelligently with the elder Doctor Burney on music and the younger on Greek. His abstemiousness about food was exceptional in his time but it would receive approbation from the medical profession now.

George III loved music and could play three instruments. He also enjoyed the theatre, if it was not Shakespeare, and would invite such actors as Kemble or Mrs Siddons to the Palace to act for him, though without fee or supper. He had a passion for clocks and telescopes and maps and military uniforms, and an interest in farming that would have provided him, in happier circumstances, with a life's occupation. He had no talent for politics or statesmanship.

For the Queen, marriage to the King of England was an amazing prize. She had been about to go into an aristocratic and, of course, Protestant nunnery and her future as George's bride must have seemed brilliant. She crossed to England in high spirits, accompanied by the Duchess of Ancaster and the Duchess of Hamilton, who had been sent to fetch her. and her faithful German attendants Mrs Haggendorn and Mrs Schwellenberg. When they succumbed to seasickness she played the harpsichord unceasingly and on arrival she resisted any attempts to improve her appearance. She was not able, however, to influence her husband. The dullness and meanness of the Court – reflected unpityingly by the cartoonists – kept the aristocracy away and she made no friends, relying only on her German attendants for company. The attacks on her husband's life, his illness, the hostility of the Regency party and even of her own children, as well as the strain of so many pregnancies had their effect on her. Silence, restraint, stoicism became her refuge but she expected the same virtues from others, even when heroics were unnecessary. Fanny Burney does not write a word of criticism of 'the sweet Queen' in her journals, but she must have been aware of the picture of coldness and self-centredness that is revealed, as if unconsciously, by what she does write.

The price Mrs Delany had to pay for the tenancy of her new house at Windsor was to have the King and Queen visiting her freely, rather as if she were the family grandmother. Because of her great age she was often allowed to sit in their presence, but their insistence on etiquette was otherwise unremitting. For a few weeks after her arrival at Windsor there were no royal visits because of the death of the Queen's brother, but even so the King came, incognito and alone, to give a mourning Mrs Delany news of a mourning Queen.

Mrs Delany's health was seriously impaired by the loss of her friend and Fanny relates several very touching stories of the affection between the two ladies. There is the account of Mrs Delany finding among her papers a packet with two dried leaves in it and labelled 'Two leaves picked at Bolsover by the Duchess of Portland and myself, in September 1756, the 20th year of our most intimate and dear friendship'. Then there is the story of the weaver-bird, which alone of her friend's belongings Mrs Delany chose for a keepsake after her death. It was found dead in its cage one morning when Mrs Delany was ill and the Queen, hearing of it, insisted on sending one of her own two weaver-birds to take its place. There were hopes of a simple substitution, but the two birds were not like enough to deceive Mrs Delany. Nevertheless she was much moved by the Queen's sympathetic gesture.

Mrs Delany continued to feel unwell. The move and her mourning for the Duchess as well as the frailty of old age all combined to restrict her activities, so that she could do no more than take walks with Fanny in the Old Park 'up and down the fine old avenue which, with the castle in view, has so grand a formality, that to alter, and even improve it, would make me think,' Fanny says, 'of Mason's expression in the English Garden, that taste here were sacrilege'. Then, since she could not visit them, the King and Queen came over to spend two hours with Mrs Delany at tea-time, that is, after the early dinner of the period. Miss Burney's writing was discussed and the possibility of her attempting a play was touched upon. The Queen called Mrs Delany to witness that Fanny's 'character, by all I hear, is too delicate to suit with writing for the stage'. Mrs Delany agreed with this view and Fanny recorded the verdict delightedly for her father's pleasure.

So far Fanny had not met the Royal Family, When they were expected at Mrs Delany's house she fled from the room, claiming that a meeting would cause her 'infinite pain'. But the Queen had made so many enquiries about Fanny, had commented on Dr Burney's good qualities, asked whether Fanny read aloud to Mrs Delany (a significant question in the light of later events) and expressed so often a wish to meet the novelist that it was becoming difficult to put the occasion off any longer. Accordingly Fanny was prepared for a royal encounter. The journal mentions only Mrs Delany's injunction against monosyllabic answers, but a letter to Hetty written at about this time summarizes the rules amusingly:

In the first place you must not cough . . . In the second place you must not sneeze . . . In the third place you must not on any account stir either hand or foot. If, by chance, a black pin runs into your head, you must not take it out. If the pain is very great you must be sure to bear it without wincing; if it brings the tears into your eyes you must not wipe them off; if they give you a tingling by running down your cheeks, you must look as if nothing was the matter. If the blood should gush from your head by means of the black pin you must let it gush; if you are uneasy to think of making such a blurred appearance, you must be uneasy but you must say nothing about it. If, however, the agony is very great, you may, privately, bite the inside of your cheek or of your lips, for a little relief; taking care, meanwhile, to do it so cautiously as to make no apparent dent outwardly. And with that precaution, if you even gnaw a piece out, it will not be minded, only be sure either to swallow it or commit it to a corner of the inside of your mouth till they are gone – for you must not spit.

After these essential preparations there came an evening when the large figure of the King, all in black and wearing the diamond star of the Garter, arrived dramatically in Mrs Delany's drawing-room and would not allow Fanny Burney to escape unpresented. He spoke to her briefly and then moved on to talk to Mrs Delany, chiefly about his children's ailments. The Princess Elizabeth, who had been ill, 'had been blooded [he said] twelve times in the last fortnight and had lost seventy-five ounces of blood, besides undergoing blistering and other discipline'. The younger children all had the whooping-cough. Meanwhile Fanny, whose feelings were being so sensitively spared by the King's manner of making her acquaintance, was amusing herself, the first shock over, with the thought that they were all playing the children's game of Puss in the Corner, standing at equal intervals against the wall while His Majesty, in the centre, beckoned each of them with a 'puss, puss, puss'.

At last her call came and there ensued one of those conversations for which His Majesty was renowned:

'But what? – what? – how was it?'
'Sir,' cried I, not well understanding him.
'How came you? – how happened it? – what? – what?'
'I – I only wrote, sir, for my own amusement – only in some odd, idle hours.'
'But your publishing – your printing – how was that?'

The conversation continues along these lines until George III has extracted every detail of Fanny's publication of *Evelina* from her, then sets out with equal thoroughness to discover what she is writing now, whether she intends to write any more, what her father is writing, whether he writes quickly, whether she plays an instrument and so on. The Queen joins him and works really hard to be amiable, revealing by her questions that the Burney family have been discussed in royal circles and some quite unexpected scraps of gossip passed on, such as Susan's being brought to bed unexpectedly at Norbury Park of her first son, the handsome and loving Norbury.

Fanny has, of course, remembered every word, particularly the compliments, and her rendering of the King's conversation reminds us that she was later to mimic the royal pair for the entertainment of the Lockes. It is an interesting portrait she has given of herself, disingenuous about the writing of *Evelina*, since they were not odd, idle hours in which she wrote, secretive about her other productions, emphasizing for effect her famous shyness and at the same time holding her own very well, especially over such questions as whether she would play to the King.

After this meeting, by slow and easy stages, the acquaintance progressed. Then in May 1786, the Mastership of the King's Band fell vacant and Dr Burney who had just, through Burke's influence, obtained the position of organist at Chelsea College, was very anxious for this higher post. On the advice of his friend Mr Smelt and with the help of Mrs Delany, he and Fanny joined the crowd of courtiers awaiting the moment when the King and Queen and the six princesses were to parade on the terrace in the evening. Fanny was able to exchange a word with the King but Charles Burney went unnoticed. That evening Mr Smelt came to tell him that the post had already been allocated without reference to the King.

Almost immediately after this, the retirement was announced of Mrs Haggendorn, one of the two Keepers of the Robes that Queen Charlotte had brought with her twenty-five years before from Mecklenburg-Strelitz. The Queen, who must have known for some time that Mrs Haggendorn was retiring and who must certainly have been giving much thought to the question of her successor, now decided to offer the post to Fanny. The dedication of Dr Burney's *History of Music* to the Queen, Fanny's probity and distinguished reputation, the interest the Royal Family liked to take in literature and the arts, their wish to please Mrs Delany, Dr Burney's disappointment, all these influenced her choice and although no word of the possibility of a post at Court could be spoken or written, Mrs Delany probably had the idea in mind when she invited Fanny to Windsor.

Mr Smelt was sent to make the first advances to Fanny. To his astonish-

117

ment, she behaved with the utmost reluctance. He and a very disappointed Mrs Delany tried to persuade her to overcome her fears. Both of them assured her of the sweetness of character of the Royal Family and Mr Smelt emphasized the great honour the Queen had shown her in choosing her out of 'thousands of offered candidates of high birth and rank but small fortunes'. More persuasive still was the attitude of Dr Burney. He equated, it was said, the Court with heaven and he also regarded it as a very valuable source of preferment. The whole family, he believed, could be enriched by Fanny's influence: James would have a ship and Charles a bishopric, while he . . . Overcome by unselfish family considerations, Fanny accepted the post.

This is the picture Fanny Burney presented in her journals and in the lengthy letter by which she kept Miss Cambridge apprised of the offer and of her unwillingness to take it. She emphasized her deep unwillingness to leave a busy happy life for the royal service. Macaulay was later to write of her wasted talent in the years when she was 'put to folding muslins'. But was that quite true? To the King's enquiries about her writing she had made a very interesting answer: 'I believe I have exhausted myself, sir.' This she described as 'plain fact' when he treated it as a joke. We should set the 'plain fact' against a letter she wrote to Hetty from Windsor soon after she joined Mrs Delany there which hints quite plainly that she is angling for a royal appointment:

> You know I told you, in my last, my various difficulties, what sort of prefer-ment to turn my thoughts to, and concluded with just starting a young budding notion of decision by suggesting that a handsome pension for nothing at all would be as well as working night and day for a salary.
>
> This blossom of an idea, the more I dwelt upon, the more I liked. Thinking served it for a hot-house and it came out into full blow as I ruminated upon my pillow. Delighted that thus all my contradictory and wayward fancies were overcome and my mind was peaceably settled what to wish and to demand, I gave over all further meditation upon choice of elevation and had nothing more to do but to make my election known.
>
> My next business, therefore, was to be presented. This could be no difficulty; my coming hither had been their own desire and they had earnestly pressed its execution. I had only to prepare myself for the rencounter.

These paragraphs, written six months before Mr Smelt 'took Fanny by surprise' with an offer of a place at Court, can only mean that her appointment as Keeper of the Robes was carefully planned for and deliberately sought after by Fanny herself. In fact, the first of the three paragraphs suggests that what she had in mind was a *pension,* in other words that she planned to serve the minimum number of years with the Queen and then rely on her influential friends to raise an outcry about her health, which, in any case, could always be described as failing. If this was so – and there seems to be no other interpretation – her behaviour on going into the Court and on coming out of it can be seen in a new light. 'A cunning little rogue,' Mrs Thrale called her. Her hesitations and tremblings, which were as much because she was giving up the idea of marriage to George Cambridge as for any other reason, served like her shyness to procure sympathy and especially considerate treatment. When the moment comes, her father is to know what family preferments will cost Fan:

> I could disguise my trepidation no longer – indeed I had never disguised, I had only forborne proclaiming it. But my dear father now, sweet soul! felt it all, as I held by his arm, without power to say one word, but that if he did not hurry along I should drop by the way. I heard in his kind voice that he was really alarmed; he would have slackened his pace, or have made me stop to breathe, but I could not; my breath seemed gone and I could only hasten with all my might, lest my strength should go too.

Fanny was apt to speak of her decision to enter the Court as if she were being urged into a nunnery. Her separation from family and friends must certainly have been grievous, but the ideas that run through her mind at this juncture are of marriage. They merge in a fashion we can follow quite clearly: a marriage (to Barlow) that she has refused, despite her father's encouragement; a marriage she was not offered (by Cambridge); and finally a post that was an establishment, a substitute for the marriage she was not offered, and that she dare not refuse, because of her father's wishes. She begins to think of herself as the bride of the Court: she writes to Charlotte, who had married Clement Francis six months before (and Francis, who was Warren Hasting's secretary in India, had returned to England with the express purpose of marrying the author of *Evelina*), 'I am now fitting out, just as you were', and describes the trousseau and excitement as being like preparations for a wedding. She is to be in attendance on the Queen only and is to have apartments in the palace, a footman, a maid, a coach shared with Mrs Schwellenberg and £200 a year. She need not envy a bride. She puts the thought into words when she writes to Susan:

I am *married,* my dearest Susan – I look upon it in that light – I was averse to forming the union and I endeavoured to escape it; but my friends interfered – they prevailed – and the knot is tied. What then now remains but to make the best wife in my power? I am bound to it in duty and I will strain every nerve to succeed.

When Fanny Burney entered the Court she was thirty-four. For eight years she had been a celebrity and had been treated with reverence by people of the most remarkable distinction. Mrs Thrale had commented on her touchiness and the trait was still with her. So her anxiety about life at Court concerned itself chiefly with the question of whether she was paid enough respect by those she encountered there. The Queen appears to have understood this perfectly and shows an almost super-human tactfulness in her dealings with Fanny. George III was his kindly self and the princesses, bored in what they too called their nunnery, were glad of someone new to talk to. Besides, they had been brought up to be exquisitely considerate to everyone they met, and such courtesy enchanted Fanny.

At the time Fanny went to Court, the Prince of Wales was twenty-four. He and his brothers were lodged in pairs, each pair with its own governors and tutors. The princesses remained with their parents, the six of them ranging in age from the Princess Royal who was twenty-three to the little Princess Amelia whose third birthday Fanny attended. The lives of the princes and the princesses contrasted sharply. The Prince of Wales had already had a most expensive *affaire* with an actress known as Perdita Robinson, which had cost his father £5000 for letters as well as a considerable sum in life annuities for Perdita and her daughter. Now Mrs Fitzherbert's name was coupled with his. The New Lady's Magazine for 1786, the year Fanny entered the Court, contains portraits of the Prince and of Mrs Fitzherbert, a short article on the lady and an account of the sale of the Prince's stud, presumably to pay his debts. Even his favourite horse, Rockingham, was sold. A carefully-worded comment laments the improvidence of it all: '. . . had the horses continued in his Royal Highness's possession, there is no doubt but they would have won him immense sums.' The rest of the princes had each their usually scandalous, always expensive and sometimes farcical affairs until the death of the Princess Charlotte sent them shopping around Europe for Protestant princesses in a race to ensure the succession.

The princesses, on the other hand, had no liberty at all. Their pocket-money was given them by the Queen and the only men they met were those employed about the Court. Perfectly suitable offers of marriage were ignored by George III, who did not care for the idea of marriage for his daughters. Charles Greville, the diarist, said they 'stayed at home with their passions boiling over, ready to fall into the hands of the first men whom circumstances enabled to get at them'. The Prince of Wales, to do him justice, helped them all he could, but their stories in later years include secret marriages to elderly commoners, or royal marriages in late middle age to fat and conspicuously ugly princes out of the German states, or, in the case of Mary, to her own cousin, William of Gloucester, 'lanky and shambling', but above all, dull: 'a lambent dullness plays about his face,' was the line from Dryden Greville quoted in comment on him.

Fanny Burney was, like everyone else in the country, well aware of the reputation of the princes. Her journal includes a very lively description of the oafish behaviour of William, Duke of Clarence, in St James's Palace at dinner one evening. She could not have been expected to foresee the grotesqueness of the romances forced upon the beautiful young princesses in later years, but it is curious to notice how little aware she is of their problems in the five years she is at Court – and later – and to observe her apparently complete acceptance of the Queen's idealized picture of family happiness. When she takes her little son to visit the Royal Family and the princesses are kind to him, she does not speculate on their lack of husbands or children. When the Princess Royal marries at last, in 1797, she tells us that every stitch in the wedding dress was sewn by the Princess herself and mentions the prospective bride's nervousness and tears. But the Fanny Burney Maria knew would have sketched in the bridgeroom – Gillray's 'Great Bellygerent' – in his wedding costume of 'silk shot with gold and silver richly embroidered'.

It would be instructive to know how Fanny had envisaged her duties as Second Mistress of the Robes before she went to Court. With her well-known lack of interest in clothes she can hardly have expected to be concerned with the actual dressing of the Queen and she certainly under-estimated the amount of time she would have to spend on her own clothes, especially for the Drawing-Rooms and Birthdays. Perhaps she saw herself as simply living in the same ambience as the Queen, leading much the same kind of life – 'a handsome pension for nothing at all'. If so, she little understood the tedium protocol imposed upon life at Court.

Fanny found her rooms at Windsor as attractive as she could desire. She had a large drawing-room facing the Round Tower on one side and the Little Park on the other. On the first morning the Queen sent her to fetch Mrs Delany, wishing, no doubt, to make her feel less lonely in her new surroundings. But it is not long before we realize that the daily routine is an exhausting one, especially for anyone as frail as Fanny had always been and as used to freedom.

At six in the morning Fanny got out of bed, dressed simply and waited for her summons to the Queen, which usually came at half-past seven. At this time she found that the Queen had had her hair arranged by her wardrobe-woman Mrs Thielky and that she was required to help her dress by taking the garments one by one from Mrs Thielky and putting them on the Queen. To anyone as sensitive as Fanny this service must have seemed both embarrassing – since it involved physical contact – and distinctly menial. It is unlikely that Fanny was particularly adroit at the task: the Queen is said to have complained to Mrs Delany that Fanny always managed to tie her back hair into the bow that fastened a necklace. By eight o'clock the Queen was usually dressed and able to proceed to family prayers. Fanny then went to her room and allowed herself an hour for breakfast with a book. From nine until ten she devoted to organizing her affairs, particularly clothes, which were a great worry to her at Court. She was then free until a quarter to twelve, except on Wednesdays and Saturdays when the Queen's hair needed curling and craping. Often she would go for a walk. At a quarter to one the Queen began dressing for the day and required the help of all her attendants. She read the newspapers while her hair was powdered by the hairdresser and often read paragraphs aloud to those about her, which must have alleviated the tedium. By about three o'clock all this was over and Fanny was free until dinner-time.

Five o'clock was dinner-time and Fanny shared a table with Mrs Schwellenberg, the senior dresser and a woman who was to give her a a great deal of misery. The Royal Family then walked on the terrace where they could be seen by any visitors who cared to watch. Fanny and Mrs Schwellenberg had coffee together in the latter's room until eight. Then they came down to the eating-room and served tea to the equerries and any other male guests. At nine the equerries and guests went off to the concert-room, but Fanny still stayed with Mrs Schwellenberg until eleven when she had her supper, of fruit, in her own room. The Queen's last summons came between eleven and twelve. This final duty took her up to half an hour, after which she looked out her clothes for the next day and went to bed.

This programme must have been immensely boring to Fanny, embodying as it it did a long-drawn time-wasting very uncongenial to anyone who had been accustomed to making good use of every hour. And if her duties often seemed menial, the feeling was intensified by the fact that she was summoned to them by a bell. Quite soon she was being required to mix the Queen's snuff, simply because Mrs Haggendorn always did, and to read to her, a task that made her unduly self-conscious. Miss Burney was tactfully reminded by 'the sweet Queen' that her voice was too low to be heard, but the snuff was a total success: 'Mama says the snuff is extremely well mixed; and she has sent another box to be filled.'

It is obvious from the outline of Fanny's day that she was forced for a great many hours into the company of Mrs Schwellenberg. She was the senior of the Queen's two dressers, Mrs Haggendorn, the junior, having been reduced to ill-health and retirement by the exigencies of her job. Mrs Schwellenberg was not a woman of any great culture and she valued the power it gave her to be so near the Queen. She made life quite intolerable for Fanny by a frank, forthright rudeness that takes the breath away. Fanny, who by no means underestimated her own consequence, was compelled to stand up to her in a tiresomely unremitting fashion that can have done her health no good at all:

> When I saw myself expected by Mrs Schwellenberg [Fanny remarks in a letter] not to be her colleague but her dependant deputy! not to be her visitor at my own option but her Companion, her Humble Companion at her own command. This has given so new a character to the place I had accepted under such different auspices that nothing but my horror of Disappointing – perhaps Displeasing – my dearest Father has deterred me from the moment that I made the mortifying Discovery from soliciting his Leave to Resign.

We are never given Mrs Schwellenberg's point of view, but certain mitigating factors come to mind as one reads. She may have wished for another German to talk to or even had in mind a friend or relative to fill the post. She was far from well: 'This poor woman was so ill, so lost for want of her party at cards and so frightened with apprehensions of the return of some dreadful spasmodic complaints from which she has many years suffered the severest pain, that I was induced to do a thing you will wonder at . . .' Fanny writes. The thing her friends will wonder at is her agreeing to play cards with the poor old woman. Cards were much despised in Blues circles. We hear nothing more about the 'dreadful spasmodic complaints' as time goes on and Fanny loses sympathy with Mrs Schwellenberg. Again and again we are told that Mrs Schwellenberg no longer comes down in the mornings or is too ill to attend the tea-table, or is holidaying for her health. But no allowance is made for the effect of illness on her disposition.

Then again, it had always been a Burney custom to mimic the foreign accents of the musicians who frequented the family house in such numbers. Charlotte especially enjoyed writing a kind of broken English in her letters. Mrs Schwellenberg had cast herself as a comic character from the beginning and her resentment of Fanny, who may not have been congenial to her, promptly promoted her to comic villainess. It is true that she was fond of her pet toads and that she tiresomely demanded the window open in a coach. Fanny wished to have it shut and found her eyes seriously affected by the draught. It is a curious thing that years after and in France Fanny describes a coach journey in which a 'gouvernante' and a highlander contend over just such a point. 'Two spirits of such fiery materials,' she says, 'both offended, were not likely to remain long without striking against each other.' Was she looking back at the journeys in Mrs Schwellenberg's coach and confessing that there had been a dispute for the mastery implicit in the wrangling that went on?

One of Mrs Schwellenberg's vanities was to preside over the tea-board at eight o'clock each evening and give the gentlemen their tea. A certain jealousy of Fanny became evident in her behaviour here, and this was unfortunate because the equerries valued the hour of leisure and Fanny valued their company. When Mrs Schwellenberg kept to her room as a result of ill-health, Fanny was perfectly happy in the company of the dull but quite personable young men who were in attendance on the King, wearing the King's Windsor uniform of blue and gold turned up with red. In an excess of discretion she gave them all pseudonyms. Thus the Queen was referred to as the Magnolia, the Princess Elizabeth as the Lily and the Princess Augusta as the Rose. In the same way we hear of Colonel Wel-·bred and Colonel Manners, of Mr Fairly and of Mr Turbulent who liked to tease and to be a great deal too familiar, even with the princesses. But Mr Turbulent had a wife and so could be regarded with detachment. Mr Fairly's wife was reported to be dying and consequently his attentions – since Fanny had reached the age for widowers – had a great deal more charm and interest. 'He is a man,' Fanny reported, 'of the most scrupulous good-breeding, diffident, gentle and sentimental in his conversation and assiduously attentive in his manners.' He was also Colonel Stephen Digby, brother of the Dean of Durham and of the first Earl Digby whose family seat was Sherborne Castle in Dorset.

Other mild alleviations of the dull Court routine included the royal birthdays of which there were a gratifying number. The first that Fanny experienced was, pleasantly enough, the birthday of the little Princess Amelia who was then three years old. 'The manner of keeping the birthdays here is very simple,' Fanny records:

All the Royal Family are new-dressed; so – at least so they appear – are all their attendants. The dinners and desserts are unusually sumptuous; and some of the principal officers of state and a few of the ladies of the Court come to Windsor to make their compliments; and at night there is a finer concert, by an addition from town of the musicians belonging to the Queen's band. If the weather is fine, all the family walk upon the terrace.

The Princess Amelia walked upon the terrace in a robe-coat covered with fine muslin, a dressed close cap, white gloves and fan, leading the royal procession because it was her birthday. Mrs Delany was there, invited by the King and Queen to the birthday breakfast. She and Fanny together joined the company on the terrace and received the curtsies of the princesses as each passed.

Just before this event occurred one of the many attacks on the life of the King. Margaret Nicholson, a poor mad-woman, struck at His Majesty with a knife under the pretext of presenting some kind of petition to him. George III, with amazing compassion, intervened between his servants and his would-be murderess. 'I have received no injury,' he cried. 'Don't hurt the woman; the poor creature appears insane.' He went in to see the Queen, who had with her the two eldest princesses as well as the Duchess of Ancaster and Lady Charlotte Bertie, and 'hastened up to her, with a countenance of striking vivacity, and said, "Here I am! – safe and well – as you see! – but I have very narrowly escaped being stabbed".'

This was all rather sudden for the Queen, who envied, at first, the tears of her attendants. The King then tried to cheer his family in his own unsubtle way: 'Has she cut my waistcoat?' cried he – 'Look, for I have had no time to examine.'

'Thank heaven,' Fanny says, 'the poor wretch had not gone quite so far.' 'Though nothing,' added the King, in giving his relation, 'could have been sooner done, for there was nothing for her to go through but a thin linen and fat.'

When the mob offered to lynch Margaret Nicholson, the King called to them, 'The poor creature is mad! Do not hurt her! She has not hurt me!' Fanny says: 'He then came forward and showed himself to all the people declaring he was perfectly safe and unhurt; and then gave positive orders that the woman should be taken care of, and went into the palace and held his levee.'

A contemporary description of Margaret Nicholson says she was

About 40 years of age, a native of Yorkshire, rather short, of a very swarthy complexion, which gives her much the appearance of a foreigner; she was dressed in a flowered linen or muslin gown, black gauze bonnet, black silk cloak, morning wire cloak with blue ribbons. Her brother is a respectable character and keeps the Three Horse Shoes public house, the corner of Milford-Lane, in the Strand.

The poor woman is described as 'a harmless creature', if not actually insane, and the knife that might have killed a king was 'an old, ivory-handled dessert-knife, worn very thin towards the point and cracked in several places in the handle'. There were to be other attempts on the King's life and on each occasion he displayed a kind of exhilaration as well as a refusal to try to save himself. 'Do you flinch, my lord?' he enquired in surprise of his travelling companion when the missiles came too near their mark. His courage was never in dispute, nor his mercy towards those demented creatures who threatened the life of a king.

The Court always moved to St James's for the Queen's birthday, the King's birthday and the Drawing-Rooms. This gave Fanny an opportunity to visit her friends and to receive visits at the Palace from her friends and family. The *Lady's Magazine* of the time devotes several columns of ecstatic description to the King 'in brown velvet richly embroidered with gold and silver', the Queen 'in a beautiful laurel-green satin, trimmed with a rich embroidered cape, in coloured foils etc. which appeared to be executed in a stile truly superb and elegant'. The Prince of Wales, needless to say, outdid even his parents. He wore 'a rich dress of silver on a light ground, of a very curious manufacture, the seams were ornamented with an embroidery that appeared like thread lace and gave a beautiful relief to the brilliancy of the suit'. In the evening, the dressing was all to do again for the Birthday Ball.

Another of the variations on the Windsor routine took the form of visits to towns or country-houses. Seldom were these visits attended by any pleasure for the royal train and we cannot believe that the Royal Family themselves found these interludes very relaxing, but any break was looked forward to for its own sake. The Oxford expedition was one of the occasions when Fanny showed herself very sensitive of her dignity and we wonder how tolerable the Royal Family found her at close quarters. The plan was to spend one day at Lord Harcourt's, at Nuneham, one at Oxford and one at Blenheim, dining and sleeping always at Nuneham. Fanny was obviously desperately anxious to make the point that she could be staying with the Harcourts as a guest, not just as an attendant to the Queen. She had met Lord Harcourt, been introduced to him in fact by Sir Joshua Reynolds, and regretted that she had missed at the time the opportunity to meet Lady Harcourt. Mrs Schwellenberg in her usual obtuse fashion tried to reassure Fanny about her wardrobe, realizing no doubt that Fanny had few formal clothes. 'When you go with the Queen,' she said, 'it is enough; they might be civil to you for that sake.' She also offered (kindly) to see to it that Fanny was kept in the background: 'There is no need you might be seen.' This was, of course, very far from Fanny's intention.

Miss Planta, the children's governess, and Fanny arrived at Nuneham to find everybody preparing for the King and Queen who were to follow a few hours later. They were not welcomed by anybody at all and could not even find a porter, so decided to look for their own rooms. The servants were far from helpful and Fanny soon began writing them down in her journal as 'yellow-laced saunterers' and wishing she had brought either her man or her maid to deal with them. But her fury was chiefly directed at Lady Harcourt who, she admits, has other things to think about at the moment but should have arranged for them to be looked after. Eventually they met a Frenchwoman, Lady Harcourt's maid, who showed them into a pleasant parlour and offered them tea. By now the King and Queen were in the park and Fanny was – or said she was – extremely anxious that they should not come into the house by the garden door leading into the parlour and find their two attendants, Miss Planta and Fanny, neglected. Fanny's dignity was at stake here it seems, not Lady Harcourt's. So, although Miss Planta, who was used to the farce behind the royal tours, was amused by the suggestion, they set out once again to find their rooms.

Miss Planta managed to find not their room but the princesses' and having made sure that everything was prepared for them decided good-temperedly to have tea in the Princess Elizabeth's room. By now Lady Harcourt had arrived and Fanny, on being introduced to her, gives her a 'cold, silent courtsey'. Lady Harcourt offers to send her sisters to them and when these ladies do not come Fanny is enraged and Miss Planta convulsed with mirth. The princesses arrive and are then obliged to placate an injured Miss Burney with light conversation and soothing words. Fanny and Miss Planta are taken to their room and left there for two hours, until a maid tells them that supper is ready. Since they have not been summoned by the ladies of the house they decide not to have supper – Fanny could always manage without eating – and this naturally brings Lady Harcourt to propitiate them. The Queen has arranged for them to join her suite the next day on the visit to Oxford. A final triumph is that when the Queen asks Fanny what gown she has brought with her she is able to say 'a new Chambery gauze', not the riding-dress she had travelled in and which Mrs Schwellenberg had suggested would do for all occasions.

The next day Fanny spends a great deal of effort explaining to anyone who will listen how slightingly she and Miss Planta have been treated and snubbing anyone who does not sympathize. The party sets out for Oxford and in the Sheldonian Theatre the King and Queen listen to loyal addresses and reply appropriately. Then follows the homage of the learned and Fanny is amused in a superior fashion by their shambling ignorance of Court etiquette. She was also pleased with the city and soothed by the gallantry of one or two of the Doctors and Professors who made such flattering remarks as, 'You seem inclined to abide with us, Miss Burney?' and 'No, no, don't let's shut up Miss Burney among the old tombs! No, no!' She was presently recognized as Dr Burney's daughter and treated with the soothing deference the visit had so far disastrously lacked. What also raised Fanny's spirits was Mr Fairly's ingenuity in finding a small parlour in Christ Church where Miss Planta and Fanny could sit down and then producing bread and apricots. The ladies of Nuneham, realizing that Miss Planta and Fanny had been included in the royal party, behaved towards them with appropriate ceremony for the rest of the visit and Fanny was pleased to revise her opinion of their moral worth as a result.

In August 1787, while she was at the Court of St James for the birthday of the Duke of York, just returned to England after seven years in Germany, Fanny read of the death of Mr Fairly's wife, formerly Lady Lucy Fox-Strangways. He returned to Court from nursing her 'thin, haggard, worn with care and grief and watching – his hair turned grey – white rather, and some of his front teeth vanished'. Thereafter he was frequently about, shepherding his sons who were at Eton and ousting Colonel Welbred from Fanny's closest favour by his philosophical disquisitions: 'Life and Death were the deep themes to which he led; and the little space between them and the little value of that space were the subject of his comments.' At tea-time it became a matter of custom for Fanny to have the two colonels one on either side and for Mr Fairly – Colonel Digby – to stay as much as half an hour beyond the time of his Court duty.

Early in 1788, when life at Court was already becoming a great deal more interesting for Fanny, the trial of Warren Hastings, so long delayed, began at last. The Queen offered Fanny two tickets for the Grand Chamberlain's box and suggested she should take her father. She also sent Fanny some cakes from her breakfast table so that she could make an early start. But at St Martin's Street Fanny found her father suffering from the effects of a fall and summoned instead her brother Charles to be her escort.

Fanny and her brother arrived at Westminster Hall between nine and ten o'clock and she gives in her papers a 'journalizing' description of the arrangement of Westminster Hall, conscious no doubt that she had been sent to the trial as a reporter and that the recipients of her journal would also expect to be given every detail. Warren Hastings was regarded by Fanny as 'an innocent and injured man', and this view – which was also the court view – she protests throughout the trial, on what evidence it is difficult to detect. Charlotte's husband, Clement Francis, may have been the source of her information or she may simply have adopted the Tory stance. Any acquaintance who is, by office or conviction, on the prosecuting side receives Fanny's coldest disapproval. This has its difficulties when she has known them for some time or when they are impressively well connected. She has also to bear in mind that if she is not friendly to anyone they will suppose that the Court has made her too grand to know them. Mr Wyndham, one of the Committee on the prosecuting side was not only a distinguished acquaintance but he had been notably kind to Dr Johnson, so Fanny could scarcely avoid his company. She did, however, make a number of attempts to convert him to her point of view, in vain: Wyndham maintained implacably that Hastings had been guilty of arrogance, oppression and tyranny. Fanny countered with the retort that she knew nothing of the case but she had met Hastings and liked him, which made it impossible for her to believe him guilty. When Mr Burke, fresh from his speech of accusation, recognized Fanny and bowed, her curtsey, she says, 'was the most ungrateful, distant and cold'. Lord Walsingham and the Streatham physician Sir Lucas Pepys were also reproved for disagreeing with Fanny's views.

On Fanny's third visit to the Hastings trial (it went on for seven years) she found Wyndham furiously declaring that the outcome was rigged: the Lords and the Chancellor were protecting Hastings. Fanny grudgingly admitted that her esteem for Hastings was diminished, but on her fourth visit when she was accompanied by James, she was still behaving very distantly to such old friends as Burke and Sheridan because they were not on Hastings' side. Wyndham, however, she was content to dispute with, believing, she said in her journal, that he could eventually be converted to her point of view. It is evident that Fanny at least enjoys her proselytizing and the conversation eventually turns to a theme upon which she and Wyndham are more in agreement, the deep respect both feel for Dr Johnson. 'His abilities,' cried Mr Wyndham, 'were gigantic and always at hand; no matter for the subject, he had information ready for everything. He was fertile – he was universal.'

'My praise of him,' Fanny comments rather priggishly, 'was of a still more solid kind – his principles, his piety, his kind heart under all its rough coating.'

The Hastings Trial dragged on interminably but Fanny had to return to her 'monastery' as she now called it. Her visits to Mrs Delany were becoming even more frequent because her old friend's health was failing and in April she 'was bereft of the most revered of friends and, perhaps, the most perfect of women'. She left Fanny her fine quarto edition of Shakespeare, a choice of one of the paper flowers, a copy by Mrs Delany of Vandyke's portrait of Sacharissa and two medallions of their Majesties.

Fanny's loneliness was now even more acute than before. Fortunately or unfortunately, Mr Fairly was on duty with the King when she returned to Court and he was very willing to be considerate, 'interesting himself about my diet, my health, my exercise; proposing walks to me and exhorting me to take them, and even intimating he should see that I did were not his time all occupied by royal attendance'. The group of equerries, including Colonel Welbred and the outrageous Mr Turbulent, had now become a group of cheerful friends. Besides, there was Mr Wyndham, who was so flattering and attentive whenever she met him at the Hastings Trial.

In July 1788 the Court set out for a holiday at Cheltenham for the benefit of the King, who had had one or two disquieting bouts of illness, the first indications of the serious malady which was to come upon him in the autumn of that year. The illness was variously diagnosed as consumption, gout flying to the head (that favourite blanket diagnosis of eighteenth-century doctors), the results of the dry, hot weather and the result of his ascetic eating and drinking habits. Lord Fauconberg, one of the Lords of the Bedchamber, lent his house, Bays Hill Lodge, also known as Fauconberg Hall, and the King combined the benefits of taking the waters ('He finds a Pint and a half the proper quantity to give him two openings') with horse-riding and country-air.

In Cheltenham the friendship between Fanny and Mr Fairly had an opportunity to develop, since away from Windsor there was much more freedom. Fanny was lodged with the King and Queen and princesses at Fauconberg Hall and Mr Fairly was lodged in the town a quarter of a mile away. He lost no time in arranging to drink tea with Fanny and Miss Planta and even brought his friends. At other times of the day he found it convenient to use Fanny's room, to read melancholy poems to her and to leave his inkstand, the gift of the Queen, so that he was able to use the room for writing. Miss Planta, who shared the room with Fanny, took herself out for tactful walks and Fanny became used to the luxury of companionship and literary discussion with Mr Fairly. He lent her books, begged her in a lover-like fashion to mark her favourite passages and urged her to keep his bookish tastes secret lest he should be accused, he says 'of bookism and pedantry'. Then he appeared with a volume entitled 'Original Love Letters' which he recommended most enthusiastically to Fanny but which for sheer self-consciousness she dared not read.

Mr Fairly contracts the gout and is unfit for his duties. He turns up, however, in Fanny's parlour with a swollen face and muffled up in a huge great-coat. The date is approaching when his year of mourning will be up and rumours abound. Fanny is asked whether she thinks he will marry again and she interprets these enquiries in a wholly complimentary sense. Has he not assured her himself that he has no interest in 'Miss Fuzilier', who was Miss Gunning, one of the Queen's Maids of Honour and generally favoured as a candidate for Mr Fairly's hand? Mr Fairly continues to visit Fanny, to insist that she reads 'Original Love Letters' or that he should read them to her and to spend peaceful hours with her on the steps of Fauconberg Hall.

The King and Queen are beginning to enquire about Mr Fairly's health and they even visit him in Fanny's parlour to see how he is. He resumes his duties and then goes on leave with the enigmatic remark to Fanny, 'We will say nothing of any regrets'. But Sir Edmund Waller, holder of one of the richest sinecures in the royal gift, dies suddenly and there comes a note to Fanny asking her to bring this to the Queen's attention. Fanny is torn between eagerness to oblige Mr Fairly and a certain diffidence about the indirectness of the request. The bold subscription 'very truly and sincerely yours' seems to her perfectly appropriate considering the intimate terms they are on and she longs to let her Majesty see it, but after some reflection decides it would be more tactful to ask the Princess Elizabeth to give the Queen the message and to leave the note upstairs. The Queen is quite obviously suspicious of the whole business and nothing will satisfy her but producing the note. Whatever her suspicions they were dispelled; the note, written quite formally but for the ending, must have disarmed her for Fanny received 'a most gracious smile' and Mr Fairly his sinecure.

Fanny by now is calmly confident of Mr Fairly's affections. She seems to have learned nothing from her friendship with George Cambridge, whose appearance of devotion was at least as strong as Mr Fairly's. She speaks in her diary of 'my acknowledged friend' and even of 'a permanent relationship. There is little doubt that Digby was either extraordinarily obtuse – he even brought one of his Etonian sons to dine with her – or genuinely attracted but dissatisfied with her family connections.

A month or so after the return from Cheltenham, Fanny went to Kew with Miss Planta, Mr Turbulent and Mr de Luc. Her relations with Mrs Schwellenberg had seldom been worse and, if we are to believe Fanny, that lady was constantly advising her that Colonel Goldsworthy or Dr Shepherd would be quite willing to marry her. Mr Turbulent teased her about flirtations in Cheltenham. Since the Court generally must have been aware that Mr Fairly's engagement to Miss Gunning was talked of as certain, both Mrs Schwellenberg and the Colonel may have been trying in a clumsy fashion to prepare Fanny for the shock to come. Early in October Mrs Schwellenberg had to be sent to Weymouth because her illness, which Fanny scarcely believed in, was worse. 'I was really very sorry for her,' Fanny records. 'She was truly in a situation of suffering, from bodily pain, the most pitiable.' There is a note here of astonishment, of vanquished disbelief. She then writes a little homily on the thought that spleen and ill-temper only aggravate disease. Mrs Schwellenberg is not to be forgiven just because she is ill; the habit of believing oneself ill-treated, which the Burney girls acquired from life with their step-mother, dies less easily than that.

In a day or two, the first warnings of a period of great misery are sounded at Court. The King is ill and the expected return to Windsor must be postponed. The Court is not equipped to remain at Kew. They are short of clothes and books. Fanny begins a tragedy, the ill-starred *Edwy and Elgiva,* to pass the time. However the King recovers, at least temporarily, and the journey to Windsor is made. Here his condition deteriorates. One of the King's pages, Philip Withers, describes the painful episode in which the King 'pulled up his horses, descended from his carriage and approached an oak tree'. He seized one of the lower branches and shook it cordially. When Withers approached the King he was able to discover that his Majesty believed it to be the King of Prussia he was talking to, and about continental politics. Fanny records:

> I had a sort of conference with his Majesty, or rather I was the object to whom he spoke, with a manner so uncommon that a high fever alone could account for it; a rapidity, a hoarseness of voice, a volubility, an earnestness – a vehemence rather – it startled me inexpressibly; yet with a graciousness exceeding even all I ever met with before – it was almost kindness.

Modern medical opinion, expressed in an article published by Dr Ida Macalpine and her colleagues, is that the King was suffering from a disease called porphyria. Whether this is to say that he was not mad or to give a name to his madness it is difficult to discern. John Brooke explains that 'he suffered physically and was for long periods in extreme pain; and . . . he was fully aware that when attacks were severe his mind was affected'. The symptoms – and we can find most of them recorded in Fanny's journal – make distressing reading: 'Attacks were ushered in by cold, cough and malaise', quickly followed in the first attack by anginoid pains ('stitches in the breast') and in all others by abdominal colic with constipation ('very acute pain in the pit of the stomach shooting to the back and sides') tachycardia up to one hundred and forty-four beats a minute; hoarseness (his voice 'croaking', 'rasping', 'hardly audible') painful weakness and stiffness making him unable to walk and even stand unaided or hold a cup or pen; tormenting 'cramps'; paraesthesiae ('complained of heat and burning'); hyperaesthesiae ('could not bear the touch of clothes or bedding, wig or tie'), hypalgesia ('scarce sensible of the Blisters applied to His legs'). One may add to these symptoms the purple urine from which the disease was named and the two afflictions Fanny is most strongly impressed by, his garrulity – he once talked incessantly for twenty-six hours – and his inability to sleep, one period of insomnia lasting as long as seventy-two hours.

Porphyria is said to run through the royal families of Europe. Mary Queen of Scots showed some symptoms of the disorder, as did her son

James. Henry, Prince of Wales who died at eighteen, had similar symptoms to Mary's but Charles I and Elizabeth of Bohemia were transmitters only of the disease, as were Sophia of Hanover, George I, George II and Frederick Prince of Wales. In George III and George IV the disease returned. Caroline of Brunswick was affected, as was the only child of George IV and Princess Caroline, the Princess Charlotte. The death of the Princess Charlotte, after giving birth to a still-born son, is attributed to 'a fulminating attack' of the porphyria from which, it seems, she had always suffered. Although some hitherto inexplicable deaths among royal people can be attributed to porphyria it does not always kill: George III at eighty-one 'blind, deaf and witless,' as T. H. White tells us, 'so that they had to lift his chair as the only signal to the imprisoned brain within – died officially as he had long been dead in practice'.

During those weeks at Windsor the King appeared to improve in health, only to relapse again, walking 'like a gouty man', never sleeping, talking until he was hoarse. Fanny had several distressing conversations with him in which he assured her that he was quite well but needed rest. The Queen, not surprisingly, was 'almost overpowered with some secret terror' and burst into a violent fit of tears as soon as she was alone with Fanny. In more public situations she remained resolutely calm, reading, working at her tapestry, playing upon the Princess Augusta's harpsichord and listening without apparent horror to that hoarse voice talking unceasingly and never pausing for a reply.

The King's physician, Sir George Baker, a society doctor who was not at this time particularly well himself, took fright and sent for Dr William Heberden, who also was unable to understand the illness. The princes were sent for and the King 'in a positive delirium' suddenly seized the Prince of Wales by the collar and hurled him against the wall. The Queen wept and the princesses wept. Mr Fairly was sent for to deal with the newspapers and Fanny again had his company in her room and his sympathetic enquiries as to whether her health would stand the strain of attendance in such an unhappy situation. At ten o'clock at night the two parted to their respective duties and for two hours Fanny sat alone in the silence of the house. She opened her door and listened: nothing was to be heard of any kind whatever. She went back and waited another hour. A little after one, a page summoned her to the Queen. The King had been told that the Queen was ill and so had consented to sleep in the dressing-room adjacent to their bedroom. Fanny and Lady Elizabeth Waldegrave, after they had undressed the Queen, offered to sit up but were gently ordered to bed. The Queen's wardrobe-women sat up, however, and the equerries and every page, both of the King and Queen.

In the morning, rising at six after a sleepless night, Fanny went to the Queen. She was in a state of considerable distress. The King had come in during the night holding a candle to make sure that his wife was there. He had remained for about half an hour, to her terror and that of Miss Goldsworthy who slept in the room. Now she dreaded the possibility of another visit and sent Fanny at frequent intervals to discover what the King was saying or doing. Fanny came back each time with much the same account of the words he uttered in his poor exhausted voice:

I am nervous [he cried]; I am not ill, but I am nervous: if you would know what is the matter with me, I am nervous. But I love you both very well; if you would tell me truth: I love Dr Heberden best, for he has not told me a lie: Sir George has told me a lie – a white lie, he says, but I hate a white lie! If you will tell me a lie, let it be a black lie!

By the orders of the Prince of Wales only four people were allowed to enter the house and they were to confine themselves to the equerry-room. None of the residents was to go out. The Queen was moved to rooms at a little distance from the King's, in the curious belief that her absence would soothe the unhappy man. Mr Fairly invited himself and one of his sons to dine with Fanny but during dinner Mrs Schwellenberg arrived and the party dispersed in confusion. Fanny, bereft of even her hated Court routine, unable to concentrate on reading, had begun to find the visits of Mr Fairly becoming not merely pleasurable but indispensable. Her confusion and excitement must have increased then when he told her that the poor rambling King, talking of everything and of nothing, had mentioned Mr Fairly's predilection for staying at Miss Burney's tea-table until he was late for his duties. He then as if irrelevantly refers to Miss Fuzilier's accomplishments and denies the rumour that he is to marry her. Fanny wonders – but briefly – whether, since the King has noticed, Mr Fairly's visits ought to cease, but decides that as no criticism has been made she ought to disregard what she has heard. 'I had no other social comfort left me but Mr Fairly and I had discomforts past all description or suggestion,' Fanny writes.

It was Fanny's custom to go to the equerries' waiting-room at seven in the morning to enquire after the King and then to take the news back to the Queen, often in a moderated form. It was usually Mr Fairly who gave her the bulletin, since he was responsible for the organization of the attendance upon the King. Late in November the decision was made to remove the King to Kew, since it was believed to be a place where total seclusion was possible. The physicians, who increased in number all the time, and the princes were in favour of the move. They believed that the King must be persuaded to go 'by some stratagem' and the trick they employed was not one calculated to calm the patient. The Queen and the princesses were to leave privately for Kew and the King was then to be told that the Queen was there. It was believed that he would then insist on following, though the Queen was afraid that the effect on his mind would be disastrous. She departed weeping, and weeping the household servants watched her. Fanny and Miss Planta followed the first party and found Kew Palace breathless with suspense. Should the ruse fail – and the King was known to dislike Kew very strongly – the Queen was determined to go back to Windsor before night.

Scarcely had Fanny found her room (which was not difficult because the Prince of Wales had ridden over and chalked on all the doors the names of those who were to use them) and rung for her servant than Mr Fairly arrived. Fanny was astonished because his period of duty was over, but he explained that he had come to tell her Majesty that the King was on his way. He promised to visit Fanny frequently in the next few days, to her delighted astonishment. Then he began to tease Miss Planta about the possibility of the King babbling out *her* secrets and Fanny, who knew that he was referring mischievously to the King's remarks about Mr Fairly and Miss Burney lingering at the tea-table, was so embarrassed that she got up and went to look out of the window to see if a carriage was coming.

Presently a carriage did indeed drive into the front court. The King had with him his aide-de-camp General Harcourt and his two equerries, Colonel Goldsworthy and Colonel Welbred. He had been persuaded to leave Windsor only with the greatest of difficulty and had been seen off by most of the people of the town. They grieved at his going and were afraid he might be shut away from them for ever, a fear which had probably occurred to the King himself. But the cruellest part of the stratagem was waiting to be discovered at Kew. He had gone there to find the Queen and when he arrived his sons and his physicians would not allow him to see her. Early the next morning when Fanny went, as was her custom, to enquire about the King's health, she was told that the night had been 'the most violently bad of any yet'.

Residence at Kew was in itself a misery. The Palace had been designed

136

for a summer residence and the floors were bare. Mr Fairly proposed buying small carpets for the princesses and when he saw Fanny's parlour he promised to do the same for her. Sandbags for windows and doors were another suggestion of his. The Queen later presented Fanny 'with a very pretty little new carpet; only a bed-side slip but very warm'. Fanny adds that she gave another to Mrs Schwellenberg, obviously feeling that Mr Fairly's kind offer has been extended a little too far. Fanny was not particularly well at Kew, and indeed the strain and fatigue must have been considerable for them all. Mrs Schwellenberg's bedroom was only thinly partitioned off hers and Mrs Schwellenberg had the habit of summoning her servants at all hours of the night, as the Queen knew from Mrs Haggendorn. As a result Fanny was tactfully given a room previously occupied by the physician-in-waiting, a room with far better furniture and carpeted all over. Another task that fell to the Queen at this unhappy time was resolving the quarrel between Mrs Schwellenberg and Fanny over where the latter should wait for a page to bring the morning bulletin. Fanny had chosen to wait in Mrs Schwellenberg's parlour and she, hearing this, had it locked. Fanny protested that the corridors were cold and damp from washing. By threatening a sore throat Fanny persuaded the Queen to rearrange the rooms, with the result that Mrs Schwellenberg's parlour was made over to the officers of state who came on business to the house and she, Fanny, was able to use it while she waited for a bulletin in the mornings. 'Everyone is so absorbed in the general calamity,' Fanny observes unctuously, 'that they would individually sooner perish than offer up complaint or petition.'

Since there was no sustained improvement in the King's condition, the princes now sent for Dr Francis Willis and his son John. Dr Willis was a clergyman who ran a small private asylum for the insane in Lincolnshire and by calling him in the princes were making it plain what manner of illness they believed their father to suffer from. The diarist Charles Greville was shocked by Willis's methods, since he believed his patients were to be broken in, 'like horses in a manège', by the use of the strait-waistcoat. The doctors brought with them three keepers. Mr Fairly, and consequently Fanny, were most enthusiastic about the honest enthusiasm of the Willises and knew or said nothing of their methods of treatment, which, to be fair, were no more brutal than the usual treatment of the insane in those days.

Fortunately for the Willises and for all the other physicians employed on the case, the King now began to recover. The general public had offered them all kinds of violence if he did not. The Regency Bill, that high hope of the Prince of Wales and his Whig supporters, was now at risk. On 19 February, when it was about to be read in the Lords for the third time, the Lord Chancellor said that 'the intelligence from Kew was that day so favourable every noble lord would agree with him in acknowledging that it would be indecent to proceed farther with the bill when it might become wholly unnecessary.' The House was adjourned.

At about this time Fanny's sisters began to be anxious about her health. The suggestion was made that she should retire from the Court and divide her time between Charlotte, Susan and her father. Sir Lucas Pepys, an old friend of Streatham days now treating the King, advised Fanny to take air and exercise regularly to safeguard her health. Colonel Welbred gave her a key to Richmond Gardens and this she used, varying her walks from Richmond Gardens to Kew Gardens according to the reports of where the King was walking. But one morning Dr John Willis told her the King would be walking at Richmond and she accordingly went into Kew Gardens. To her surprise she caught sight of figures, one of which she recognised as His Majesty's. She ran in alarm. The King ran after her calling her name. The Willises begged her to stop. The King, starved so long of conversation, poured out all that was in his mind from complaints about his pages to reminiscences of Mrs Delany. He even tried to sing some of Handel's oratorios in his hoarse voice. He ended by saying, 'I shall be much better served; and when once I get away, I shall rule with a rod of iron'.

T. H. White called Fanny a 'middle-aged, maidenly and short-sighted Alice' and suspected that her meeting with the King was not entirely accidental. Was she capable, now that he was recovering his health, of contriving to meet him, out of kindness or so as to be able to take a report to the Queen? He had held many a conversation with her in the early days of his illness and, like most elderly men, he found her easy to confide in. She may have intended simply to give him that pleasure again. His promise of promotion for her father and help against Mrs Schwellenberg may have been gratitude. In his friendless state even a King may have been anxious to please. When a bulletin of his physicians declared. 'There appears this morning to be an entire cessation of His Majesty's illness' and the Court returned to Windsor, Fanny was there moralizing on the scene: 'All Windsor came out to meet the King. It was a joy amounting to ecstacy; I could not keep my eyes dry all day long. A scene so reversed! sadness so sweetly exchanged for thankfulness and delight!'

Fanny at once succumbed – as she could hardly afford to do before – to the effects of strain and the depression that had so long surrounded her. The King remarked that she looked a little yellow and on the following day she accepted Mrs Schwellenberg's offer of a coach airing. This was reckless of her because there was an old feud between them about whether the windows should be up or down. As always, Mrs Schwellenberg insisted that they should be down and Fanny caught a violent cold which afflicted her for five days. She continued in attendance on the Queen and when opportunity arose, mentioned the window. The Queen – rather tartly – said that an airing with Mrs Delany had never inconvenienced her, but Fanny had grown much more independent lately, perhaps on account of Mr Fairly. Mrs Locke, Mrs Thrale and Mrs Delany, she asserted, had all left the opening of the coach window entirely to her. She followed her cold with neuralgia, for which she tried, in vain, a blister and then leeches.

The Royal Family now planned to visit Weymouth for the King's convalescence. On the way they stayed at Lyndhurst in the New Forest and passed through Salisbury, Blandford and Dorchester to stay at Gloucester House in Weymouth. Everywhere they went the crowds were massed, singing *God Save the King* and cheering him enthusiastically. The towns were decorated with slogans and arches of flowers. Green-clad bowmen with hunting horns who had met them at Lyndhurst accompanied them as far as Salisbury, where the clothiers and manufacturers of the area met them, dressed in white, loose frocks with flowers and ribbons. In Gloucester House Fanny slept in the attics. The men of the party were lodged nearby and the servants further away still. The town was illuminated and every man, woman or child, Fanny says, had a bandeau round the head printed with the words 'God Save the King'. The bathing-women had it on girdles round their waists. The King bathes and 'a machine follows the royal one into the sea, filled with fiddlers who play God Save the King as His Majesty takes his plunge!'

During this tour of Dorset there is no record of happy evenings spent in the company of Mr Fairly. Fanny learnt later that he had written a proposal to Miss Fuzilier from the great house at Saltram and, in November, the engagement was announced. Miss Fuzilier, or Miss Gunning, had £10,000 and the marriage took place in 1790. Fanny comforted herself with the Queen's remark that he looked melancholy and even with Mrs Schwellenberg's suggestion that there was something odd about the marriage. But she grieved so much that she neglected her journal and

139

also her tragedy-writing. And in May, when her father took her to hear *Messiah* and she had the opportunity to talk in confidence, she broke the news to him of her unhappiness at Court.

The conversation arose from the question of one of the French ladies who were anxious to make acquaintance both with Miss Burney and with the Court. She enquired whether Fanny ever had holidays and the answer to this made Dr Burney realize a great deal that he had never thought about. He confessed that he had heard complaints of Fanny's 'seclusion from the world' and Fanny, owning her respect for the Queen, explained why Court life was particularly distasteful to her. She lived like an orphan she said, and the Queen's servants, though their mistress behaved so kindly to them, had neither liberty nor social intercourse nor repose.

Fanny stopped talking because of her father's total silence and, glancing at him, saw that he was almost in tears, his head sunk low with dejection. 'I have long,' he cried, 'been uneasy, though I have not spoken . . .but . . . if you wish to resign – my house, my purse, my arms shall be open to receive you back.' It is curious to notice that almost immediately after she has been given this permission to come out of her nunnery, Fanny mentions in her journal that she has kept up her correspondence with the Cambridges. Her unquenched hopes appear to be almost the first thought she has of life outside the prison of the Court.

Before she left that prison, Fanny decided to test her father's assumption that there was advantage to the whole family in her employment by the Queen. Accordingly she forced herself to beg two favours. James, who had been so long without a ship, longed for a frigate of thirty-two guns. Charles, who had just been passed over for the headmastership of the Charterhouse, wanted the Archbishop of Canterbury to give him a mandate degree in place of the Cambridge degree forfeited by his theft of books. Neither favour was granted and so she was able to resign from Court without feeling that she was robbing her family of useful patronage by doing so.

Her conversation with her father took place in May. It was October before she drew up a tactful letter of resignation in her father's name and her own. She was ill and exhausted, and her friends, Miss Cambridge, Mrs Ord, Mr Wyndham and her sister Charlotte had all expressed their indignation. Even Boswell, come to beg for her letters from Johnson to use in his coming book, told her she should resign, though he appears to have been more concerned with her loss of literary earnings than her health. His invitation to Fanny was tempting: 'I want to show him in a new light,'

Boswell declares. 'Grave Sam and great Sam, and solemn Sam and learned Sam – all these he has appeared over and over. Now I want to entwine a wreath of the graces across his brow; I want to show him as gay Sam, agreeable Sam, pleasant Sam; so you must help me with some of his beautiful billets to yourself.' When Fanny unaccountably refused his request, saying that she had not the time to look out her letters from Johnson, he exclaimed: 'But, ma'am, as I tell you, this won't do – you must resign off-hand.' But although her journal became shorter and her health more precarious, Fanny could not bring herself to present her resignation to the Queen.

At last Fanny wrote to Charlotte and her husband, the physician Clement Francis, mentioning her symptoms and asking for advice. 'The only actual and continued evil,' she said, 'is want of sleep – of which I have early lost the power, even for the time I can give to it. My eyes keep wide open and I rise in the morning as if I had not been to bed, unrefreshed, heavy, wearied and listless.' Fanny mentioned also a complete loss of appetite, 'Without taking bitters I had rather not eat at all.' She was consequently weak and thin, afflicted with pains in her side and chest, and jaundiced. Interestingly she suggested that there seemed to her two possibilities. Her constitution was 'essentially altered and injured' or alternatively she was exhibiting 'symptoms of an approaching long fever'. Either would provide honourable release from Court. Clement Francis was to reply to her father, but Fanny mentioned to the Queen that he had been consulted, believing this would help in the delicate negotiations that lay ahead of her. She was by now in a wretched state 'half dead with real illness, excessive nervousness and the struggle of what I had to force myself to perform'. As a result she found it impossible to explain to the Queen, when she expressed her solicitude, exactly what it was she wanted to say. She offered to put it into writing, referring no doubt to the lengthy memoranda already drawn up on the subject of resignation. The Queen accepted the suggestion gladly.

The Queen conferred with Mrs Schwellenberg who complained that Fanny was not apt to confide in her. As a result Her Majesty suggested that the memoranda should be given to Mrs Schwellenberg. It was a drawing-room day and the Court was at St James's. The King, the Queen and the princesses were all most solicitous for Fanny's health. The Queen asked for Mr Francis's opinion and when she heard that he was unable to give it without an examination she suggested that Fanny should see Dr Gisburne before they went back to Windsor. He ordered her opium, three glasses of wine a day and a great deal more freedom to visit her friends. Mrs Schwellenberg, by a happy coincidence, then called her in and offered her six weeks leave for visiting, after which she would be quite well and able to return to Court. Fanny promised demurely to convey this message to her father. She presented the paper containing the memoranda to Mrs Schwellenberg as requested, and when pressed to say what it contained told her that it was her resignation. Mrs Schwellenberg's rage was unbridled, but she was obliged to carry the message to the Queen.

Mrs Schwellenberg had 'uttered the most furious expressions of indignant contempt,' Fanny says. The Queen expressed no anger, only the more formidable emotions of sorrow and disappointment. Apart from that she did not commit herself in any way and, having waited so long to present her memorial, Fanny now had a further wait for an expressed reaction to it. In April, nearly a year after her first conversation with her father on the subject, the Queen decided to discuss the matter with Fanny. She may have allowed time to pass so that Fanny could recover her health and recover, perhaps, from Mr Fairly's marriage. She has paid Fanny some charming compliments: 'True as gold', she said of her to a friend, Mrs De Luc, 'and in point of heart, there is not, the world over, one better.' The qualities required by Fanny's successor were discussed, particularly the need to keep friends and acquaintances away from the Palace. For this reason, the Queen decided, a foreigner might be preferable.

Since Fanny's friend, Mrs Ord, was anxious to plan a holiday tour for the restoration of Fanny's health, another conference with the Queen was necessary. Fanny's successor, a Mlle Jacobi, was sent for and a few weeks after the King's birthday she left the Court. The Queen had promised her half her allowance as a pension, £100, and never in the course of her long life did it fail. On 7 July, her last day at Court, she took leave of everyone she had known there, of the equerries, of Mrs Schwellenberg, who suggested she might one day succeed to her own place when it was vacant, of the dressers and her servants, of the King and Queen and the princesses. The Court then set out for Kew and Fanny stepped into freedom almost five years after she had entered upon her life of royal servitude.

I I

MISS BURNEY MEETS
LE COMTE D'ARBLAY

The home that Fanny Burney returned to from Court was not the familiar house in St Martin's Street but the rooms in Chelsea College that went with Dr Burney's appointment as organist there and that were commodious enough for Dr and Mrs Burney and the one child living at home, Sarah Harriet. James and Charles came instantly to visit her, the Lockes came and so did Miss Cambridge who made Fanny promise to visit Twickenham when her holiday tour was over. Dr Burney, who understood the value of his friendships, called on a number of the people who had advised Fanny to leave Court, Sir Joshua Reynolds, Miss Palmer and Mr Burke among them, and wrote to others, to Mr Walpole, Mr Seward, Mr Crewe, Mr Wyndham and the Worcester uncle. A flood of congratulatory letters arrived and some calls.

A week before the end of July Mrs Ord called for Fanny on a rainy morning and they took the road to Staines, which was also Fanny's usual road back to Windsor from St James's. They went out into the west country, Farnham, Winchester, Southampton to Salisbury and Stonehenge and on to Exeter, Wells and Bath.

Bath was, Fanny says, trebled in size from the days when she used to visit it with Mrs Thrale. She admired it, but considered that it had an unfinished effect: 'Yet in truth,' she says, 'it looks a city of palaces, a town of hills and a hill of towns'. She made a nostalgic tour of the town, revisiting Mrs Thrale's house on the North Parade and the houses of other friends and acquaintances. Gloomily she listed the names of those now dead and remarked that in ten years' time another writer might make another list. She decided that she had no acquaintances left in Bath but, somewhat to her surprise, received a call from Lady Spencer, mother of the invalid Lady Duncannon and the spectacular Duchess of Devonshire, who were both with her in Bath.

Lady Spencer was a progressive woman, a patron of Sunday Schools, which, in the days before compulsory schooling, taught children to read, and of the Schools of Industry whose growth Hannah More worked so hard to encourage. She arranged to take Fanny to see one of the Sunday Schools and Fanny admired them greatly. The schools, she considered, 'must at least impress them [the children] with a general idea of religion, a dread of evil and a love of good; it was indeed a sight to expand the best hopes of the heart'. She was invited also to witness on the following day the celebration of Lady Harriot's sixth birthday. Lady Harriot was the daughter of the Duchess of Devonshire and Lady Spencer's grand-daughter. Six little girls were to be new-clothed and toys distributed to the children by lot. There was also a picnic in the garden. Lady Georgiana, Lady Harriot's elder sister, begged to join the party of poor children and on her grandmother's assuring her mother that she was not likely to catch anything, she was allowed to go. Their younger brother, the Marquis of Hartington, was not in evidence since he was never allowed to move away from the Upper Walks, near his house in Marlborough Buildings. 'He has a house of his own near the Duke's,' Fanny says, 'and a carriage entirely to himself; but you will see the necessity of these appropriations when I tell you he is now fourteen months old.'

Meanwhile Fanny was introduced to the Duchess of Devonshire and, 'as if unavoidably', to Lady Elizabeth Foster. The situation was one which might have been expected to outrage Fanny's notorious prudery. Georgiana, Duchess of Devonshire had been married when an open-hearted, attractive girl of seventeen to her chilly Duke. Fanny says, 'I did not find so much beauty in her as I expected, but I found much more of manner, politeness and gentle quiet.' She possessed, it seems, that warmth and animal magnetism that makes beauty irrelevant. Unhappiness had driven her to gambling, the obsessive eighteenth-century vice, and her debts had become horrifying. The Duke had paid them (far more easily than he pretended) and had also and at the same time installed Lady Elizabeth Foster, an irresistible charmer, under the family roof. Two children were born to Lady Elizabeth, a girl and a boy, and after the death of his first Duchess the Duke was to marry her. Although Georgiana did not appear to resent the presence of Lady Elizabeth – considered her in fact a good-luck bringer since while she was living with them the heir, Hartington, was conceived and born – still the curious situation at Devonshire House gave rise to much speculation and may have accounted for the unhappiness Fanny thought she detected in the Duchess.

Mrs Ord was horrified by Fanny's acquaintance with the Duchess and Lady Elizabeth because they were leaders of the Whig faction and so had agitated very strongly for a Regency during the King's illness. Fanny herself was politically opposed to the Duchess and was naturally a champion of the King and Queen. It would have pleased the Devonshire House faction if Fanny had been willing to depict herself as a victim of royal tyranny but she was aware of that and on her guard. At no point does she comment on the scandals connected with the ducal house and progeny, and she rates Mrs Ord severely in her journal for her narrow-mindedness in this respect.

Fanny had begun her tour in July and by the middle of September she was delivered to Mickleham and Susan, Mrs Ord returning to Bath. When this visit came to an end, she was welcomed back home. Her father was usually at home now and seemed disposed to keep her in his company:

> Indeed I now live with him wholly; he has himself appropriated me a place, a seat, a desk, a table and every convenience and comfort and he never seemed yet so earnest to keep me about him. We read together, write together, chat, compare notes, communicate projects and diversify each other's employments. He is all goodness, gaiety and affection; and his society and kindness are more precious to me than ever.

The carefully-structured sentences of Fanny's journal contrast oddly with the Doctor's casual tone: 'The great grubbery will be in nice order for you as well as the little; both have lately had many accessions of new books. The ink is good, good pens in plenty and the most pleasant and smooth paper in the world.' It is easy to see that the Court had done Fanny's literary style no good at all, and that was a pity because she must have intended to live by writing now. Not writing novels; the Queen distrusted novels. *Camilla,* her next work, was described by *The Monthly Review* as 'a guide for the conduct of young females in the most important circumstances and situations of life'. It was dedicated, by her permission, to the Queen.

But, meanwhile, between the Court and *Camilla,* came the most unexpected chapter in all Fanny's eventful life, her own romance and marriage. She was forty and so far as it is possible to tell, no man had proposed to her since Mr Barlow. The inexplicable but wounding Cambridge affair and the curiously shoddy behaviour of Colonel Digby were fresh in her mind. She must have lost her sexual confidence. Then the French *émigrés* arrived in Surrey and were welcomed by Susan and Mrs Locke, who spoke their language and sympathized with their sufferings and deprivations.

It was Susan who gave her sister the important news:

We shall shortly, [she wrote in September] I believe, have a little colony of unfortunate, or rather fortunate since they are here safe, – French noblesse in our neighbourhood. Sunday evening Ravely [a neighbour] informed Mr Locke that two or three families had joined to take Jenkinson's house, Juniper Hall, and that another family had taken a small house at West Humble, which the people very reluctantly let, upon the Christian-like supposition that, being nothing but French papishes, they would never pay.

Fanny was then busy with a round of family visits, a return to Court for the King's birthday and attendance at the still unconcluded trial of Warren Hastings. She liked to think of herself as leading a grander, busier, social life than her married sisters and it is unlikely that they grudged it to her.

In October she accepted an invitation to stay with Mr and Mrs Arthur Young at Bradfield Hall. Mrs Young was the second Mrs Burney's sister. Sarah, her youngest half-sister who was already staying at the house, came running out to meet her and Mr Young followed, 'with both hands full of French newspapers'. Despite Arthur Young's conviction that the French ruling classes had brought about their own downfall, he was quite willing to invite to dinner the nearest example of the species and so give Fanny her first, preliminary experience of the dangerous attractiveness of these exiles. This was the Duc de Liancourt whose tall, well-proportioned figure, aristocratic deportment and seducing manners (Fanny was always very easily impressed by manners) quite bowled her over. The Duke rode over on horseback bringing with him his favourite dog, just retrieved from France by his groom, and he gave a great deal of attention to curing Sarah of her fear of the animal. Then, as if he had not already made a quite favourable enough impression, he drew his chair near Fanny's and began to talk freely, sensibly and knowledgeably about *Cecilia*. Fanny sums him up in a sentence that might have been spoken by Jane Eyre: 'He has all the air of a man who would wish to lord over men, but to cast himself at the feet of women.'

It was from the Duc de Liancourt that Fanny first heard the name she was to carry for the next forty-eight years of her life. She writes to Susan: 'He enquired very particularly after your Juniper colony, and M. de Narbonne, but said he most wished to meet with M. d'Arblay, who was a friend and favourite of his eldest son.'

Soon after this meeting, Susan wrote to Fanny: 'It gratifies me very

146

much that I have been able to interest you for our amiable and charming neighbours.' She had been taken by Mrs Locke to Juniper Hall and had had an opportunity to see for herself how the *émigrés*, all noble and almost all titled, were living in their rented accommodation near Norbury. In a house at West Humble, Madame de Broglie and her party were occupying a workman's cottage with a dirt floor. Juniper Hall was rented by a larger party, including La Marquise de la Châtre, M. de Narbonne, formerly Minister for War who was 'about 40 – rather fat but wd be handsome were it not for a slight cast of one eye', M. de Montmorency, Charles and Theodore Lameth, Jaucourt and, a little later, M. d'Arblay. In a very few weeks, such was the friendliness of the *émigrés*, the Phillips were paying frequent informal visits to both houses and the French nobles were calling freely on them in return, often using the derelict old carriage which was the joint property of the community.

Susan's visit to Madame de la Châtre resulted in an introduction to the newly-arrived M. d'Arblay, formerly adjutant-general to M. Lafayette, *Maréchal de Camp* and, in fact, the chief in military rank of Lafayette's followers. Her first impression was most favourable: 'He is tall and a good figure, with an open and manly countenance; about forty, I imagine.' Every meeting confirmed her good opinion: 'He seems to me a true militaire, franc et loyal, open as the day – warmly affectionate to his friends – intelligent, ready and amusing in conversation, with a great share of gaieté de coeur and at the same time of naïveté and bonne foi.' It is interesting, when one considers the long, close affection between the two sisters, to find Susan so enchanted with Fanny's future husband.

Fanny writes back to Susan with gentle patronage about the Juniper Hall colony. She has been on a week's visit to Mrs Rishton and the old friendship has revived to such an extent that 'our parting was a tragedy on her side. On *mine*, the calls away predominated too forcibly for such sympathy.' She had met Maria's Mrs Coke, the equivalent in her life of Fanny's Mrs Thrale, or Susan's Mrs Locke. Mrs Coke was, it is almost superfluous to say, 'one of the sweetest women, on a short acquaintance, I have ever met with'.

Fanny had also been staying with Charlotte at Aylsham. She had missed meeting Mr Wyndham because of the illness of her brother-in-law Clement Francis. She was to make Charlotte a second visit soon and find her with a new baby in her arms and her husband dead of the apoplexy. Like any other spinster aunt, Fanny took over the household and cared for her sister. Then, announcing rather importantly to Susan that she will be with her soon, but she cannot leave town before the Royal Birthday, she adds; 'Your French colonies are truly attractive – I am sure they must be so to have caught me, so substantially, fundamentally, the foe of all their proceedings while in power. But the Duc de Liancourt taught me how little we can resist distress, even where self-incurred'.

On 28 January Fanny writes from Norbury Park to her father. She has arrived to find the *émigrés* in such mourning for the execution of Louis XVI that all their gaiety was lost. M. de Narbonne and M. d'Arblay, 'two of the most accomplished and elegant men I have ever met', have been 'almost annihilated' with shame at the disgrace of being French. M. d'Arblay, 'from a very fine figure and good face, was changed, as if by magic, in one night, by the receipt of this inexpiable news, into an appearance as black, as meagre and as miserable as M. de la Blancherie'. Fanny's sympathy is absolute: 'O what a Tragedy!' she writes: 'how implacable its villainy and how severe its sorrows!' Ashamed of being out of mourning she begs Sarah Harriet 'to take from my last Drawer but one, in our joint Bed Room, my round black Gown and my new black Linnen, and some black ribbon from my small Dressing Table Drawer and to make them up in a brown paper parcel and send them *immediately* by the stage . . . I am distressed how to appear.'

Despite their loss of spirits, M. de Narbonne and M. d'Arblay impressed Fanny at least as favourably as they had her sister. In a letter dated 4 February, an answer to Charles Burney's written to both his daughters, gloomy with the conviction that only war against France will stem the tide of anarchy, she speaks of a private letter Madame de Staël, daughter of M. Necker, has received giving pitiful details of the King's execution. Then, as if in their defence, she praises her two newly-made friends. M. d'Arblay, Alexandre-Jean-Baptiste Piochard d'Arblay, is 'one of the most delightful characters I have ever met, for openness, probity, intellectual knowledge and unhackneyed manners'. M. de Narbonne is almost as admirable. She stays on at Norbury, claiming disingenuously that Susan's temporary widowhood (Phillips is away in Ireland, where insurrections are breaking out inconveniently close to his property) 'has spelled me with a spell I know not how to break' and giving her father another enthusiastic account of M. d'Arblay. He is to teach her French and she is to teach him English. Madame de Staël, who has all Mrs Thrale's good qualities, has invited her to stay at Juniper Hall for a month before she returns and her father's permission is begged by both. In her letters to Mrs Locke, Fanny makes no attempt to conceal her

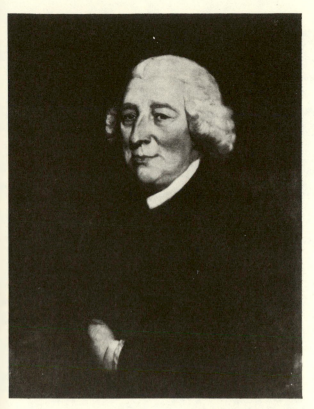

Samuel Crisp by Edward
Francesco Burney (*National
Portrait Gallery*)

Mrs Thrale (Hester Lynch
Piozzi) by G. Dance
(*National Portrait Gallery*)

Queen Charlotte in court dress by Gainsborough (*By permission of H.M. The Queen. Copyright Reserved*)

delight in the company of the *émigrés,* though she had not known M. d'Arblay for more than a fortnight.

Fanny's letter draws a sharp rebuke from Dr Burney who begins, 'Why Fanny, what are you about and where are you?' He goes on to declare that his nights are feverish, his eyes and head weak. He proceeds to advise her against any friendship with Madame de Staël, saying that her house was the centre for revolutionists before 10 August and hinting that her reputation among her compatriots is not good. It is strange that such an accusation should be made. She had been brought up in Paris in a home where learning and liberal ideas were the climate. Her philosophical beliefs included 'unshaken fidelity to the principles of liberty and to the "rights of man" and through all the vicissitudes that these ideas involved her in she never wavered'. But after she married Baron Staël de Holstein and became Swedish Ambassadress in Paris, the Embassy was used as a hiding-place for many of her friends whose lives would otherwise have been forfeit to the Terror. She used great sums of money to bribe the employees of the Commune and to obtain false passports. Her great-granddaughter Baroness Elizabeth de Nolde, who edited the correspondence between Madame de Staël and her lover Benjamin Constant, claims that she saved the lives of Narbonne, Talleyrand, Montmorency, Beaumetz, the Vicomtesse de Laval, Jaucourt, the Duchesse de Broglie and many others. When she joined the *émigrés* at Juniper Hall it was to be reunited with a circle of friends she had helped, sometimes at considerable risk to herself. Here she found Narbonne, the real object of her journey, with whom her relationship at this time was close enough to give rise to scandal. Dr Burney's objections to her may, of course, have been prejudiced by the stories he had heard of her private affairs. But she was a woman whose friendship it was a privilege for Fanny to have. 'She was the bright particular star of this circle, as she had been in Paris, and as she continued to be wherever she went throughout her life.'

Dr Burney came very near to forbidding Fanny to pay a visit to Madame de Staël and mentioned various invitations that had come for them both, presumably to draw Fanny away from the undesirable company she was mixing with and back to civilized life. Fanny obediently succumbed and gave a definite date for her return with Susan and her husband. Since Fanny and Madame de Staël had become closely acquainted at Juniper, a certain embarrassment was inevitable. Madame de Staël was astonished, as she might well be, and perhaps a little incredulous, at the constraint put upon unmarried women, even of middle age, in England. It was obvious that Fanny would have been delighted to stay for a month at Juniper Hall, yet here she was recalled to be company for a sick father, or so she said, like a girl of fourteen.

On Fanny's side the embarrassment was rather more serious. If Madame de Staël's politics were totally unacceptable to her father and his friends, she must find out whether d'Arblay shared them. She knew him to be a Constitutionalist, very nearly a democrat. He believed that laws should be made 'après la volunté et l'interêt de tous'. Did this rank him with those who, like Madame de Staël, incurred the obloquy of her father's friends? He had called on her immediately before she left Susan's cottage at Mickleham and asked if they could continue to exchange themes, even though she was in London. Mrs Locke had confirmed that stories were circulating about Madame de Staël and M. de Narbonne, and Fanny managed to drop some hint of this to M. d'Arblay. She intended to investigate his attitude further in the themes.

To Fanny's consternation she had scarcely been a fortnight in London when Madame de Staël called on her, first at Chelsea, where Mrs Burney received her pleasantly, and then at Sloane Street, where Fanny was staying with Charlotte. What was worse, Mrs Ord, so very rigid in her views about the Duchess of Devonshire, had found Madame de Staël at Chelsea when she called and, going on to Sloane Street only to find her carriage there, had sent a message but would not go in. Then M. de Narbonne's letter arrived, suggesting that he should spend a day with Fanny and she was racked with alarm. News of her disreputable acquaintanceships might reach the Queen. At this juncture, when Fanny was being made to realize the political difficulties of such a match, d'Arblay wrote a tentative and exploratory letter that can only be construed as a proposal of marriage.

M. d'Arblay's proposal was made under the serious disadvantage that he could not keep a wife. He had no likelihood of being employed in ·England and in any case he was trained as a soldier, not for any other profession. He had, however, been considering the formation of a corps of Horse Artillery which would be used for the defence of the English coast in the event of an invasion. Mr Locke had suggested that he might become an Agent for one or several battalions of Frenchmen then beginning to form in England. It was Fanny's interest he solicited and her approval; in fact he wanted Fanny to share in the project by obtaining the support of the Queen while he tried to interest John Villiers, 3rd Earl of Clarendon, an acquaintance of M. de Narbonne. He did not mention marriage in so many words but he did make it clear that he was trying to find a way of earning a living in England and that the reason for his wishing to do this concerned one particular person – *une personne*.

Fanny's response to this letter, written immediately to Susan, is a flurry of emotion. He deserves a younger partner, she says. She has never met a man she admired more and certainly the character of M. d'Arblay, his delicacy and gallantry, his diffidence and at the same time the irrepressible gaiety he wears, the panache that so becomes a military man, these qualities put him firmly among the romantic heroes she has read and written of. On the same day she writes a guarded little note to M. d'Arblay giving him good reason to believe in her affection but making no promises. This lead to a pleasant and characteristic episode. She and her father were working in the study when the maid came in carrying a rose tree and a note. Luckily Fanny assumed, since it was the day Mr Locke usually sent a cart to town for provisions, that the gift was from Mrs Locke and she said so, with conviction because she believed it. But the note, she found, was in M. d'Arblay's hand and she was forced to tell her father that she believed it was a theme, though in so stammering a voice that her 'dear guileless father' must have been curious. The tree had not, in fact, arrived by cart but had been delivered by d'Arblay himself who had ridden to town on horseback and then, his note says, lacked the courage to call because there would be too many witnesses to their conversation. He wanted a more definite answer to his proposal than Fanny's slightly encouraging note. A more definite answer was precisely what Fanny was unwilling to give. 'My sole wish, at present,' she writes to Susan, 'is to be spared from entering upon the subject, yet to keep his friendship, quiet his disturbance and give him confidence in my faithful – but not fervent – regard.' But d'Arblay called at Chelsea for his answer and only the arrival of Mlle Cuénod, a Swiss governess, described by Fanny as 'that wearisome gossip', prevented a tussle of wills.

If it is true that romance depends for its existence on frustration, then Fanny's love story owed a great deal dramatically to the lack of money on both sides. It took no more than two months from the first meeting for M. d'Arblay to realize that he wanted to marry Fanny. Four months later the wedding took place. At no point were their mutual feelings ever in doubt. Only money stood in the way. And yet their financial situation was a very serious concern, so much so that Fanny is racked with doubts as to whether M. d'Arblay will not regret the poverty marriage will plunge him into and refuses to discuss his proposal of marriage until she has considered it at some length.

Two days after the interview of 8 April, when Fanny was saved from being forced to give an answer to her lover's question by the arrival of the Swiss governess, she was fetched from the study by Sarah Harriet on the arrival of M. d'Arblay. Mrs Burney and Sarah disappeared, leaving Fanny alone with the importunate suitor. At once he began his petition and though Fanny attempted to delay, she soon found herself at bay.

> His look, then, half made me draw back: 'une grace! – une grace!' he cried, 'c'est une grace que j'aye a vous demander – que – '
> He stopt – – and hid his Face upon my Hand, which he would not suffer me to loosen – I felt half gasping with apprehension of what was to follow – and he was long still in his exordium –
> 'C'est – c'est que – puisque vous ne voulez pas que je vous parle – '
> 'Oh no, no, no,' I cried.
> 'Eh bien – puisque vous ne me permettez pas – puisque vous me defendez de vous parler – – puisque absolument, vous – – '
> I repeated my negative warmly –
> 'Eh bien, donc – permettez, au moins – – que je parle – a quelque autre! – a une – – que vous aimez bien! – '

In short, M. d'Arblay wanted Fanny's permission to talk to Susan about his feelings. The emotional tension of the scene is quite out of proportion to so mild a request and hints at the frustrated passion of both participants. We have only to compare it with any of Fanny's interviews with Mr Barlow to realize that, unlike her first suitor, M. d'Arblay was able to match Fanny's style and that indeed was the chief reason for the success and happiness of their life together.

Since he had proposed marriage in honourable fashion, even though the proposal was contingent upon an unlikely scheme for making an income, it was proper that d'Arblay should meet the Burney family, should become 'a gentleman whose calls are admitted'. Dr Burney, faced with the choice of allowing him a morning visit or an evening visit, grudgingly allowed him the latter. So an evening when Fanny and M. d'Arblay were both dining with the Lockes at Portland Place was fixed upon and then the problem arose of making an unselfconscious exit from the dinner-party together. It was resolutely solved. Fanny sat in her father's coach ready to go home while the coachman folded away the steps. M. d'Arblay came out as if to say goodbye, leapt over the side of the coach and sat down opposite her.

Fanny's step-mother had gone to her room with a headache. Dr Burney's welcome for once lacked warmth. But Sarah was enthusiastic about her sister's suitor and it was Fanny's impression that the Doctor liked him too, apart from his politics. D'Arblay followed up the visit by asking if he could come to tea. He and Dr Burney became very companionable over books, but still he was a Constitutionalist, while the Doctor was in favour of hereditary authority, like Piozzi he was a Catholic and he had no money whatever. To the Doctor, brooding resentfully on the splendid marriage his daughter ought to have made, it must have seemed ironic that it was her Court pension that made the thought of this marriage possible. Fanny had £100 a year from the Queen and about £20 from the invested profits of *Cecilia*. It was a very comfortable income for a single woman, but between them they would have no more. John Burnett, the economist, writes in his *History of the Cost of Living* that by the end of the eighteenth century skilled craftsmen were earning about fifteen shillings a week, but that these were 'the aristocrats of labour'. Wordsworth, who was left £900 in 1795 by his friend Raisley Calvert, was able to consider himself independent for the rest of his life on the interest of this, which at five per cent would have been £45. But Dr Burney expected his family to rise in the world, and the Comte d'Arblay had certainly not been used to an income of that level.

The ritual of courtship continued. Mrs Burney could be relied upon to behave in a way that made everybody feel selfconscious and she now hastened out of any room M. d'Arblay came into. Sarah was persuaded to stay and witness M. d'Arblay's most formal behaviour, designed to convince her or anybody else that he and Fanny were no more than social acquaintances. In public, too, M. d'Arblay's behaviour was impeccable: 'He made me a distant and ceremonious bow,' Fanny reports of the Lockes' dinner-party, 'but never once spoke to me, except absolutely forced by something incidental . . . At Dinner, also, he never any way addressed me, save once to pick me out an orange!' Notes were passed, however, from one to the other, dropped into a chair and snatched up quickly, read behind a newspaper, answered and snatched as quickly back. D'Arblay, who had so little, gave her a pen he had had for twenty years. She valued and dramatized the giving. Later she was to give him a writing-box and allow him to call her Fanny, but not yet. She had not finally made up her mind to marry, though of her feelings there was no doubt. She decided to go to Chessington.

D'Arblay, distressed by Fanny's absence, begged her address from Susan and arranged to pay Chessington a visit. Fanny writes a charming description of the preparations in rural Chessington for a visit from a

French noble. A half-ham was boiled. Chocolate was made, but had to be drunk by the family because it began to spoil. Miss Kitty Hamilton trimmed up her best cap but was caught in 'her round dress, nightcap and without her roll and curls'. Mrs Hamilton, who had put on a silk dress in expectation every noon for four or five days, 'was seen in her linen gown and mob'. Mrs Hamilton and Kitty, listening to their visitor talk, become at last convinced that there really has been a revolution in France. And in her dear Chessington Fanny comes to the most important decision of her life. She will marry M. d'Arblay. There is only one stipulation. They must be sure that the Queen will not withdraw her pension. Fanny writes to Susan begging her for suggestions on how to deal with this most important matter.

Almost as if he knew of her decision (but then, he knew the importance of Chessington in her life and could deduce the rest), Dr Burney wrote to his daughter at this juncture drawing her attention to the very problem that had been troubling her for months. His concern was not unreasonable, though he heightened the colours somewhat: 'I have for some time seen very plainly that you are éprise and have been extremely uneasy at the discovery,' his letter begins. 'You must have observed my silent gravity, surpassing that of mere illness and consequent low spirits,' it goes on pathetically:

> I had some thoughts of writing to Susan about it and intended begging her to do what I must now do for myself, that is, beg, warn and admonish you not to entangle yourself in a wild and romantic attachment which offers nothing in prospect but poverty and distress, with future inconvenience and unhappiness.

If Susan was not employed as an intermediary between her father and Fanny, she was used by the newly-affianced couple to explain to Dr Burney just how they proposed to live on their income. No doubt she mentioned M. d'Arblay's hopes of recovering some of his former property and Fanny's intention to earn by writing. Dr Burney gave his unwilling consent to the marriage but could not bring himself to attend the ceremony. James gave his sister away when, in front of a tiny congregation, she was married at St Michael's Church, Mickleham on 28 July 1793. Two days later another ceremony was performed in the Sardinian Chapel in London so that they would be married by Roman Catholic rites as well as Protestant. This was important if Fanny was ever to be able to claim her legal dues in France.

The congratulations pour in. Charlotte and Sarah Harriett express astonishment. Maria Rishton, still teasing Fanny about her old reluctance to marry, writes one of her most endearing letters. She describes the incredulity with which she heard the news read to her from a newspaper by a friend. A letter from her mother confirmed the almost unbelievable tidings. She had, she says,

> a large Company to dine with me or in the Agitation and Delirium of the Moment I believe I should have been inspired and Actually have written an Epithulanium – but I was drag'd back from the regions of Fancy to the form and Ceremony of entertaining a Set of people perfectly uninteresting to me and while my whole thoughts were taken up with what I had just heard I call'd down to say I had not a Spit that cou'd roast the Bustard Mrs Coke had brought me the day before the fire of the Muses was instantly damp'd and I was obliged to be fertile in expedients to facilitate the dressing of the Bird, as the Company were invited expressly to eat this rare and Elegant dish – this was happily Accomplished – but All the loves and graces – fled from so vulgar an Event – the Lilly of France and the Rose of England which I had Entwined in the beautiful wreathe All faded before my large kitchen fire – the Laurel and the Myrtle – were used to Singe the Fowl with, and I returned to the Drawing Room a mear Mortal engrossed by Culinary Cares – Ah my dearest Fanny Shall I ever have the happiness of seeing you again.

The *émigrés* generally and severally sent their warmest good wishes. Madame de Staël, who seemed incapable of bearing a grudge, told her: 'Je ne connais pas un caractère meilleur à vivre que M. d'Arblay et je sais depuis long-temps combien il vous aime.' Burke wrote and so did Queeney Thrale, but the most important of the letters was undoubtedly Mrs Schwellenberg's sending the Queen's good wishes. This was an implicit promise to Fanny that the Queen would continue her pension and since her matrimonial budget depended upon the comparatively small sum no other letter could possibly mean so much.

Dr Burney, though he had refused to attend the wedding, could be relied upon to soften as soon as it was accomplished. The couple were living in rooms in Phenice Farm, along the Dorking Road. 'The name derives,' Mr Fortescue, the local historian, writes, 'from the days when grapes were grown as an annual crop in Southern England, almost certainly introduced by the Romans. An ideal Southern slope for a vineyard lies between the farmhouse and the bottom of Blagdon Hill. Phenice is probably a corruption of "Voenace", a vine-growing area.' In November of the year of their marriage the d'Arblays were able to rent a house,

known then as Fairfield because it adjoined the field of that name where
the fair was held. It was later re-christened The Hermitage, perhaps
because of Fanny's frequent references to it by that affectionate name, and
it consisted then on the ground floor only of a parlour, dining-room, hall
and scullery. The house was considerably enlarged in Victorian times but
it is still used as a residence. The 'little square parlour', with its hushed
atmosphere is untouched; one feels that Fanny would recognize it. The
size of the original garden, as far as can be estimated from the old trees
behind the house, may have been as much as two acres, a sizeable enough
plot for M. d'Arblay to serve his apprenticeship upon. To Phenice Farm
and later to Fairfield Dr Burney's gifts of books rumbled by cart:

> To encourage M. d'Arblay in the study of horticulture, I have the honour to
> send him Miller's 'Gardeners' Dictionary' – an excellent book, at least for the
> rudiments of the art.
>   I send you, my dear Fanny, an edition of Milton, which I can well spare,
> and which you ought not to live without; and I send you both our dear
> friend Dr Johnson's 'Rasselas'.

At Fairfield, which Dr Burney soon visited, the d'Arblays were about a
mile and a half from Norbury Park, the Lockes' fine new mansion, and
two miles from Mickleham and Susan's cottage. This was an encouragement to country walks, though in bad weather Fanny would accept Mr
Locke's offer of a carriage. During the five years they lived there Fanny
occupied herself happily in revising *Edwy and Elgiva,* her tragedy, and
writing *Camilla,* with which she hoped to earn a significant addition to the
family's income. Mr Locke had generously offered to lease them a plot
of land in Norbury Park to build on and it was with the profits of *Camilla*
that their first real home, Camilla Lacy, was built there. The d'Arblays also
produced a son, Alexander, in December 1794, and he was christened in
Great Bookham Church across the road from Fairfield, almost certainly
by the Rev. Samuel Cooke, Jane Austen's godfather, who was rector there
for twenty years.

They were almost idyllic days in Great Bookham:

> Here we are tranquil, undisturbed and undisturbing . . . He works in his
> garden or studies English and mathematics, while I write. When I work at my
> needle, he reads to me; and we enjoy the beautiful country around us in long
> and romantic strolls, during which he carries under his arm a portable garden
> chair, lent us by Mrs Locke, that I may rest as I proceed.

Charles was at Greenwich and James at Kingston. Dr Burney was at Chelsea. The family reunions which the Burneys valued so much could often be arranged and then they would walk over to Mickleham to see Susan. M. d'Arblay, who had taken over the garden as his particular task, was planning to provide almost all the food for the house. Unfortunately he was totally inexperienced:

> After immense toil in planting and transplanting strawberries round our hedge, here at Bookham, he has just been informed they will bear no fruit the first year and the second we may be 'over the hills and far away' . . . Another time, too, with great labour, he cleared a considerable compartment of weeds, and when it looked clean and well and he showed his work to the gardener, the man said he had demolished an asparagus bed!

This was just the period, as Fanny writes to her father, 'for a blow of sorrow to reverse the whole scene'. Mercifully the blows of sorrow that disturbed their tranquil way of life were not strong enough to disrupt it, worrying though they may have seemed at the time. The first and probably the most distressing alarm for Fanny came about two months after the wedding. A call had gone out for French royalists to rally at Toulon and defend it against 'the regicides'. M. d'Arblay felt it his duty to volunteer. Fanny could not bring herself to offer any opposition, but was thankful when, for reasons we do not know, his offer was not accepted. At this time too, the d'Arblays were made unhappy by contemporary events that had power to penetrate even their sanctuary. Marie Antoinette's execution was one such, and the poverty of the exiled French clergy, on whose behalf Fanny was induced to write a fund-raising pamphlet, was another. But the most humiliating event, and even now it is impossible to read of it without unhappiness, was the abortive production of *Edwy and Elgiva*, Fanny's tragedy. Her brother Charles, anxious to help the d'Arblays make some money, had persuaded Sheridan to read the play and, while Fanny was engaged in producing her first child, an anxious business at her age, had handed over the single uncorrected script. The actors disliked the play and the audience found it farcical. Fanny, with Susan and Charles and her husband watched the play from Sheridan's box. She was well wrapped up because feeding her baby had given her an abscess of the breast, and a fever, which almost cost her life, was to develop. The following day she asked to have the play taken off. 'That was done like a woman of an exalted Spirit,' Mrs Siddons commented approvingly.

At this time in Fanny's life, when her domestic happiness was so profound, Susan's life began the turning towards catastrophe. Molesworth Phillips took her from the quiet country happiness of Mickleham and her friends there to London. He had, it seems, grown bad-tempered and unkind, a strange contrast to the cheerful friend James had known in his sea-faring days. The weapon he used against Susan was separation from her elder son Norbury, in whose developing talents the whole family took so much delight. He owed Dr Burney money and did not even bother to make excuses when he could not pay the interest. He resigned his commission in the English forces and consequently fell ever more deeply into debt. Soon he was to insist on taking Susan to live on his property in Ireland, where her health deteriorated while her husband paid unwanted attentions to a girl called Jane Brabazon.

Meanwhile, with a resilience it is impossible not to admire, Fanny was writing *Camilla* and planning to print it by subscription so that there might be fewer profits for the booksellers (who were also publishers) and more for little Alexander. When Mr Burke had suggested such a plan previously she had not cared for it, but now she was willing to overcome her sensitivity for the sake of her child. She was given permission to dedicate the book to the Queen and made a journey to Windsor to present her with a copy. This presentation was not as simple as it might have been, because the work was in five volumes and M. d'Arblay accompanied her laden with ten books, a set of five for the Queen and another for the King.

Fanny and her husband had arranged with Mrs Agnew, formerly Mrs Delany's housekeeper, to find them rooms for one day and night. She was in touch with Miss Planta, the English governess, who had been her companion on many a royal expedition. Fanny had rather supposed that she would be sent for the next morning but Miss Planta came with a message saying the Queen would see her at once. The King had gone to walk on the terrace, but the Queen had stayed indoors to receive Fanny. The sensitive courtesy shown to Fanny by the Royal Family and the princesses did not diminish one jot after she had left the Queen's service and married a Frenchman. It was, of course, essential to give no grounds for stories that Fanny had left the Court on bad terms with the Royal Family, but that precaution by itself would not account for the ready welcome the Queen always gave her and the air of near equality with which the princesses talked and behaved.

There was a great bustle to be ready, since Court dress and the accompanying elaborate hair-dressing had never been comfortable to Fanny and now she had almost forgotten their use. Mrs Agnew, Miss Planta and

160

the landlord, who was fortunately a hairdresser, all played their part and soon the small figure in all its finery was at the Queen's House, M. d'Arblay carrying the books. Miss Planta felt a great deal of private alarm lest he should fail to understand that he was not invited in, but at the door he was persuaded to hand over the books and go.

The King had returned from 'terracing'. Miss Planta feared they were too late to see the Queen. But here again the royal indulgence was marked. The Queen received Fanny in her dressing-room briefly and promised her that the next morning she should see the princesses. Since Fanny was still carrying the weighty set of books intended for the King, the Princess Elizabeth was dispatched to summon her father. A typical interrogation by the King took place, sympathetic, banal and detailed, and then after a reassuring word from the Princess Elizabeth, Fanny went back with Miss Planta to her lodgings. The next morning Fanny's old footman came with a message from Mlle Jacobi, her successor, inviting her to dine at the Queen's Lodge. She was to be there by twelve, which allowed more time than on the previous day. So M. d'Arblay was shown his wife's former apartment – from the outside – and Fanny conversed amiably with Mlle Jacobi until she was summoned by the Queen. Her Majesty had just sat down to her hairdresser so long hours stretched ahead for conversation. While the hairdresser and servants were in the room the topics were general, but when they had gone and Fanny was alone with the Queen the talk turned to people, Queen Charlotte displaying her astonishing capacity for what in anyone other than a Queen would have been called gossip.

The Queen spoke of her new house at Frogmore with evident pleasure and said that she spent all her mornings there, arriving at Windsor just in time to dress for dinner. Today she was earlier, to receive Fanny. At two o'clock the princesses claimed Fanny. The Princess Royal was sitting for her portrait and Miss Planta was there to read to her, though she and Fanny had so much to talk about that reading was unnecessary. After an hour she was passed on to the Princess Augusta, who brought her up to date with the exploits of her brothers over the past year, in itself a lengthy discourse. The Princess Augusta, now in her late twenties, was popular with her brothers and they with her. Through them, she had a glimpse of the free world she longed to inhabit. The conversation next turned to the French royal family and M. d'Arblay's impression of their characters, then passed on to Fanny's small son Alexander, of whom the Princess encouraged Fanny to boast a little. M. d'Arblay was sent for to dine at

Fanny's old table and though we are told nothing of what they ate – for Fanny never mentions food – we are told that the meal was pleasant.

Just before dinner, Mlle Jacobi drew Fanny into a room alone and gave her a packet from the King and Queen. It contained a hundred guineas and was accompanied by the odd but well-meaning message that 'it was only for the paper – nothing for the trouble'. Fanny's sensitive pride, alarmed at once, was assuaged by the decision to use the money as a kind of Windsor fund, to enable her to visit the Royal Family more often. Later in the day when she had, presumably, had more time for financial calculations, she was able to promise the princesses a yearly visit.

M. d'Arblay had hopes of seeing the Royal Family walk on the terrace, but the weather was poor. They stayed another day in case it improved and were again invited to dinner. The weather had not improved and it seemed that M. d'Arblay was to be again disappointed, but then it was announced that a small party, the King, Princess Amelia and Mlle Jacobi, were to walk. After playing for half an hour on a raw cold evening the musicians were just going when they were recalled and, perhaps for Fanny's pleasure, the King, the Duke of York and all six princesses appeared. To make the occasion more memorable the Princess Royal pointed Fanny out to her father and he desired M. d'Arblay to be presented to him, making his usual kindly, unexciting enquiries 'with a sweetness,' Fanny says, 'an air of wishing us well, that will never, never be erased from our hearts'.

The rest of the evening was all welcome and conversation about *Camilla,* which the Princess Elizabeth had, even before her mother's inspection of it, been given permission to read. The next day the d'Arblays set out for home, visiting on the way Mrs Boscawen, who had worked so enthusiastically at the subscription list for *Camilla,* and then dining with Mr Cambridge at Twickenham. At eleven o'clock they reached home and the precious sleeping baby.

At the same time as the Burneys were grieved by Major Phillips' removal of Susan to Ireland, Fanny and her husband now had the delightful employment of planning and building their cottage. Mr Locke had offered them a plot in his park to build on, but with far-sighted prudence Fanny decided that if ever Alexander should be in such employment that he lived elsewhere (and there cannot have been many suitable jobs available in West Humble) he could hardly install a tenant in Mr Locke's park. So M. d'Arblay rented a field from Mr Locke on a ninety-year lease in the beautiful valley between Norbury Park and Dorking and believed that they were leaving their child a generous inheritance. Some day they planned to buy the field. It was a pity their means were too stringent ever to do this, because when Mr Locke's eldest son inherited he decided to sell Norbury, and the cottage they built had to be sold at a very disadvantageous figure.

Camilla Lacy, as Fanny called the cottage in compliment to Polesden Lacy, was paid for by the profits of the book, which amounted to a sum between £2,000 and £3,000. The building of the cottage is said to have cost about £1,500, but M. d'Arblay was his own architect and surveyor and also superintended the workmen. The rest of the money was put into the funds for Alexander. In November 1796 Fanny writes of three workmen preparing the ground and laying out the gardens. The foundations had been dug and so had the well which went down, in the end, about one hundred feet deep and cost nearly £22. In March the building would begin and by the next November they were installed. A plan drawn by Mr d'Arblay for Susan Phillips survives and shows some surprising details. There is a comparatively large book-room over the sitting-room; a single small room for three maidservants, since a nursery maid had been added to the two domestics on Alexander's birth; Alexander's room adjacent to the servant's room, not his parents'; a small laundry next the kitchen, mentioned by Fanny as one of her husband's novel ideas; and a cabinet de toilette pour Madame in the master bedroom, reminding us that Fanny washed all over in cold water every day for the sake of her health. The kitchen grate, Fanny says, waited for Count Rumford's next pamphlet (he published an essay 'On the Construction of Kitchen Fireplaces', bringing it out in three parts between 1799 and 1802). There was no roasting spit (but then, they ate little meat). The walls were bare. Four of the windows had to be blocked up after the Window Tax, to the chagrin of the architect. M. d'Arblay had planted trees, some evergreen, some for firewood in years to come and some fruit trees. He was also building a ha-ha to keep their one cow out of his garden.

By the end of 1797 the cottage was ready to move into and Fanny, whose letters have regained the lightheartedness of her early years, writes an idyllic account of the housewarming:

My mate, striding over hedge and ditch, arrived first, though he set out after, to welcome me to our new dwelling; and we entered our new best room, in which I found a glorious fire of wood and a little bench, borrowed of one of the departing carpenters, nothing else. We contrived to make room for each other and Alex disdained all rest. His spirits were so high on finding two or

163

three rooms totally free for his horse (alias any stick he can pick up) and himself, unincumbered by chairs and tables and such-like lumber that he was as merry as little Andrew and as wild as twenty colts. Here we unpacked a small basket containing three or four loaves, and, with a garden-knife, fell to work; some eggs had been procured from a neighbouring farm and one saucepan had been brought. We dined, therefore, exquisitely, and drank to our new possession from a glass of clear water out of our own new well.

There was no affectation in the d'Arblays' poverty: both the love and the poverty were real. And yet it is interesting to notice how faithfully (though unconsciously) Fanny remains in harmony with her times and, at a period when Wordsworth and Rousseau were drawing poetry from cottage living, how naturally the circumstances of her life combined to put her there.

As soon as she had joyfully moved into her new home, Fanny received her summons to visit the Queen, this time in London. Her only regret was that the Princesse d'Hénin and M. de Lally were expected at Norbury and both she and M. d'Arblay were too busy with preparations to meet them. But to their grateful delight the two visitors came through the mud to inspect their little cottage and the Princess even lifted the lid of a *pot-au-feu,* so interested was she in the tiny kitchen. Fanny had learned to cultivate for M. d'Arblay each and every link with his own country.

The next day, Saturday, she set off for town, without her husband who had to oversee the workmen who were finishing the outside of the lath and plaster building. She took young Alexander with her and Betty, one of the maids, and deposited him with her father at Chelsea. The Court had recently suffered the loss of the Princess Royal who had been married to the Hereditary Prince of Württemberg since her first visit. The bridegroom, a widower, was fat and ugly. Everyone cried at the wedding, except him. The King cried, the bride cried, her sisters cried, throughout the three-hour service. But the Princess Royal seems to have been happy in her new role and her sisters envied her good fortune.

Fanny was first received by the Princess Augusta who was in the hands of her hairdresser. The Princess's indifference to her appearance impressed Fanny considerably, but she might have paused to wonder whether it was altogether healthy in a young and beautiful girl. When she was taken to the Queen, Fanny was a trifle ill at ease, because, on Mrs Schwellenberg's death, which had taken place recently, and the retirement on grounds of ill-health of her own successor Mlle Jacobi, the Royal Family had entertained some hopes that she would take up her old position with them. For her it was quite out of the question and she hoped the Queen had not been offended by her attitude. But the conversation passed on from Mrs Schwellenberg and Mlle Jacobi to little Alexander, and to the Princess Royal's wedding dress, of which she had sewn every stitch herself, and to the cottage. It was gossip of a pleasant, familiar kind, a formal edition of what might quite easily pass between any two women who were friends. Then, the King, newly returned from a review at Blackheath to dress for a levee, was able to spare a moment for Fanny. Before she went, Fanny received the Queen's invitation to call on her whenever she was in town.

But Fanny's life was by no means an alternation of country peace and royal favour. The Burney family was suffering a period when some of its members brought real unhappiness to Doctor Burney, who was hard put to it to keep his courage and health in good repair even without such additional anxieties. The first problem was perhaps Charlotte's second marriage to a Mr Ralph Broome, a former captain in the Bengal Army and editor of *Simkins' Letters* and other political pamphlets. Hetty was not impressed by Broome's appearance and Maria Rishton, whose marriage had now completely broken down, could not believe that Charlotte would give up a comfortable independence for 'so disgusting a Being, both in mind and person'. Charlotte remarried without the approval of either her father or James and was soon to find her new husband possessed of an over-dramatic temper and given to extreme depression. Fanny lamented her sister's lost contentment and did her best to reconcile her father to the marriage.

More worrying still was the unusual behaviour of James and his half-sister, Sarah Harriet. Sarah was in 1798 twenty-six years old and James forty-eight. He had married Sarah Payne, daughter of the bookseller, and had had three children of whom two survived. He had separated from his wife more than once and his attentions to Sarah Harriet had caused Mrs Burney in her lifetime to make him an unwelcome visitor at Chelsea. After her death, when Fanny was rejoicing in the thought that he would now be able to come and go freely in his father's home, the reason for Mrs Burney's disapproval became clear. James proposed leaving his wife and lodging near Chelsea, boarding with the Burneys. When Dr Burney refused to allow this he eloped with Sarah Harriet, who left notes behind informing the family of her actions. Maria Rishton, staying with Dr Burney because she had left her husband, wrote instantly to Fanny asking her to come to Chelsea. Together they made plans to conceal this distressing secret from the world. For five years the Burney family offered forgiveness and help to the delinquent pair, whose liaison seemed in some curious way to ape or even parody the romantic views of the time. Fanny in her cottage may have been Wordsworthian: there was something mock-Byronic in James and his half-sister living in one slummy lodging after another while his wife and children were cared for by the family.

But if this was hard to bear, the fate of Susan was almost intolerable. She had been snatched off to live on the Major's family property at Belcotton. Major Phillips had inherited Belcotton and the townland of Termonfeckin, County Louth. In Louth alone it is said that a hundred and eighty houses of Protestants were entered and plundered. Although by 1817 he had lost all his inheritance by borrowing on it, the Major believed that he could save his property from the insurrectionists by living on it. There they inhabited a house formed of two Irish cabins the Major had found standing together. Some smaller buildings facing the front of the house had been transformed into stables, stores, a carpenter's shop and a blacksmith's. The front of the house was singular in that it had no windows, only an entrance. The parlour was reached through two small rooms, one of which contained the staircase. Unfortunately it was a dark room. It was warm, however, and had two cupboards, a recess with five shelves for books and bare walls, which could not be papered or painted until the spring. Susan hung them with drawings done by the Burney family to remind her perpetually of home. This room, the parlour, had one long narrow window, and it was only when standing and quite close that anyone was able to see a view through it. In Susan's depressed state the lack of light was painful and she complained that she was either cold from sitting by the window or reduced to working by firelight.

In her letters to Fanny, Susan broaches the subject of Miss Brabazon, the girl whom Molesworth Phillips was attracted to. She describes her as tall and rather large, with a brilliant complexion, small white teeth and blue eyes. Miss Brabazon calls on Susan and criticizes Phillips for bringing his wife into an unfinished house in January. Her kindness to Susan, her letters, flowers, newspapers and affectionate stories of the child Norbury helped to create a situation in which Phillips' wife and the girl he wanted to make his mistress were on the closest terms.

Susan's health, never very robust, now began to fail, and her family began to beg the Major to let her return to them. Phillips owed so much money that Susan was reluctant to take up the offers made by Charles and other members of the family to pay for her journey home. The Major's

General Alexandre
d'Arblay by Carle and
Horace Vernet (*from the
Collection at Parham
Park, West Sussex*)

Alexandre d'Arblay
(*National Portrait
Gallery, artist
unknown*)

(*above*) The Hermitage
(extended since Fanny Burney
lived there) (*Kindly lent by
S.E.D. Fortescue, Esq*)

(*right*) Fanny Burney's
handwriting in old age
(*Egerton M.S. 3693 f209.
Reproduced by permission of
the British Library*)

arbitrary and procrastinating decisions made it impossible for Susan to have an idea of her future and she began to feel a total despair. While her husband had possession of Norbury she could do nothing that might make her separation from the boy more prolonged. Dr Burney had offered her a home at Chelsea – for Sarah Harriet was not there – but until she could take Norbury with her she refused to leave the country. As her health and spirits deteriorated her brothers and sisters became more and more alarmed until Fanny obtained M. d'Arblay's permission, if the Major would not let Susan come to England, to travel herself to Ireland and nurse her sister there. Meanwhile Charles – whose school was prospering – wrote offering to pay the whole expenses of the journey home and to take the boys into his establishment. James was to meet Susan when she landed and conduct her home. The Lockes sent a draft for £100 and a promise of £50 more. The negotiations were delicate and the need to propitiate the Major all-important.

At last the Major consented and only Susan's weakness stood in the way of her return. In December, not a very favourable month for a sea-journey, she was able to travel to Dublin. The yacht was expected to put in at either Parkgate or Holyhead, and when Charles reached Chester he was told that it had been driven into Holyhead. Ninety miles of travel through the Welsh mountains brought him to Holyhead only to find that the yacht was now at Parkgate and there it was confirmed that Susan was in lodgings. She was terrifyingly ill and it seemed to Charles that she needed to be left quietly to herself, so he took Phillips and the children to Liverpool for the weekend. When they returned the situation deteriorated fast. Charles was with her for an hour while her husband and daughter were shopping and they returned to find her dying.

Neither Charles nor Major Phillips could write to Fanny. Mr Locke was asked to break the news and this he did. Her grief was agonizing and was to last her all her life. Because of the winter weather it was impossible for the d'Arblays to attend the funeral, though they set out intending to make the four-day journey to the coast. Phillips was stigmatized by Fanny as an unfeeling monster who had contributed to Susan's illness by taking her to Ireland and then concealed her condition from the family until it was too late for them to help. Fanny Phillips went to live with her grandfather Burney, Willy was sent to a nautical school to follow his father's profession and Norbury was educated in Ireland though he made visits to the Burney family in England when it was possible.

The family solidarity revealed in the attempt to rescue Susan was now

169

shown in happier circumstances. A friend of M. d'Arblay's, Antoine Bourdois, had managed to salvage a fortune from the reverses of the Revolution and now wished to find a wife. M. d'Arblay suggested that Marianne, the eldest of Hetty's five daughters would do admirably. She had no dowry, but that was one thing M. Bourdois did not need. And the task of bringing the young people together, judging of their compatibility and advising them on their behaviour would be very congenial to Fanny. M. d'Arblay had tried desperately to calm Fanny's grief, but in vain; this stratagem of his devising was to provide a valuable distraction.

First Fanny begs Hetty's permission for M. Bourdois to visit her, so that he may carry back to Joigny favourable impressions of Burney family life. Fanny cannot resist mentioning how useful Marianne will be in entertaining him and how important it is to be hospitable to M. Bourdois. A week later she writes a full account of M. Bourdois for Hetty and her whole plan spills out, in confidence of course, as well as all the reasons why this marriage would be very pleasant for absolutely everybody. She invites Marianne to West Humble to stay with her and the acquaintance flourishes, but a serious difficulty arises. M. Bourdois' agent has died and there is some uncertainty about the state of his financial affairs. It will be six weeks before the uncertainty is over and Fanny advises sending Marianne on a visit to her Worcester relations for that length of time (but no longer). M. Bourdois, however, overcome by the approaching separation, makes Marianne a declaration, explaining at the same time the financial situation and its hampering effect. Everything turns out well and the engagement is announced throughout the family. Fanny's joy at being able to give her sister pleasure has gone a long way to assuage her grief for Susan, whom she can now mention in a letter almost without pain. Fanny and Hetty themselves knew the difficulties of marrying without a dowry and of Hetty's five penniless daughters only Marianne found a husband.

This was to be the last instance of Fanny's active solicitude for her family for many years. After visits to London to gather news of his family from travellers returning from France, most of which reports left him disturbed and unhappy, M. d'Arblay was told that his name had been removed from the list of emigrants and that there was a possibility of saving what was left of his property. Accordingly he went to Holland, a country at peace with France, and there made out his legal claim and had it witnessed and authenticated. By this means he was able to avoid visiting his native country, which he had sworn not to re-enter until it was at peace with England. He was back within a month, a month of great loneliness and anxiety for Fanny. But a longer separation awaited them and greater anxieties. On 1 October 1801 came the conclusion of hostilities between France and England, the Peace of Amiens, opening a door into France which, soon after they had passed through it, closed for twelve years behind them.

1 2

MADAME D'ARBLAY IN FRANCE

The Peace of Amiens, concluded in October 1801, meant a great deal to M. d'Arblay and to Fanny. He had promised himself never to visit his country while it was at war with England and there is little doubt that his resolution was taken at Fanny's behest. For the Queen's pension, that ever-important £100 a year on which they depended all three for their basic necessities, might be risked if M. d'Arblay made himself at home in an enemy country. Fanny knew however that the Queen approved of M. d'Arblay's visiting his country when it was at peace with England and, since it seemed likely that a peace would not last long, it was important to waste no time.

Before October was out M. d'Arblay had embarked from Gravesend in a storm, alone because the illness of little Alex, who suffered frequent bouts of worm-fever, had kept his mother at home. The last visit to Europe he had made had been over in a month but this time, as they both knew, the separation would be longer. D'Arblay was determined to claim what he could of his old possessions and was drawn – naturally – to the idea of establishing himself in France the better to do so. Fanny was totally unwilling to leave her first real home where she had been so happy. Besides, she was writing again and comedies at that, not the fearful tragedies of her Court days. Just when she had begun to hope that they might stay safe in the cottage while she wrote them into prosperity, the peace and not the war disrupted her every plan.

M. d'Arblay, desperate to become the family breadwinner, was negotiating furiously with that in view. He had no chance, it seemed, of claiming his family property. There was a chance of becoming a retired half-pay officer, but only if he served another year in the French forces. Even the possibility of a command in Santo Domingo, an unsettled and unhealthy French colony, was acceptable to him, if not to Fanny. This opportunity was annulled, however, by a letter he wrote to Napoleon stipulating that he should never be called upon to fight against England. For this he lost the appointment and his commission. Advised by the

172

Government that he should remain in France at least a year, M. d'Arblay begged Fanny to join him and she, racked by loneliness, let the cottage, waited for the next instalment of the precious pension and then, stipulating only that they must have a place of their own, packed away her recent writings and set off for France.

Fanny had arranged to take with her little Adrienne de Chavagnac, who had been staying with Mrs Locke and whom she was to return to her father, the Comte de Chavagnac. Fanny describes – never forgetting that she is a 'character-monger' – the coach journey from Piccadilly to Canterbury with special reference to the unlovable characters travelling with her. The crowds at Calais impressed Fanny by their gentleness, some lingering fears of the Terror remaining with her, but bureaucracy was as unbending as ever at the municipality where their passports were to be produced. The dresses of the women, their jackets always of a different colour from their petticoats, their great wing-caps and always their ear-rings whatever other jewellery they wore, these things fascinated Fanny and so did the fairness of hair she saw on many women and children.

M. d'Arblay, always gallant, waited four hours for the coach from Paris that brought his wife and son. He had found a comfortable apartment in the Hotel Marengo, overlooking the gardens of the 'ci-devant Hôtel Beauvais' now in their spring beauty. His friends began at once their visits to Fanny, in some instances renewing acquaintance begun in England. First came the business, always faintly amusing to Fanny, of revising a rustic wardrobe to suit Parisian fashion. She speaks of 'the exclamations which followed the examination of my attire! This won't do! That you can never wear! This you can never be seen in! That would make you stared at as a curiosity! Three petticoats; no one wears more than one! Stays? everyone has left off even corsets! Shift-sleeves? not a soul now wears even a chemise!' Fanny solved the problem characteristically by wearing what she had always worn, regardless of the mode.

Madame d'Hénin and Madame Lafayette called upon Fanny when, exhausted after her journey, she was resting on a bed, barefooted and wrapped in a dressing-gown. They took her to the Opera Buffa, having borrowed from M. de Choiseul his family box, the largest and best in the theatre except for the First Consul's. Still tired from travelling, Fanny fell asleep and her hostess and her husband removed her before the third act. In return for her hospitality the d'Arblays were able to take Madame d'Hénin to the Tuileries to see the military parade. The crowds were overwhelming, but thanks to the assistance of General Hulis, an old friend of

M. d'Arblay, they were put into the window of a room next to that in which Bonaparte was holding a levee. M. d'Arblay's plain, worn clothes contrasted painfully with the showy uniforms of the officers in attendance, but Fanny was impressed and touched to see how eagerly these officers welcomed him and how distinguished he looked.

When the First Consul emerged at last from his audience chamber, Fanny was fortunate in being close enough to see him very clearly:

> I had a view so near, though so brief, of his face as to be very much struck by it. It is of a deeply impressive cast, pale even to sallowness, while not only in the eye but in every feature – care, thought, melancholy and meditation are strongly marked, with so much of character, nay, genius and so penetrating a seriousness, or rather sadness, as powerfully to sink into an observer's mind.

Fanny's first impression of Bonaparte was that he had 'far more the air of a student than a warrior', but later, as she watched him take part in the review, she was impressed with his horsemanship. On 'a beautiful and spirited white horse', which he managed with easy negligence, his look was changed 'to one that was highly military and commanding'. The review over, he changed again, became a tired man harassed by the importunities of those who had favours to beg and passed on to hold his monthly audience of ambassadors and ministers while the crowds departed.

In Paris little Alexander, who was always thin, had two bouts of the worm-fever that had kept his mother in England when his father first set out. Since the air of a city was considered unhealthy, the d'Arblays found a place at Monceau, very near a public garden that had formerly belonged to the Duc d'Orléans. Here Fanny was able to rest and the boy to recuperate. All too soon, however, their peace was, for the kindest reasons, disturbed. M. and Mme Bazille, M. d'Arblay's nearest relatives left in France, came as was only courteous to welcome Fanny to that country. The d'Arblays then spent a fortnight with them at Joigny where the hospitality was such that Fanny was completely overcome. The aunt and uncle themselves, she says, were so charming that she could have remained with them for months, but the hospitality of a country town demanded a way of life which was 'utterly at war with all that, to me, makes peace and happiness and cheerfulness, namely, the real domestic life of living with my own small but all-sufficient family'.

The intrusion upon Fanny's time was, of course, no more than the 'open arms and open heart' with which Joigny greeted its returned exile.

174

M. d'Arblay was 'related, though very distantly, to a quarter of the town and the other three quarters are friends and acquaintances,' Fanny claims, 'and all of them came, first, to see me; next to know how I did after the journey; next, were all to be waited upon in return; next, came to thank me for my visit; next, to know how the air of Joigny agreed with me; next, to make a little further acquaintance; and finally to make a visit of *congé*.'

On her next visit to Joigny at the end of year, Fanny made two acquaintances she thought it well worth describing in detail for the benefit of the Queen and princesses, since the one represented the new rulers of France and the other was able to give her details of the afflictions suffered during the Revolution by the old nobility. Colonel Louis Bonaparte, the youngest brother but one of the First Consul, was quartered at Joigny with his regiment. His first formal visit in the town was to M. Bazille, Fanny was happy to note. She, who was always impressed by a civilized manner, was enthusiastic: 'He is a young man of the most serious demeanour, a grave yet pleasing countenance and the most reserved, yet gentlest manners.' He discouraged gaming (by playing low) and never allowed his servants to stand behind his chair while he dined. Though he was only twenty-three, Fanny was able to comment favourably on his conversation, which was 'sensible and well-bred, yet uncommonly diffident', and his 'good sense, forbearance and propriety in such a delicate situation as his'. To add to the high merit of his character 'he was very kind to my little Alex, whom he never saw without embracing, and he treated M. d'Arblay with a marked distinction extremely gratifying to me'.

Fanny's second interesting acquaintance was a lady, an authoress in fact, Madame de Souza. She had met the Queen and princesses, so she and Fanny were able to share their ardour for the Court. She lived a little way out of Joigny in the modest château of la ci-devant Princesse de Beaufremont, whose much grander château – 'one of the most considerable in France' – had been burned to the ground during the Terror. All her genealogical papers had been consumed in the fire. The effect upon her daughter had been considerable and the Princess attributed her death, just before she was seventeen, to the shock of the event. The grounds of the Château de Cesy where the Princess was living now had been laid out in the English style and here Fanny was shown a memorial urn, surrounded by cypresses and weeping willows and dedicated to the memory of this daughter.

Before the second visit to Joigny the d'Arblays had bought an odd little house at Passy, built into the side of a hill, in which they could enjoy the country air while Paris was raked by *la grippe*. Fanny speaks of the 'dreadful want of cleanliness in that city', and adds 'the air of our house at Passy is perfectly pure and sweet'. It is not easy to imagine the style in which this house was built, for it is described as 'an up and down, queer, odd little building which we entered by the roof and of which we could only furnish the first floor, but which had two or three magnificent views from the sides of the windows and from a terrace built up to our first floor from the garden'.

It was not within the means of the d'Arblays to furnish the whole house or even allow the workmen to finish the woodwork and decorations. Indeed we rather wonder, anxious as we become for their finances, where they found the capital to buy it at all. But the house suited them and it was only two miles from the city, which proved very convenient when M. d'Arblay began to work in Paris. For, robbed of his hopes of regaining his inherited land and disappointed in the amount of pension awarded him, no more than £62.50 annually, M. d'Arblay obtained a Ministry post at £100 a year, working from 9.30 to 4.30 every day. Fanny seems astonished at the idea of his going off regularly to the office, something that had never been the custom in any circles she moved in.

At the end of April 1803, Fanny's letters reveal the consternation that the likely end of the Peace of Amiens had brought her. D'Arblay's acceptance of an army pension carried the condition that he would not leave his country in wartime. And now, when the year they were required to spend in France was half over and the prospect of living again in their cottage drew near, the end of the peace put an end to all their hopes. It was to be a decade before Fanny saw her family again.

For the next few years Fanny's letters to her father had to be taken to England by any traveller she could find. Nor was she able to receive answers containing the news she longed for, news of her father's health or her family's activities. 'My last intelligence was that you were well, my dearest father, and that the family at large, in that at least, imitated you. But details – none, none reach me! I have a bitter anxiety of suspense upon some subjects very near my heart.'

Meanwhile little Alexander was growing up in Passy as a true descendant of the scholars among his mother's family. In the spring of 1805, when he was nine years old, he was presented with Thomson's *Seasons* in French prose as a prize for good conduct and also with a crown of laurel and oak. He had three other first prizes, none of them entirely suited to a nine-year-old, Florian's *Gonzalo,* Voltaire's *Charles XII of Sweden* and Tasso's *Jerusalem,* each accompanied by a crown. Then came a time when M. d'Arblay tired of the long daily walks between Passy and Paris and moved into the city. Here Alexander was sent to a much larger school, of two hundred pupils, and here he again excelled at every subject, collecting seven first prizes and the same number of crowns. Fanny was to complain in after years that such a success was the ruin of Alexander and to look back on his seven first prizes as the beginning of his idleness. This was because Alexander had discovered that to work hard was to be unpopular with his fellows, but that it was in any case unnecessary: a few weeks' study at the last moment would usually prove just as effective. The rest of his life as a student was to be puctuated by intervals of inertia and there were times when even he found it difficult to retrieve the time lost.

It would be impossible to read the life of Fanny Burney – for it never seems comfortable to call her Fanny d'Arblay – without being impressed by her courage. This small, frail woman who all her life had needed regular rest and quiet, who lived, as her family said, upon turnips and a little water, had, even by eighteenth-century standards, indomitable strength of will. Yet in 1810 when the specialists revealed to her that the metastatic abscess, probably a cancer, in her breast would yield only to an operation, she must have needed all the reserves of courage she could muster. There were no anaesthetics available for use, no operating theatre but a room in the house cleaned and made ready by the patient herself and no analgesics could be provided to mitigate the pain during the post-operative period. Surgeons had to be prepared to work on through the patient's screams and also through the welcome periods of unconsciousness that even the hardiest patient experienced. The prognosis, had Fanny known it, was almost totally discouraging: Baron de Larrey, first surgeon to Napoleon, was the only one of the team of seven distinguished surgeons who entertained any hope at all. But she recovered and her friends in Paris were so deeply impressed by the bravery with which she had endured this nightmare experience that they referred to her admiringly as *l'Ange.*

At such a time Fanny's thoughts turned even more urgently towards her family. In the spring of 1812, six months after the operation, M. d'Arblay heard of an opportunity for her to visit England. An American captain was to sail from Dunkirk and land illegally at Dover. Since Alex at seventeen was approaching military age and Napoleon was known to be planning a Russian campaign, Fanny's anxiety was easy to understand.

The boy was a child of the Romantic period:

> He is terribly singular and more what they call here sauvage than any creature I ever beheld. He is untameably wild and averse to all the forms of society. Where he can have got such a rebel humour we conceive not; but it costs him more to make a bow than to resolve six difficult problems of algebra or to repeat twelve pages from Euripides; and as to making a civil speech, he would sooner renounce the world.

In 1810, before her operation, Fanny had come very near a visit to England. Her passport was made out for Canada, or some such place; certainly not for England, she says. Then came news that not a vessel was to leave the coast. In the interval all correspondence with England was forbidden on pain of death. One letter only reached her, announcing the death of the Princess Amelia, the death of Mr Locke and the total madness of the King. Distressing news, only sufficing to increase her anxieties.

Fanny's passport for the next voyage, which may have been, she thinks, for Newfoundland, was more difficult to obtain. She managed a licence of departure for herself and Alexander. She dared carry no letters but was requested by a number of friends in France to write for them when she arrived giving news it was impossible to transmit in any other way. The ship, sailing under American colours, hung about at Dunkirk for six weeks, hoping for more passengers as the news went round that the voyage to America was to be broken at Dover. Fanny, who could not bear inactivity, sent to her husband for the uncompleted manuscript of *The Wanderer,* only to find herself unable to concentrate on it while her situation was so uncertain. Her crossing was made more difficult to endure by seasickness, which kept her prostrate in her hammock while Alexander, restless to an irritating degree, rushed in and out informing her that the ship had been captured by British officers. War had been declared against America the previous week and the captain's dilatory tactics had led to his being taken prisoner, fortunately by the British. Leaning on the arm of a naval lieutenant, Fanny stepped ashore at Deal and pressed the nearest pebble to her lips in rather dramatic thankfulness. She was home after twelve years.

Fanny and her son set out for Canterbury *en route* for Chelsea. They stopped upon some common, she says, to water the horses and a 'gentleman on horseback' passed them twice before he ventured to speak her name. It was Charles, who had been 'watching for several hours and three nights following through a mistake'. They arrived at Chelsea at nine o'clock at night and Fanny demanded to see her father alone. He had arranged for precisely that and was waiting in his library by himself. His weakness, his head hanging down, his cruelly impaired hearing were distressing to Fanny. But soon her courage re-asserted itself and she was able to be cheerful. She had come, she could see, not a moment too soon.

Fanny was touched to find how welcome the Queen made her at Court on her return. Three days out of the five they were in town Fanny was invited to spend with them and when they went off to dine with one or other of the princes, between seven o'clock and eight, she stayed at the Palace to dine with her successor. She was still under the necessity of spending long periods resting in her room and any bouts of strenuous activity had to be compensated for in this fashion.

In the spring after her arrival in England, Fanny was excited beyond measure by the election of her son to a Tancred scholarship at Cambridge. Charles, for whom his family had done so much in the bad days, now managed to secure the votes of five out of seven of the board and Fanny's influence was able to secure the other two. The scholarship was worth £120 a year, more than d'Arblay's income, and it was to be supplemented with the £3000 advance on *The Wanderer* that Fanny had been promised. At first all went well and Alexander won a scholarship in classics, to Fanny's very real pleasure, since she did not consider mathematics a broad enough study. But the old bad habits reasserted themselves. By Christmas Alex had shown himself to be totally unable to organize his time, and in spite of Fanny's hiring a tutor for him and a gyp to get him out of bed in the morning, he failed the summer examination completely. His mother's profits from her new 'work' were almost wholly allotted to the cause of educating her son.

Because there was a shortage of rooms in Dr Burney's Chelsea apartments, Fanny and her son arranged to live nearby. At first they took lodgings but later they lived with Charlotte in Bedford Square sharing the housekeeping expenses. The family congregated frequently at Chelsea for evening parties where Alex was able to meet his cousins and Fanny to catch up on the news of her brothers and sisters, news that she had so yearned for during the long exile. They were ageing in 1814, Dr Burney's children. Hetty, the eldest, was about sixty-five. She had had ten children, of whom seven survived, and since her husband was no businessman and fashions in harpsichord or pianoforte were unpredictable, they were always short of money. To add to her problems she had had a number of illnesses and family anxieties. Only one son survived, Richard Allen, who was now in holy orders in Dorset. Of the daughters one, Fanny, had become a governess, while the eldest, Marianne, who through the good offices of her aunt d'Arblay had married the prosperous M. Bourdois, was now independent, widowed and childless in Bath.

James, who was sixty-four, had been, since 1783, without a command, despite his eager canvassing. He had a reputation for democratic or Whiggish principles and this may have made him unpopular in some quarters. His protests to the Admiralty about his crew being 'prest men, almost destitute of clothes' and the supply of 'portable broth' for the 'sick and hurt' being only one-fifth the requisite quantity, and the ammunition being 'such as does not fit our guns, and after firing, sticks so fast as to render the gun for some minutes useless', all these implied criticism of the Admiralty's organization that may well have been resented. In 1821, a few months before he died, James was to receive the promotion his friends believed he deserved, but at the time of Fanny's return he had been twenty-one years on half-pay. In 1785 he had married Sally Payne, a motherless girl and daughter of the well-known bookseller. The only picture we have of her is in middle age, as 'a small exquisite figure in black velvet and gold lace, with a pale face and tiny feet in French slippers'. The strange, wild love-affair with his half-sister, Sarah Harriet, had caused James to leave his wife more than once, but they were together again now. Charles Lamb, who knew and loved both the James Burneys, wrote of their home in terms we recognize as probable:

> I do not know a visiting-place where every guest is so perfectly at his ease; nowhere, where harmony is so strangely the result of confusion. Everybody is at cross purposes, yet the effect is so much better than uniformity. Contradictory orders; servants pulling one way; master and mistress driving some other, yet both diverse; visitors huddled up in corners; chairs unsymmetrised; candles disposed by chance; meals at odd hours, tea and supper at once, or the latter preceding the former; the host and the guest conferring, yet each upon a different topic, each understanding himself, neither trying to understand or hear the other; draughts and politics, chess and political economy, cards and conversation in nautical matters, going on at once, without the hope, or indeed the wish of distinguishing them, make it altogether the most perfect concordia discors you shall meet with.

James used the abundant free time forced upon him by the Admiralty to study and write. He had been sent at the age of ten to the *Princess Amelia,* a man o'war with a school for boy sailors established on it, and the academic training so many of his family had enjoyed was certainly not part of his early years. But four years after his last command – 'wretched weather, much danger, infinite sickness and no prize! but he is *safe* now . . . in the Humber, 50 of his men sick with Fever, from wet, hard watching and fatigue!' – he tells Fanny, on a country walk, what he is studying. His studies include 'Law, Physic, Politics and History, besides French and Latin. He has set himself a task for a year, I think, to read a certain number of pages a day, I believe he said a hundred on an average.' In 1797 he brought out two political pamphlets, *A Plan of Defence against Invasion* and *Measures Recommended for the Support of Public Credit*. Then followed in 1803 the first volume of *A Chronological History of Discoveries in the South Sea or Pacific Ocean* and the four other volumes followed over the next fourteen years, so he was able to meet Fanny after her absence as a fellow-author, one of the literary Burneys.

James had been a friend of Captain Bligh and had edited his books *The Mutiny on Board HMS Bounty* and *A Voyage to the South Sea on HMS Bounty*. More surprising was his attachment to Charles and Mary Lamb. But Charles Lamb and he had in common puns, whist and a certain irrepressible unconventionality. The card meetings at the Burneys, or on Wednesdays at the Lambs, led to an affectionate and life-long friendship. *Mrs Battle's Opinions on Whist* is a splendid celebration of Mrs James Burney at her favourite game. James Burney's pamphlet *An Essay by Way of Lecture on the Game of Whist* is a seamanlike summary of the rules of the same mystery. Even James Burney's son, Martin, was a devoted whist-player. He had had some kind of paralysis which affected one side of his face and his speech, but he too was greatly loved by Charles Lamb who describes him as 'one of the poor gentry' reading *Clarissa* on a street barrow, 'venturing tenderly, page after page, expecting any moment when he [the barrow-boy] shall interpose his interdict, and yet unable to deny themselves the gratification, they "snatch a fearful joy" '.

It was Charles Lamb who wrote in his sonnet on Martin Burney the lines

> In all my threadings of this worldly maze
> (And I have watched thee almost from a child)
> Free from self-seeking, envy, low design,
> I have not found a whiter soul than thine.

The affection in these lines must surely have been mutual; we hear how Martin, at Mary Lamb's funeral, wept bitterly for her loss and would not be comforted.

Martin's sister Sally was a talented musician as well as a lively, attractive girl. It is her wedding that Lamb is writing about in his essay on that title. He incorporates in it a splendid description of James, promoting him a little before his superiors in the navy chose to do so:

> My friend the Admiral was in fine wig and buckle on this occasion – a striking contrast to his usual neglect of personal appearance. He did not once shove up his borrowed locks (his custom ever at his morning studies) to betray the few stragglers of his own beneath them. He wore an aspect of thoughtful satisfaction.

Charles, after his expulsion from Cambridge, had taken his M.A. at Aberdeen and had then stayed in the north much longer than his family expected. Some kind of love-affair may have been the reason but it all added to the impression many of his family had of him, that he took his situation with far too much levity. The fact that he was in debt only confirmed their view. He was refused ordination by the Bishop of London, as they feared, and the Cambridge scandal so told against him that he was to go on being refused ordination for some years. The luck that often goes with levity stood by him, however, and midway through 1783, only eighteen months later, he married the daughter of a Dr Rose and became headmaster of a school at Chiswick. He prospered, of course, and in three years was opening his own school at Hammersmith. He was a keen disciplinarian, a flogging master of the kind already considered old-fashioned, but his reputation for scholarship was growing impressively.

His publications began to bring him in honorary degrees: Aberdeen and Glasgow both gave him an LL.D. He was made Professor of Ancient Literature at the Royal Academy, elected a Fellow of the Society of Antiquaries and then Fellow of the Royal Society. Then, to his father's delight, in 1807 he was re-admitted to the books of his former college and after the publication of his work on Richard Bentley, awarded an honorary M.A. of Cambridge University, after thirty years in the academic wilderness. More publications and some research for the Archbishop of Canterbury on the Greek Testament brought him a D.D.

The time was ripe. He handed his flourishing school, now at Greenwich, over to his son Charles Parr Burney and was admitted to holy orders. At once he was appointed to a plurality of livings and preferment followed with such speed that by 1812 he had become Prebendary of Lincoln and Chaplain to the King. Marianne Francis, his niece and Charlotte's daughter, a girl of strong evangelical leanings complained in a letter that Charles would have more than £2000 a year preferment, after having been but two years in the Church. 'Not Theology but Scholarship raise a man to a Bishopric now.'

Charles in his prosperity collected so famous a library that, reading about it, we realize at once the attraction of the Elzevir Editions he stole from the library of Caius College. His collection of the classics was more complete than that of the British Museum:

> Few men, with such limited means, have achieved so much in this way; no obstacles prevented, no sum, however large, obstructed, no difficulties, however formidable, deterred him in his pursuit. By devoting nearly the whole of his fortune to this particular propensity, he was enabled to achieve great things; and some of the richest of our nobility were startled at a competition in which a private gentleman, with but very scanty resources, fairly outbid the proprietors of large hereditary estates.

As well as his classical library, each text represented in all available editions, Dr Charles Burney had a magnificent collection of English theatrical material, a link with the Burney family's passion for the stage. He is said also to have collected the best wine in the best vintages and to have detested draughts.

Charlotte, fifty when Fanny returned, had married Clement Francis, a surgeon to the East India Company and secretary to Warren Hastings. By him she had three talented and lively children, Clement, Marianne and Charlotte. Six years after his death she had made her unfortunate marriage to Captain Ralph Broome. He left her with one delicate and much-loved son, Ralph, known as Dolph, who was at this time still alive, though his condition necessitated frequent changes of air and a great deal of nursing. Clement was at Cambridge and Marianne was of all her generation the most generously gifted, having inherited her grandfather's passion for languages. She read Latin and Greek and spoke French, German, Italian and Spanish. She was also learning Hebrew and Arabic, 'understood' algebra and geometry and played the pianoforte well enough to impress her grandfather. Charlotte, the younger, had married at sixteen, a Mr Barrett, some years older than she was and quite unwilling to wait. She lived at Richmond and, after Fanny's death, edited the *Diary and Letters of Madame d'Arblay*.

One of Dr Burney's first family, and the one Fanny would most fervently have wished to find there, was missing from the reunion gatherings. Susan had been dead since 1800, though her sister still dedicated every sixth of January to her memory. Molesworth Phillips had remarried in less than a year after her death and then deserted his second wife and family for a mistress. He was constantly in debt. He was an ogre to the Burney family, to Fanny a 'murderer', but still welcome at James Burney's house and at the Lambs. Plainly there was an incompatibility between his seamanlike virtues and the almost excessive sensitivity of the elder Burney girls, but James's tolerance is remarkable in this instance. Of Susan's children only the beautiful Fanny Raper was there to meet Fanny. William had gone to Charles Parr Burney's school in Greenwich and then to sea. The delightful and intelligent Norbury, musical as his mother and grandfather were, had graduated from Trinity College, Dublin, been ordained and was to die in 1814.

Of the second family, the children of Dr Burney and Mrs Stephen Allen, the good-looking Richard Thomas, known to the family as Bengal Dick because of his association with India, precocious in everything had died at thirty-nine after a life of notable piety, leaving eight children. The eldest of his sons managed to obtain leave from the East India Company long enough to take a degree at Cambridge.

Sarah Harriet, the youngest of Dr Burney's children, was forty-four years old by now, unmarried, and a fairly ineffective housekeeper to her father. She had published three novels anonymously, partly in an effort to earn a little money of her own, and they enjoyed a certain popularity. Her romantic *affaire* with her half-brother James had, by now, burnt itself out, though the affection between them remained. She is interesting on the subject of Fanny, her half-sister and fellow-novelist:

> That there is still considerable vanity [in the Diary] I cannot deny. In her life she bottled it all up and looked and generally spoke with the most refined modesty and seemed ready to drop if ever her works were alluded to. But what was kept back and scarcely suspected in society, wanting a safety valve found its way to her private journal.

To be the progenitor of so talented a range of children and grand-children must have given Dr Burney immeasurable satisfaction in his lonely hours, as he looked back over his amazing life and forward to that plot in Chelsea College burial ground where he expected soon to rest. Peacefully and with tired resignation Dr Burney dies, at the very moment when the sky was illuminated for the victory over Bonaparte and the end of the war that had separated him from his favourite remaining daughter. His will, made on principles that seemed to him eminently just, combined two ideas. One was that where there was no need there should be no legacy, a principle that removed Charles and Charlotte from the beneficiaries. The other was that where education or professions were given to the sons, property that was personal rather than hereditary might without any injustice be given to the daughters. Hetty and Fanny were accordingly made residuary legatees, to share equally in the proceeds from the sale of his library and in what remained after debts and bequests were paid. It must have seemed to James inequitable that he, who had given his father no expense from the time he was ten years old and who had been so poorly rewarded in his profession should receive the same as Charles. He interpreted his father's action as criticism of his past behaviour and grieved accordingly. No offers from Hetty to share her inheritance were acceptable to him. Charles, the most successful and prosperous of Dr Burney's brood, posed no such problems but then he had been sure of his father's regard for many years and had no kind of reconciliation to make with the dead.

Fanny's grief for the loss of her father was balanced a little by pleasant news from France. M. d'Arblay had discovered that the political side his moral scruples demanded he should take was now the winning side and grateful for his service. He was summoned by the Duc de Luxembourg to be a member of *La Garde du Corps de son Roi*. Fanny, a fortnight after the defeat of Bonaparte, was presented to the French king in London. We are not often told what Fanny wore on any occasion, but for this ceremony she had on, in mourning for her father, a 'black bombazien and crepe' dress with an 'enormous train' and a small white cap. She carried a bouquet of fleurs-de-lis, a charming compliment to her husband's country. The king was, like almost everybody Fanny was ever introduced to, one of her constant readers. To her delight the Duc de Duras, who was presenting the audience to his majesty, now made a flattering reference to M. d'Arblay and the king, perhaps reminded of the former title by hearing the name, now took Fanny's hand and added to his farewells a title she had never been used to receive of anyone: *Bon jour, Madame la Comtesse*. A week or two later M. d'Arblay arrived, totally unexpectedly and Fanny's happiness for all her mourning, was restored after the long separation.

M. d'Arblay could stay no more than four weeks in England and then he must return to his duties, to his new uniform and to mounted guard duty after twenty-one years without riding. Fanny was pleased by the restoration of his military position and especially so when, on the petition of his friends, he had conceded to him the rank he formerly held in the army of *Maréchal de Camp,* an award dated back to 1792 when Louis XVI first promoted him. Nevertheless she hoped that as soon as the situation became more settled she would be able to persuade him back into civilian life, since he was sixty-one and not really of an age to re-embark upon a military career. But the escape of Napoleon from Elba was to lay much heavier burdens upon the ageing Comte than mounted guard duty, and before he could retire into domesticity he was to face some of the most strenuous and exacting events of his life.

Fanny was not able to return with her husband, though she must earnestly have wished it. There were two reasons and both of them were anxious ones. The first was the enforced sale of Camilla Cottage. It had been built on land that belonged to Mr Locke at the time but had now been inherited by his son. The d'Arblays paid an annual ground rent. Now Norbury Park was to be sold and young Mr Locke, very reasonably, offered to buy the cottage at valuation. It was estimated that Camilla Cottage had cost £1,300 to build and M. d'Arblay considered an offer of £1000 would be acceptable. Unfortunately the independent valuation was £640 or £650. Some ill-feeling was engendered by the fact that Mr Locke employed lawyers to act for him, whereas M. d'Arblay believed these matters should be dealt with between gentlemen. Fanny, knowing that they were being fairly – indeed generously – treated, had first to pacify her husband and then to remain in England to see the sale through. The inheritance they had planned for Alexander had proved a disappointment.

Camilla Cottage itself passed out of the hands of the d'Arblays but it is pleasant to note that it was described in 1892 as belonging to a Mr and Mrs Wylie who had given over one small room to be the 'Burney Parlour'. Here, we are told, were manuscripts of 'her three celebrated novels', under glass, and a splendid collection of portraits of Fanny and her intimate friends. Below each portrait and also enclosed in a glass case were manuscript letters written by the person depicted and addressed to Madame d'Arblay.

All this was destroyed by fire in 1919. Later the house was rebuilt. One would say that another and totally different house had been built on the site, but for the insistence on 'The Burney Garden where Fanny Burney is reputed to have written her books', for the place was by 1931 'a modern Tudor-style residence with fifteen bed and dressing-rooms, five bathrooms and complete offices'. Dr Percy Scholes, who quotes from a sale advertisement in *The Times,* mentions also the 'spacious lawns shaded by magnificent forest trees, sports grounds, hard and grass tennis courts, large covered riding school, ranges of garages and stabling, and the wonderful rock garden'—the Burney Garden, in fact. How Fanny would have laughed. And we, remembering the day the d'Arblays moved in and sat on a borrowed bench in front of their own fire, drinking to their new home in clear spring water, hardly know whether to laugh or not.

Fanny's other task was the resettling of Alexander to his studies. It is no unusual temperament, the kind where there is the ability to learn quickly and easily, but not the motivation. She was able to supervise him in the long vacation, to make sure he got up in the mornings and spent some time working under a tutor. With her watchful eye upon him he might perform exceedingly well. Without it he might fail as he had done before. His father saw the solution to the problem in his joining the French army – no other career in France than the army would do his family credit – and wrote to him suggesting he choose between Cambridge and *La Compagnie de Luxembourg*. Alexander chose Cambridge. His mother, whose health demanded the warmer climate of France as much as she herself desired to be with her husband, left him there and went back with M. d'Arblay in November.

The sea journey was bound to be rough at that time of the year and Fanny was so enfeebled by her usual seasickness that she had to be carried in a chair to the grateful warmth of a fire in an inn. While he was tending her, M. d'Arblay was struck in the chest by the shaft of a cart and had to be taken to the inn and blooded into a salad bowl. After that, and in strict contrast, we read of the presentation of Fanny to Her Royal Highness, the Duchess of Angoulême. The Duchess had, like everybody else, been reading Fanny's latest book, but in a French translation. M. d'Arblay accordingly sent her a copy of the English edition and also took his wife to an exhibition of pictures where she could see a portrait of Madame d'Angoulême. In Fanny's opinion Madame's face was deeply interesting but deeply melancholy. These preliminary overtures completed, Fanny was escorted to the Tuileries and received there by the Dowager Duchesse de Duras, whom she had, in fact, met before. She was passed on to Madame de Choisy and shut into a room where she found a lady standing at the other end. This lady curtseyed slightly and began the formal ritual of enquiries about her health and expressions of delight at meeting her. Fanny, whose mind was totally preoccupied with the whereabouts of M. de Montmorency, who was to introduce her to the Duchess, hardly glanced at her companion and, when invited to sit down, plumped down beside her in an informal way.

While Fanny focused her short-sighted eyes on the door, watching for M. de Montmorency, her companion made a remark about her last book. She then followed it up by asking if she could keep the copy she had been sent. As in a nightmare Fanny realized that she had behaved towards royalty with an indifference that must have suggested an extreme of bad breeding. Reluctant to explain to the Duchess that she had not taken her for royalty, a remark she might not have construed as a compliment, Fanny merely changed her mode of address to one suited to very high rank, but in other respects chatted on as if to an ordinary acquaintance. Fanny told the story of her clandestine voyage to England and emphasized the loyalty M. d'Arblay had maintained towards the royalist cause. The conversation then moved on to the admirable qualities of the English Royal Family, a subject on which Fanny could always speak with enthusiasm, and came to a close only when the Duchess was summoned to the King's dinner. Fanny confidently expected that this meeting might lead to such respectful friendships with the French royal family as she had had for so long with the English. But before any further meeting with the Duchess could take place, Bonaparte returned from Elba and there followed the Hundred Days.

Fanny wrote a connected narrative telling the story of Napoleon's return and the first idea she expresses in it is astonishment at how little the people of France expected it. She had lived ten years under Napoleon's rule and had known many friends who spoke confidently of him. 'The greatness of his power, the intrepidity of his ambition, the vastness of his conceptions and the restlessness of his spirit' – all these were known to her and to others who had lived in France at the time. Despite this, even after Bonaparte had entered France, the d'Arblays continued to drive in the Bois de Boulogne in the light calèche the General had bought when he was restored to his former army position. Like the rest of France they assumed that Napoleon would be taken prisoner or driven out of France and before they felt any kind of alarm he was reported to be at Lyons.

M. d'Arblay now, if he had not before, realized quite clearly the dangers of the situation. He took on double duty, acting as artillery officer at the barracks and *officier supérieur* in the King's Body Guards at the Tuileries. When it became evident that Napoleon was advancing to Paris and that a civil war was likely to ensue, M. d'Arblay began to make plans to remove Fanny to safety. He would have liked her to go back to England and when she refused he obtained a passport *pour Madame d'Arblay, née Burney,* so that she could escape if necessary from a beleaguered Paris.

Marshal Ney went out confidently to meet Napoleon, promising the King that he would bring him to Paris in an iron cage. At first the frequent notes by means of which M. d'Arblay, on duty almost all day and all night, kept in touch with his wife expressed confidence and optimism. Well-informed persons, including the Princesse d'Hénin, thought much the same, though the latter also promised Fanny to include her in her party if the situation should deteriorate and flight become necessary. She was totally unwilling to move away from her husband and desperately anxious because M. d'Arblay, in his sixties and after twenty years of country life, was preparing for active service. Then all hope disappeared and Fanny received from her husband a note begging her to leave the capital, a note that only a Frenchman would write: 'Il est présumable que nous ne pourrons faire aucune resistance . . . Tout parait perdu, "hors l'honneur", qu'il faut conserver.'

13

MADAME D'ARBLAY AT WATERLOO

Madame d'Arblay later identified as 'one of the most dreadful days' of her life, 19 March 1815, the last day before the triumphant return of Bonaparte to the French capital. Her husband came home at about six in the morning, exhausted but, worse than that, furious at the inefficiency of those around him. He begged Fanny to leave Paris and she, recognizing that to stay would only add to his problems, recognizing perhaps that he was here facing the kind of situation that all his training had pointed towards and that he should be left to deal with it single-mindedly, consented to go with the Princesse d'Hénin. M. d'Arblay was going on active service and 'he called upon me,' Fanny says, 'to exert the utmost courage lest I should enervate his own'. The two of them prayed briefly together and parted with a brave attempt at cheerfulness. Then it occurred to Fanny that she might catch one last glimpse of him through the window and so, in fact, she did. The General, as he should now be thought of, was mounted on his war-horse and his servant Deprez was preparing to mount another. An effect as of the White Knight in *Through the Looking-Glass* is given by the fact that d'Arblay's horse is 'loaded with pistols and equipped completely for immediate service on the field of battle', while the family cabriolet was filled with baggage and implements of war. 'Bayonets, lances, pistols, guns, sabres, daggers – what horror assailed me at the sight,' Fanny cries. He rode off into a Paris street made preternaturally silent by the apprehension in the city, and she was left to keep her word and leave Paris with the Princesse d'Hénin.

While Fanny was locking up her house and selecting those valuables she intended to take with her, a message came from the Princess saying that she must bring nothing but a small change of linen and one band-box as the news inclined her to believe that they would be back in two or three days.

In the interval before she had to join the Princess, Fanny went in search of her friend, Madame de Maisonneuve. She was to be found at the house of General Victor de la Tour Maubourg, who was, despite the amputation of his leg and thigh, about to equip himself in full uniform and wait upon His Majesty. The entry into the room of an officer of the King's *Garde du Corps* in the uniform d'Arblay himself was wearing startled Fanny momentarily. When she recognized the wearer, she realized that it was Count Charles de la Tour Maubourg, the youngest brother of her friend Madame de Maisonneuve. As soon as he saw her he produced a note from her husband which read: 'Ma chère amie – Tout est perdu! Je ne puis entrer dans aucun détail – de grâce, partez! le plutôt sera le mieux. A la vie et à la mort, A.d'A.' At that moment the message came that the Princess was ready for her.

When Fanny reached Madame la Princesse d'Hénin, she found her in a state bordering on hysteria. Fanny had seen her always at her most 'elegant, rational and kind'. Now her opinion of the situation fluctuated wildly between alarm and confidence. Worst of all she suggested plainly to Fanny that her inclusion in the party was inconvenient, and yet Fanny, notoriously touchy, could do nothing but stay with her, since there would be confusion enough without General d'Arblay having no real idea what company she was in.

The Princess made matters very much more embarrassing by quarrelling spectacularly with M. le Comte de Lally Tollendal, the Cicero of France, as Fanny calls him. It was believed by some, including Fanny, that the two were secretly married and certainly they seem to have been on very intimate terms. Yet if we make allowance for the discretion of Fanny's language it is easy enough to perceive that between the two of them on this occasion were almost operatic scenes of unbridled emotionalism and violent temper. With them was Madame la Comtesse d'Auch whose husband, like Fanny's, was in the King's bodyguard. She sat in silent meditation, resolving the question whether or not to try to travel the two or three hundred miles to her château at Auch with her babies and servants so that she might save her husband's property from confiscation.

M. de Lally went off to find out what was happening. The Princess paced up and down the room. People came and went. She interrogated them shrilly, calling them abusive names when they replied and never pausing to hear what they had to say. La Comtesse d'Auch resolved her fearful question in silence, at least on her part. A message arrived from M. de Lally for the Princesse d'Hénin to announce that Napoleon was within a few hours' march of Paris. She was to leave the capital without delay and he would follow.

As soon as the Princess had ordered her berlin she was told that the Government had requisitioned all horses and Fanny, in utter despair, imagined that she would be detained in Paris and imprisoned where no news of her husband could ever reach her. Madame d'Auch went away to make her own arrangements for flight. However, the Princess's valet Le Roy managed to persuade a friend to lend him horses for the first stage from Paris. Since things were now going well, the Princess's temper changed abruptly and she took leave of her servants with dramatic and memorable sweetness, the women kissing her cheek and the men the hem of her robe. Between ten and eleven at night they left the city, Fanny huddled speechless in the coach, thinking of her husband, the Princess exchanging occasional exclamations with her maidservant.

At Bourget, where they intended to change horses, it was almost impossible to obtain a room and M. de Lally, riding after them, and the servant Le Roy, sent back to Paris on horseback to obtain news, both brought seriously discouraging information. Bonaparte's advance was now totally unresisted. The King, preceded, encircled and followed by his bodyguards, including General d'Arblay, had left for an unknown destination. The woman slept out the night three in a bed, the Princess, Fanny and the maid, while the menservants slept on mattresses in the kitchen. In the morning they went on to Amiens. There was no going back now.

At Amiens Madame d'Hénin and M. Lally were entertained by the prefect, M. Lameth, but Fanny was passed off as a *femme de chambre* for her own safety and perhaps for M. Lameth's, since, as the wife of a member of the King's bodyguard, she was no suitable guest for a man who must, like everyone else, very soon pretend loyalty to Bonaparte. M. Lameth gave the Princess new passports, merely including Fanny in the party and not mentioning her name. He helped them obtain fresh horses and advised hurrying on to Brussels via Arras, since at any moment (Bonaparte now having reached Paris) he might be ordered to detain them.

At Arras, M. Lameth's note of introduction secured a warm welcome for the party and they were entertained to 'an elegant breakfast' at which the guests included several officers who were in Arras for a review. The coolness of temper with which everybody present behaved surprised Fanny a little but presently the commander of the troops under review came in and broke the news to the Prefect of Napoleon's advance. It seemed that whole bodies of troops were defecting or at least remaining inactive and the party from Paris were anxious to be on their way.

They went through Douai and hoped to reach Tournai before stopping for the night, because there they would no longer be on French territory. They changed horses at Orchies, where small parties of troops caused them some anxiety. It was safer, they thought, to continue to travel although it was past eleven o'clock. They were scarcely out of Orchies when they heard a cry for help and found that the cabriolet in which M. de Lally was travelling ahead had broken down. The groom was sent to find a blacksmith who said that the repair must wait for daylight. The party now began to be seriously concerned with their safety, even if they returned to the inn, where, in any case, there were no beds to be had.

By very great good fortune a door now opened in a small house nearby, and an old lady appeared with a candle in her hand. She drew them silently into the house and made a fire, found food and wine and tea, and when they refused to accept the bed she offered them – probably her own – gave them pillows and a chair at head and feet.

When they tried to sleep they were aroused by the sound of trumpets and of the trampling of horses coming in their direction. It turned out to be a party of pro-Bonaparte Polish Lancers looking for accommodation. The old lady was able to assure them quite calmly that she had relatives staying. They believed her and rode away, leaving Fanny's group of refugees listening in terror for the next assault on the door. Another party of horsemen arrived almost as soon as the refugees had drifted into sleep and from that time on they abandoned the attempt and lay awake until five in the morning when their carriages were ready for them. They passed through suspicious groups of military and across the frontier to Tournay where they heard that Louis XVIII was at Lille, waiting for permission to enter the Netherlands. His safety was, to Fanny, the safety of her *cher ami* and consequently she was somewhat heartened by the news.

While Fanny was tramping the streets of Tournay, trying to find someone who would deliver a note to Lille, since the post was discontinued, a carriage with the royal coat or arms arrived. For a moment, so great was her eagerness to see her husband, she imagined that the King was there in Tournay and his bodyguard with him. She was told, however, that the Prince de Condé had just arrived.

While she was making plans for obtaining information from one so near the throne, Fanny came upon Madame d'Hénin, 'sauntering up and down while holding by the arm of a gentleman I had never before seen'. To avoid any frustration of her purpose, Fanny tried to slink past, but the Princess called her loudly and clearly and she was compelled to stop.

Desperate to know how her husband was faring, Fanny begged her for the names of some of the gentlemen who had just arrived, so that she might make enquiries of them.

The Princess mentioned M. le Comte de Vioménil, who, together with Victor de Maubourg had been appointed to raise volunteers for the King. Here was a name she could use. Victor de Maubourg was, of course, brother to her dear friend Madame de Maisonneuve and that almost constituted an introduction. The gentleman whose arm the Princess held now offered Fanny his assistance 'in a tone and with a look of so much benevolence that I frankly accepted it, and we sallied in search of a person known to me only by name'.

M. de Vioménil was duly found, dining by himself in an upper room of the inn, but he had no news except that his Majesty was in Gand. Madame d'Hénin later introduced Fanny's guide to her as M. de Chateaubriand, a writer very much in disfavour with Bonaparte who had blocked his election to the French Institute. Fanny had read and admired his book *The Itinerary to Jerusalem* and was glad of the opportunity to praise it to the author.

The party arrived at last at Brussels. Here they drove to the house of Madame la Comtesse de Maurville who had kept a French school in England while she was an emigrant and now lived on a small pension in Brussels. 'She received us in great dismay, fearing to lose her little all by these changes of government.' Here Fanny was ill for several days, a circumstance hardly surprising after the strain of parting from her husband and making so arduous a journey. Dr James's powders and determination overcame her fever, however, and after she had 'kept to her bed a day or two', she was well again and ready for her main task of finding out where her husband was and what state his health was in.

Madame de Maurville endeared herself to Fanny by her admiration of Susan, whom she had met in London. Fanny appreciated also her vein of satire and her shrewdness. She soon found the party a house near the cathedral and not so very far from her own. Fanny took what we would call the ground floor, the Princess the first floor and the one above was for M. de Lally.

It was impossible at first for Fanny to discover anything at all about the fate of the King and his bodyguard, but eventually Madame la Duchesse de Duras, whom she had formerly met in Paris, wrote around to various of her friends to try to calm Fanny's anxiety. Fanny visited her in true *émigrée* conditions, a shabby hotel without servants, her daughter obliged to bring in the wood for the stove. She told Fanny that the King's body-guard had been disbanded by the Duc de Berry on the frontiers of Belgium, since the King could not enter the country with a military guard. They had been given liberty to go wherever they pleased, and that was certainly information that would trouble Fanny, since it left her without any means of knowing where her husband might be.

Fanny chafed hopelessly for days until Madame de Maurville, in a state of pleased excitement, brought her a letter from General d'Arblay in which he enquired of her for news of Fanny. 'The joy of that moment,' Fanny exclaims, 'oh! the joy of that moment that showed me again the handwriting that demonstrated the life and safety of all to which my earthly happiness clung, can never be expressed and only by our meeting, when at last it took place, could be equalled.' A whole series of letters followed. Fanny had already written, at hazard, to almost every town in the Netherlands. News came that the King had gone to Gand and had been followed there by his bodyguard, so she wrote there as well, under cover to the Duc de Luxembourg, captain of the corps. Her joy in his safety made her willing to forget all the things she had left in Paris and she wrote to her son and her friends telling them the glad news. A letter from General d'Arblay came by post from Ypres and another from Bruges. He had heard through the Duc de Luxembourg that Fanny was safe in Brussels. Then her door was opened, Fanny says, by General d'Arblay himself.

M. d'Arblay had undertaken feats of endurance that would have taxed the strength of a much younger man and his 'shattered frame', according to Fanny, was held together only by 'mental strength and unconquerable courage'. Yet he had now pledged himself to serve the King even in the perilous circumstances the King found himself in. Accordingly he was liable at any moment to be recalled to Gand. While he was able to be at Brussels, however, a social circle was set up. A new friend, Madame de Beaufort, wife of Le Colonel de Beaufort, 'a warm, early friend of General d'Arblay', was visited and so were Madame de la Tour du Pin, a lady of English origin, her daughter Madame de Liedekirke, Madame de Maurville and Madame de Merode, the Duchesse d'Ursel, M. de Carbonnière and the Boyd family. The d'Arblays boarded with the Princesse d'Hénin by 'picnic' contract, that is, each paying his or her own expenses, and M. de Lally, when he was not at Gand with the King, did the same.

The summons came for M. d'Arblay from Gand. His posting was cruelly disappointing and held out no possibility that his wife might join him. He was to go to Luxembourg and there collect and interview all soldiers who were willing to leave Bonaparte to serve with the King. With him were to be Colonel Comte de Nazancourt, M. de Premorel and his son. Eleven other posts were to be set up, all on frontiers, and very unattractive they must have been to officers yearning only for active service.

Now that General d'Arblay was restored to her and engaged in work that could be considered important, Fanny decided they must leave the Princess and live on their own. She had lived for a month in La Rue de la Montagne and they now found a house in the Marché aux Bois where they could have the first floor, the drawing-room being appropriated by the military and the rest left for Fanny. In seventeen days Fanny knew all there was to be known of d'Arblay's staff officers, the number of their children, the names of their brothers and sisters and their degree of affluence or poverty.

Plans were made for the forthcoming campaign while Fanny maintained her calm with difficulty, knowing as she did the dangers of the months to come. Then d'Arblay decreed a morning's jaunt for recreation. In their new cabriolet with their new horses they drove to the Palais de Lachen, which Napoleon had given Josephine at the time of their divorce. There Fanny was pleased with the park and enamoured of the Gobelin tapestry. They went also to a benefit for the singer Catalini, where Fanny observed the good spirits of Lord Wellington and watched too how diplomatically he behaved. When a chorus from *Rule, Britannia* by Arne, Dr Burney's old music teacher, was sung he listened without applauding and when his officers began to demand an encore, his smiling mood changed to one of such complete disapprobation that they stopped at once.

In May, on his birthday, came M. d'Arblay's recall to Gand and thence to his frontier post at Trèves where Fanny could not join him. She kept up her spirits by visiting friends, though the Princesse d'Hénin was now too busy with politics to be very sociable, and, of course, in writing letters, since even the best library in Brussels could not provide anything that interested her and she was in no mood for serious writing. While she was drifting through her days, bored and lonely, the Battle of Waterloo came upon her unawares.

The premonitory signs of the battle passed Fanny by without alerting her. There was a bugle at dawn, lights, a few hurrying soldiers: no more. Then, finishing a letter to her 'best friend', she decided to post it herself for safety, though her breakfast had already been brought in. On the way back from the Post Office she heard military music and saw a complete corps, 'infantry, cavalry, artillery, bag and baggage' marching in time. They were in the black uniform with white death's-head insignia of Brunswick. Byron speaks of this nephew of George III, 'Brunswick's fated chieftain', as attending the ball that was held for officers the night before Waterloo and there hearing the first gunfire. 'He rushed into the field,' Byron relates, 'and foremost, fighting, fell.' Most of the Brunswickers were killed with him and Fanny's macabre vision on a June morning was only a prelude to the slaughter that followed, the 'hills of dead' who had to be buried by three thousand peasants in some haste before epidemics of disease resulted.

The Battle of Waterloo, by Fanny's account, followed three days of inconclusive skirmishes. The Belgians, whom Fanny had previously described as 'slow, sleepy and uninteresting', crowded into their doorways and windows to watch the soldiers go by. 'Placidly, indeed, they saw the warriors pass; no kind greeting welcomed their arrival; no warm wishes followed them to combat. Neither, on the other hand, was there the slightest symptom of dissatisfaction.' The news that Bonaparte had already broken into Belgium and taken Charleroi was known to almost everybody except the solitary Fanny and it was universally believed that he must win. Friends such as the Princesse d'Hénin offered Fanny hospitality during the conflict that was certain to follow.

All Fanny could think about was Trèves. On 17 and 18 June she watched the wounded being dragged back from the front on improvised ambulances to be cared for in the city and almost more painfully saw the 'ready-armed and vigorous victims that marched past my windows to meet similar destruction'. Bulletins from the battlefield were sent every hour, quite often from the Duke of Wellington to Lady Charlotte Greville who gave the news to other ladies with relatives fighting and so spread it about Brussels. It was often possible, too, to obtain news from the lightly wounded and those who helped them from the battlefield.

Madame d'Hénin had arranged with Fanny that in the event of defeat they should go by barge to Antwerp for safety and on 18 June at six in the morning Fanny heard the sound of hurrying feet and then a rapping on her bedroom door. It was Miss Ann Boyd, daughter of old friends of Fanny's, and she brought the news that Bonaparte was making straight for Brussels and that Fanny must be ready at eight to go to Antwerp, or, if Antwerp was threatened, to sail to England.

Fanny wrote to her husband, paid her bills and packed her necessaries.

There were no carriages, so she set off on foot, her maid and her landlord carrying the baggage, and soon joined the Boyds. It was an unpleasant walk:

> Though the distance was short, the walk was long because rugged, dirty and melancholy. Now and then we heard a growling noise, like distant thunder, but far more dreadful. When we had got about a third part of the way, a heavy rumbling sound made us stop to listen. It was approaching nearer and nearer and we soon found that we were followed by innumerable carriages and a multitude of persons.

They reached the wharf where they saw the barge they were to go in, but while Mr Boyd was on his way to arrange last-minute details, and they were ordering breakfast in a nearby inn, he was told that military evacuation of Brussels had been ordered:

> ... all the magazines, the artillery and the warlike stores of every description, and all the wounded, the maimed and the sick should be immediately removed to Antwerp. For the purpose he [the Duke] had issued directions that every barge, every boat should be seized for the use of the army and that everything of value should be conveyed away, the hospitals emptied and Brussels evacuated.

The canon reverberated more loudly than ever before and now Fanny's party began to imagine the guns directed against Brussels and against them. There were no land carriages to be had and no horses: no escape from Brussels by water or by land. However, when the barges returned the next day, they were to be allowed a passage, if they were at the wharf by six o'clock. Fanny was to spend the evening and night with the Boyds, but meanwhile she returned home to write to Trèves where her hosts greeted her with the same impassivity that they showed to all the events of the war.

It was while she was writing that shouts reached her ears. The Belgians, their impassivity totally demolished, cheered the news that the tide of war had been reversed and Bonaparte was taken prisoner. When she rushed to the window she was able to observe in detail an officer in a 'high, feathered, glittering helmet', seated on a war-horse 'in full equipment'. She had seen Bonaparte and knew this was not he. Did that mean that the rumour was totally unfounded or merely that the 'crew of roaring wretches' surrounding the prisoner had exaggerated the importance of their prize?

Scarcely a quarter of an hour later Fanny was again distracted from her letter, this time not by shouts of delight, but by a more blood-curdling sound. It was 'a howl, violent, loud, affrighting and issuing from many voices'. When once more she went to the window she saw the Marché aux Bois filled with hurrying people.

> Women with children in their arms or clinging to their clothes ran screaming out of doors; and cries, though not a word was ejaculated, filled the air, and from every house, I saw windows closing and shutters fastening; all this, though long in writing, was presented to my eyes in a single moment and was followed in another by a burst into my apartment, to announce that *the French were come.*

Fanny pushed her papers and money into a basket and put on a bonnet and shawl, intending to join the Boyds as had been arranged. But she could not cross the stream of people and decided on Madame de Maurville instead. That lady had become hardened to revolutions and the loss of a husband and three sons had left her with few personal anxieties, so she received Fanny with calm and cheerfulness. Her example of sangfroid was particularly valuable in the midst of such terrifying rumours as swept over the city.

This proved to be the darkest hour. The French in Brussels were prisoners, not conquerors. News now gave praise to the Duke of Wellington and hoped almost confidently for his victory. But the issue was by no means certain and Fanny, escorted by Madame de Maurville's servant, set off to join the Boyds that evening as had been arranged. The crowds were less terrifying than they had been, but the sight of wounded soldiers distressed Fanny: '. . . officers of high rank, either English or Belge and either dying or dead [were] extended upon biers carried by soldiers. The view of their gay and costly attire, with the conviction of their suffering or fatal state, joined to the profound silence of their bearers and attendants, was truly saddening.' Another and less poignant sight was a British soldier exhibiting the tall war-horse he had looted from the field, quite contrary to his Commander-in-Chief's orders.

At the Boyds Fanny found a determination to leave for Antwerp and a pessimism about the outcome of the battle. No land-transport at all was available and the hope of travelling by barge was all that remained. Better news came, however and a friend of the Boyds assured the party that the Bonapartists were flying in all directions. On the strength of that news, Fanny, when roused at four or five the next morning to set off for

Antwerp, decided to stay in Brussels where letters from Trèves could not fail to reach her. The Boyds, no doubt surprised, left without her.

It was not until the 20th that the victory was announced as certain. Bonaparte was said to be 'totally defeated, his baggage all taken, even his private equipage and personals'. He was a fugitive and in disguise. The Duke of Wellington boldly sent a message to the King suggesting that he should move to Tournai. The wounded were to be sent to Brussels, which in his opinion was safe against invasion now.

The cost of the victory was something Fanny had every opportunity to assess:

> I never approached my window but to witness sights of wretchedness. Maimed, wounded, bleeding, mutilated, tortured victims of this exterminating contest passed by every minute: the fainting, the sick, the dying and the dead, on brancards, in carts, in waggons, succeeded one another without intermission.

It was nearly a week before the doctors could work through to the prisoners and by that time blood had dried on their bodies and their clothes smelt ominously of pestilence. All Fanny's friends were occupied in nursing, some by the medium of their servants, some personally. The official end of the fighting, declared on the 26th, was a matter on which all her French friends expressed to Fanny their congratulations. Only one thing remained to complete her joy.

On 19 July, while Fanny was waiting to know where she could join her husband and was writing one of her copious letters to him at Trèves, the Princesse d'Hénin and Colonel de Beaufort came into the room with the air of people who bring bad news. A letter had arrived from General d'Arblay. While Fanny waited, wondering to what height of calamity their news was building, they told her that M. d'Arblay had received on the calf of his leg 'a furious kick from a wild horse' and was confined to bed by his injury. He hoped Fanny would be able to travel to Trèves to join him.

Fanny was immeasurably alarmed to discover that the letter was not in her husband's handwriting. A surgeon, determined to mend matters, had made them decidedly worse and M. d'Arblay had now added a nervous fever to his original injury. Without waiting for servants or a guide, Fanny now set out on what must have been a terrifying and exhausting journey. There were no horses to be had so she was compelled to travel by diligence and via Luxembourg. The diligence for Luxembourg had left on the previous day and there were six days to wait for the next. By great good fortune her friend the Baroness de Spagen was able to recommend that she go by Liège, travelling to that city under the protection of her brother-in-law who was going by the night coach. Fanny was delighted, booked her seat and was in the act of setting off when the Princess d'Hénin's servant arrived with a message from his mistress suggesting an alternative and, in her opinion, safer plan. Fanny refused to delay, but as a result of the time spent dealing with the message was three or four minutes too late for the coach. The next coach would give her a week to wait and, of course, no Comte de Spagen.

The booking-clerk had a suggestion to make. If Madame were to hurry to the Allée Verte, two miles away, she might catch the diligence at a stop there, where it usually halted for parcels or fresh passengers. And so she did. But when she asked for le Comte de Spagen she was told he had caught an earlier coach. She wanted to go to Trèves, she said. Ah, said the booking-clerk, she had come the wrong way then. She should have travelled by Luxembourg. Couldn't he suggest anything at all? Well, if she would go to Aix, she might, possibly, pick up a connection. But to leave Liège was impossible without a passport. Fortunately she had hers with her, though quite accidentally. At Aix she was told that a diligence to Juliers, even further north, was the only possible conveyance. It left Aix at four the next morning.

Fanny had no heart for the tourist attractions of Aix-la-Chapelle, for the tomb of Charlemagne or the famous cathedral. In her misery she was conscious only of the 'misty, mizzling rain' and the sandy, heavy roads. She took a room and lay all night without undressing, shutters and curtains open while she waited for the coach. She woke at three and wandered about the house, finding no one. Every quarter of an hour after that until four o'clock she went to see if it was time and at four climbed thankfully into the coach standing ready. They went into Cologne through a seven-mile avenue of lime trees. An officer in a Prussian uniform came to examine passports and when he saw Fanny's he asked in a low whisper if she were French. When she said yes and explained her anxiety to reach Trèves quickly, the officer said that he would take her passport to the magistrate and get it signed and could recommend a respectable French couple who would put her up, so that she might be spared going to an inn.

Fanny was then conducted to a house not very far away where a couple of elderly gentlefolk, probably of the former provincial nobility, and served by an equally elderly domestic, received her. Fanny describes the vast, scarcely-furnished room and the rickety, threadbare arm-chair she was given to sit in. The ceremonious behaviour of her host, both to his wife and to her, did not go unnoticed. Tea was served by the domestic. When a little halting conversation began and Fanny explained the reason for her haste, they told her how they had lost their sons and their property and were now in penury. An 'economical but well-served and well-cooked' little supper appeared at eleven and since Fanny had to catch the coach at four she was then encouraged to retire for the night.

Again Fanny lay down in her clothes, striking the repeater of her watch throughout the night. At half past three she set out, leaving what money she could spare for her host to find, knowing he would never accept it if offered directly. The tottering domestic carried her luggage and she reached the diligence just before it set off. To her great regret she had no money left to give the servant, much as she wanted to reward him for his kindness. There followed a two-day journey along the Rhine to Coblentz and from Coblentz to Trèves. For the first time since she set out Fanny became aware of the beauty of the scenery. The Rhine and its banks, the rocks and hanging woods delighted her. Almost every hill 'was crowned with an ancient castle or fortress', many of them ruined by the depredations of war.

Then she arrived at Trèves, terrified of what she might find but overwhelmingly glad to have arrived. It was important to avoid giving the sick man a dangerous shock. She had written to her husband's aide-de-camp to prepare him for her coming and now she wrote a brief note to General d'Arblay's valet, asking him to come for her luggage. In five minutes he was with her, running, she said, like a greyhound although he was a staid and composed German. She could hardly force herself to ask him what she wanted to know, but he told her instantly. The General was out of danger; both surgeons said so. She went in at once.

Dreadfully suffering, but still mentally occupied by the duties of his profession, I found him. Three wounds had been inflicted on his leg by the kick of a wild horse, which he had bought at Trèves, with intent to train to military service. He was felled by them to the ground. Yet, had he been skilfully attended, he might have been completely cured! But all the best surgeons throughout every district had been seized upon for the armies . . .

General d'Arblay was billeted on a private gentleman of Trèves and there was no room for Fanny in the house. The next day her husband entered upon a private 'picnic' plan for her with a friend, a Madame de la

Grange. There she breakfasted, had dinner and slept, escorted to and fro by kindly gentlemen who happened to be available. D'Arblay had already set in motion the tedious business of having himself recalled and discharged from service, and eventually, though only by the intervention of the Duc de Luxembourg, they received their orders and passports. Then they made their slow journey back to Paris and there took leave of their friends before embarking for England.

14

MADAME D'ARBLAY RETURNS
TO ENGLAND

Last night, my ever dear friends, we arrived once more in Old England. I write this to send the moment I land in London. I cannot boast of our health, our looks, our strength; but I hope we may recover a part of all when our direful fatigues, mental and corporeal, cease to utterly weigh upon and wear us.

So wrote Fanny to her friends Mrs Locke and her daughter Mrs Angerstein. The sea voyage (and Fanny was never a good sailor) had been unusually rough. She was nearly unconscious with seasickness and both she and the General had to be carried ashore. His wounds had re-opened under the strain of the crossing and Fanny was anxious to install him comfortably in Bath, which was restorative for invalids and inexpensive considering its advantages. It was quite possible to be sociable in Bath without keeping a carriage and there were still sedan chairs to be hired. Living was cheap and the town was visited by all kinds of distinguished people. The streets were clean and safe. For the genteel poor – and when had the d'Arblays ever been anything else? – it was an ideal place to live and Fanny was hoping to persuade her husband that they should make their home there.

On the way to London from Dover the d'Arblays had visited Charles, then well on his way to become a bishop, had not apoplexy intervened and carried him off at almost the peak of his success. They met Alexander and then James with whom he had been staying, had two royal visits and saw Esther and Charlotte again. The brisk round-up of all those dear to her must have made Fanny feel at home again, since home was always her family wherever it might chance to be.

In Bath Fanny had first to find lodgings cheaper than those Marianne Bourdois had ready for her in Rivers Street, and then to pay a round of visits that would have her circulating in Bath society as soon as she was recovered from the ordeal she had so recently endured. One of the first visits she paid was to Mrs Piozzi, a very stiff, uncomfortable affair that did nothing to restore the two women to their old friendship. Several calls followed, but always when the lady called on was not at home. Two years later when Fanny called however she was taken to the boudoir and engaged in intelligent conversation, not like a friend but at least like a welcome visitor. In Mrs Piozzi's common-place book she notes the visit and describes Fanny as 'always smooth, always alluring'. At seventy-six Mrs Piozzi had not forgiven her old friend, but she could not resist, she says, the pleasure of her conversation. Her own conversation had become celebrated in Bath and visitors came to hear her talk as they had once come to Streatham to hear Dr Johnson. Sir William Pepys and Hannah More, Mrs Garrick and Mrs Piozzi were all that was left of those days. And now Madame d'Arblay; but Mrs Piozzi was not inclined to make her one of them.

One of the griefs of Fanny's life was the loss of Camilla Cottage. It had held for her the idea of retreat from society into personal happiness, into an egoism for two. But at the end of her life her choice was for a modified town life in Bath. One need not dig the garden, but intelligent society and civilized amusements were comfortable and soothing. She had reached a compromise now between her frenetic season of London society after Streatham, when she was fêted as authoress of *Cecilia,* and the extreme simplicity of living in her cottage.

Not least of the advantages of Bath was that it was attractive to Alexander d'Arblay, Fanny's son, in a way that a remote country place could never be. That made it easier for Fanny to persuade her husband to stay in England and easier for her to keep an eye on the studies of that unambitious young man. He had a curious innocence, a lack of worldliness that is not to be wondered at when one considers his parents and upbringing. Fanny was able to impose her will on his and make him work, and she felt it her duty to see that he acquitted himself as well as possible in the Cambridge examinations. At times this makes her letters to him educative in the most unattractive sense, and at times it makes her tone sharp and governessy when she writes. But he was to take his degree as tenth wrangler because of her supervision of his studies and no one could deny that he needed guidance.

In August, leaving Fanny to superintend her son's vacation work, General d'Arblay went back to France to arrange various business matters connected with his pension and there, it seems, he reverted to the ideas of his own class and nationality and picked out a bride for his son. It is curious to note how unlike d'Arblay's own marriage this choice is. Fanny sums her up by intuition and what little the General has told her:

> A darling daughter – an only child, nursed in the lap of soft prosperity, – sole object of tenderness and of happiness to both her parents; rich, well-born, stranger to all care and unused to any control; beautiful as a little angel and (be very sure) not unconscious she is born to be adored; endowed with talents to create admiration, independently of the éclat of her personal charms and indulged from her cradle with every wish, every fantaisie . . . Will such a young creature as this be happy with our Alexander?

Fanny's description of the girl M. d'Arblay had picked out for his son gives off a sardonic contempt which shows how clearly she realizes the difference between such a young creature and herself as a bride. She realizes too that in her husband's opinion there is still only one career for Alexander in France and that is a military one quite unsuited to his temperament. This marriage is not for him, she tells d'Arblay. One cannot go backwards in time. Her son's life could not be regulated by the ideas prevailing when her husband was young.

Alex, at twenty-one, was, as usual, in trouble with his tutors. He was to take his degree in January and then decide on his career. The Tancred scholarship was at an end because he had decided against medicine and he was totally dependent on his parents. Since General d'Arblay's small pension was very uncertain indeed during those uneasy days after the war, it was important to have him settled as soon as possible. If he took a good degree – became a wrangler – Fanny believed he would be offered a fellowship. She was probably right in thinking that some such life would accommodate his peculiarities. But she constantly wrote him letters such as she wrote to nobody else, prodding and jocular, and wise with the wisdom of the great men whose names she so perseveringly dropped. If he reacted against her advice it is not surprising.

Early in July Fanny took Alex to Ilfracombe where he was to be tutored by a man called Jacob and she was to try the effect on her constitution of fresh air and rest. She longed to be with her husband, but to take Alexander to France would be to distract him from his work. She believed too that she could manage her son by means of patience and forbearance, while his father's greater forcefulness would agitate and alienate the boy.

Fanny describes the harbour at Ilfracombe and the master of a Spanish vessel who is waiting to be tried for 'piracy or smuggling or aiding the slave trade'. He is on parole and has kept with him only a minimal crew.

She watches his cook, dressed all in white, make the daily *pot-au-feu*. He has the meat cut, she thinks, into pounds

> for I see it all carved into square morsels, seemingly of that weight, which he
> inserts bit by bit, with whole bowls, delicately cleaned, washed and prepared,
> of cabbages, chicory, turnips, carrots, celery and small herbs. Then some
> thick slices of ship ham and another bowl of onions and garlic; salt by a
> handful and pepper by a wooden spoon full. This is left for many hours; and
> in the interval he prepares a porridge of potatoes well mashed and barley well
> boiled, with some other ingredient that when it is poured into the pan bubbles
> up like syllabub. But before he begins, he employs two lads to wash all the
> ship.

This is the only time we find Fanny interested in cooking and it was doubtless the curious circumstances of the making of the *pot-au-feu* rather than the food itself that drew her attention.

There is a hurricane – even in July – and a ship lost. News of the General is not particularly encouraging and even Fanny, who does not care what she eats, finds the meals a little unsatisfactory. The General would not like it: 'When he comes, if I am so happy as to see him return while we are here, I must endeavour to ameliorate these matters.' She has moved away from the harbour because of unhealthy smells at low tide, but she misses the interest she found there. It is all slightly dull if the truth is told, and she is glad of the unexpected arrival of Mr Bowdler, whom she had met often at Blues parties and who begged leave to call on her.

When she agrees to receive him, Mr Bowdler changes very quickly into 'a toilette of great dress, such as would have suited the finest evening assembly at Bath' and calls on Fanny at once. Alex is enchanted beyond measure, for Mr Bowdler was considered the finest chess-player in England and he had a passion for the game. They are invited to dine with Mr Bowdler and his two sisters, whom Fanny knew in the old 'Ting-mouth' days, at the hotel the next evening. Fanny is anxious not to disrupt Alex's routine, and especially for anything or anyone connected with chess, but since it is seven years since Mr Bowdler has played she thinks there is little danger. So she and Fanny Bowdler remembered the past while Alex and Mr Bowdler talked chess, and the very pleasant break in the monotony of the routine Fanny had instituted was doubtless good for both of them.

There was another break in the routine before the summer was over, and this time it was a much more unpleasant one. Since they were soon to leave the coast Fanny decided upon devoting a morning to inspecting it and collecting souvenirs. She set out with M. d'Arblay's favourite little dog Diane and a large silk bag to hold any addition to M. d'Arblay's 'mineralogical stores' that she might find. The wind was high and she was quickly compelled to leave the cliffs for the edge of the sea where she collected some especially fine pebbles. Fanny had no idea whether the tide was in or out but wandered on, increasing her collection and admiring the rugged coast-line, until Diane tugged at her dress in some dismay and she found the sea had risen unnoticed. It was impossible to return by the way she had come.

Diane managed to find a small hole which led to the upper sands, but her mistress could get no more than her head through it and after wailing in despair the little dog vanished. A storm was rising now and the waves were noisy and violent. Fanny noticed on top of one of the highest of the small rocks around her a tuft of grass, clear evidence that it was above tide level. She decided she must aim at that point and with the sharp edges of the rock tearing her clothes and cutting her hands and feet she managed to gain a ledge a quarter of the way up and sit down for a moment. But the waves mounted higher and Fanny, always a realist, knew that her life depended on reaching the top pinnacle where she would be safe. About two-thirds of the way up, when her head was nearly level with the tuft of grass she aimed at, the only tuft of grass to be seen anywhere, she was forced to stop. She could grip on to a great slanting slab ahead of her and balance her weight on one foot. It was hardly a rest, but it was a position she could hold for a little while.

It was calmer now and the wind was still, but when Fanny watched the tide 'with my near-sighted glass' she saw to her horror that the water was still rising. She looked hopefully for a boat, at which she might wave her parasol, but in vain. At this moment of despair the little dog Diane reappeared by the very hole she had escaped through. It was easy for her to reach the rock Fanny was on, but to climb up to her was almost impossible. At last she reached the slab of slate and Fanny was able to hook the curved handle of her parasol in the little dog's collar and lodge her safely in a niche. She was happier not to be quite alone, but had scarcely recovered from the excitement of the moment when she saw that the tide now broke on her rock and was rising fast. A huge wave dashed violently against it, but at the very moment that she thought she was to be drowned, she realized that that wave was the last of the rising tide. Uncomfortable as she was, clinging to her rock and trying to soothe the terrified little dog, at least she was out of actual danger.

Fanny made her position a little less contorted by finding crevices for her feet and a spot where she could occasionally lean one of her elbows. She made a cushion for Diane with the pebble-filled bag and caressed her continually. The sun went down. The dark came and a light rain began to fall. There was no moon, only a pale brightness reflected from the sea. It would be several hours before Fanny could go back across the sands.

Then suddenly a movement, a shadow, appeared before Fanny's short-sighted eyes. She could see nothing at first, then at last, on the opposite side of the bay she made out two small dark figures. They saw her and called out. She answered, 'I am safe'. Her son's voice cried, 'Thank God. O thank God', and her first concern was to tell him to wait, not to take risks too soon.

Figures surrounded her. An old sailor who knew the rocks reached her with a coat, which she refused to put on because it was Alexander's and she thought he should be wearing it. Almost at once he was with her himself, following the sailor's route at some hazard to be with her quickly, and took her in his arms. Two days later the rock to which Fanny had clung was broken off at its apex; in its new form it could not have saved her from the waves.

Early in October, the return of General d'Arblay from France provided Fanny with fresh cause for anxiety. He was 'altered – thin – weak – depressed – full of pain – and disappointed in every expectation of every sort that had urged his excursion'. He was never to recover fully from the damage done by the kicks on his leg from the wild horse that he suffered at Trèves, or the treatment by inefficient doctors that followed it. The strain he had endured during the fighting had now begun to affect him adversely and though Fanny nursed him most solicitously, she must have begun to realize that the first signs of his fatal illness were upon him. Fanny stayed at home with him, admitted no visitors and was glad to be his only company in his illness.

While Fanny was thus engaged, a momentous occasion for the city of Bath was being organized. George III had longed to bring the Queen to visit the city and to take the cure for her health. He had had three houses rented for him in the Royal Crescent to accommodate his family, who included the Princess Elizabeth, and a civic reception had been arranged. But the King was suddenly struck by blindness. He had endured so much but there was to be no end, it seemed, to his afflictions. The Queen, with her customary stoic resolution, or a sense of thrift, since the arrangements were made already, decided to come with the Princess alone. They were to appear in all the splendour they were accustomed to parade at Court and go through the whole programme as it had been arranged.

At the moment that the Queen was having the diamonds placed on her head for the civic reception, news was brought to her of the illness of the Princess Charlotte. The Princess was in childbirth and the child she was to bear carried with it the hopes of the nation since there was no other heir to the throne. Labour had been unduly prolonged and she and her baby were to die of it. When the Queen heard how seriously ill she was she considered (for the second time) cancelling or postponing the festivities. But it was, she thought, too late. Everybody had arrived and the money had been spent. She and the Princess Elizabeth, who was also loaded with jewellery, put out their best efforts to make the occasion splendid and the dinner began.

By the curious eighteenth-century custom, the Queen, the Princess Elizabeth and the Queen's party ate at a table by themselves. The Duke of Clarence was at another table with the Marquis of Bath and all the Queen's suite. During the meal the Duke received an express containing news of the Princess Charlotte's death. 'He rose from table and struck his forehead as he read them and then hurried out of the assembly with inexpressible trepidation and dismay.' The Queen shut herself up alone to grieve. Her doctor advised against her returning to Windsor the next day, but the day after she left the city where so friendly a welcome had been given her and such tragic associations had now been formed. She returned stoically after the funeral and took the cure as she had meant to do. Fanny d'Arblay called on her daily to enquire about her health. Charlotte Barrett comments in a letter that 'the Queen's visit to Bath put all the inhabitants in a fever of curiosity, expence or attendance. She kept my aunt d'Arblay standing for three hours every morning during her stay and never gave her a pinch of snuff.'

A few months after this, at the beginning of the year 1818, another stately, tentative *rencontre* between Mrs Piozzi and Madame d'Arblay took place by letter. Fanny had stayed on friendly terms with Queeney, now Lady Keith, and was glad to feel that there was no animosity lingering between herself and Mrs Piozzi, especially since they were all ageing and Bath was an enclosed society. Mrs Piozzi refers to the General's illness ('Who attends the General?' 'And why do you think him so very bad?') Fanny in answer says that she has been led to expect a long, slow recovery. Her postscript, with its touch of swagger, has also its pathos: 'I hope you were a little glad that my son has been among the high Wranglers.'

210

Fanny has left an account of the General's last illness. He had returned from Paris in the autumn of 1817 jaundiced and feeble. After the Queen's first visit to Bath he had recovered somewhat and when she returned for the cure it was arranged that he should be presented to her. He wore his military honours and he and Fanny were taken in sedan chairs to the Pump Room. The Queen arrived by the same kind of conveyance and, if we are to believe Fanny's rather partial account, her charm overcame her age, illness and unimpressive size. The British Museum portrait of her at this date (after L. Gahagan) shows us how 'the Celebrated Modeller' saw her in the Pump Room and so it lacks, of course, the dress and ornaments that would take the viewer's eye away from her features, which were never handsome. The strained amiability on the face reminds us of the life she had led and of how often, when tragedy struck the Royal Family, she had had to put on her diamonds and that pinned-back smile and over-come it with regality (which was charm enough for many).

A royal conversation was held, the Queen introducing suitable subjects tactfully chosen and the General commenting eagerly and non-committally upon them. As soon as the audience ended, he was overcome with the pain of his illness and compelled to go home and rest.

The Queen and Princess ended their visit to Bath by making gifts to Fanny. From the Princess came a pair of camp candlesticks, so that Fanny could by their light research among her father's papers which the Royal Family wished her to edit with a prefatory memoir. The Queen sent a small collection of books including a privately-printed book of prayers. 'In this she had condescended,' Fanny says, 'to write my name, accompanied by words of peculiar kindness.'

The Queen died in late 1817. The General began, in 1818, quite early, to talk about his approaching death. Life had never been so pleasant, he declared constantly, but he felt that he must prepare for death. To Mr Hay, who had long been his physician, was added at Charlotte's suggestion Mr Tudor. After Mr Tudor had examined him, his expression was 'for-bidding', Fanny says, and she adds that 'Mr Hay had lost his air of satisfaction and complacency'. The General had a stoppage of the bowels: his end would be soon and most miserable. He wanted to discuss his situation calmly and even cheerfully. It was Fanny who clung unreason-ably to hope.

By April the state of the General's health suggested to his friends that he should see a priest. Fanny, who believed that he had in all important respects become a Protestant, nevertheless left him the decision. He chose

211

to die in his former religion. With the utmost agony in her heart, Fanny brought him Dr Elloi, who stayed with him about three hours. The patient, however, was left calm and placid. If General d'Arblay knew he was to die, he was reconciled to that experience.

Fanny had called in a Catholic priest, somewhat against her own convictions and was glad to have pleased her husband. Now, unfortunately, Dr Elloi visited every day and at all hours of the day, kneeling at the bedside for two hours with his prayer book even when General d'Arblay was in an opium-induced sleep. The priest had obtained the General's promise that he should administer the last rites and this too Fanny allowed and witnessed, painful as the ceremony was to her.

After he had received the Last Sacrament, the General tried to bring Fanny to realize that she must go on alone. He told her that she must talk about him, as she had not talked about Susan after her death. Alexander, especially, must not be allowed to forget his father. He put the hands of his wife and son together in a firm grip, signifying that they must support each other after his death. He agreed with his wife that he had had enough of priests. He had made his last confession and had no more to say. He should be left in peace now.

General d'Arblay now begged Fanny to pray with him and then to allow him uninterrupted meditation, which was, in the event, to continue for an evening, a night and very nearly the whole of the next day. She was 'not to utter one word to him, even in reply, beyond the most laconic necessity'. After that he had a conversation with Alexander, offering him advice and consolation. In the morning he had the shutters opened and the curtains drawn back and stared through the window at the beauty of what was to be his last day. Fanny, later, made some remark about his 'heavenly resignation', but he repudiated the idea sadly: 'Résigné?' he repeated, 'mais . . . comme ça?' And then in a voice of the most touching tenderness he added, 'Te quitter!' 'I dare not even yet,' Fanny comments, 'hang upon my emotion at those words!'

The last words of M. d'Arblay to his wife were spoken with the singular grace that attended all his relations with her. He bent forward and took her hand and said: 'Je ne sais si ce sera le dernier mot . . . mais ce sera la dernière pensée – Notre réunion!' He fell into a sleep so calm that Fanny believed a crisis had arrived, a crisis that might well end favourably. Those about her knew that no such outcome was possible, but she insisted on believing what she did. The sleep continued. Hour succeeded hour. Presently Fanny discovered that his hands were cold and covered them.

She took new flannel to roll over his feet. Still he did not move and still he grew colder.

Alexander, guessing what had happened perhaps, fetched Mr Tudor. Fanny continued her desperate refusal to accept the truth, putting sal volatile on M. d'Arblay's temples, his forehead and the palms of his hands, avoiding always the betrayal of pulse or lips. Mr Tudor, coming in, put a hand on his heart and told her what she could not bear to know.

For weeks after her husband's death Fanny looked to her son Alex for support and, curiously enough, received it. The young man, whose innocence of heart was combined with total unreliability, was kind to her in her grief. Together they read the Bible and Alex, who had recently decided to take Holy Orders, was able, no doubt, to turn her thoughts to the reunion of which his father had spoken. Two months after General d'Arblay's death she gave Alex the choice of where they were to live, realizing that she would keep his company longer that way. He chose London.

The letters began to come in from friends and family offering Fanny some tenuous hold on life, some glimpse of the consolation she would in future obtain from slighter relationships than the one she had lost. Madame de Maisonneuve and Mrs Frances Bowdler were among these early sympathizers, and James, her brother, renewed his contact with her, meeting her when she arrived in London and, when Alex went to Cambridge early in October, taking over the responsibility of helping her with practical matters. Her sorrow at leaving the house where she had lived with her husband was augmented by a message she received from Court, to the effect that Queen Charlotte was dying. Her life must have seemed to be crumbling about her.

Like any other compulsive writer, Fanny turned now to her trade for comfort. The Princess Elizabeth's camp candlesticks had been given her to encourage research into her father's papers. These papers the d'Arblays had lugged about with them across Europe and back again, trunk-loads of papers, which were fondly believed to be of the utmost interest. The names of Dr Burney's acquaintances alone, it was believed, would sell the book Fanny would make of her father's memoirs. But at Ilfracombe in 1817, when a little leisure gave her the opportunity to examine the papers, Fanny was grievously disappointed. Dr Burney, like so many men and women of his century, had been a fascinating talker, a raconteur his friends had delighted to listen to, but the notes he had made had either been on topics uninteresting to the reading public at large or had been very scantily recorded. 'My dear Father has kept, unaccountably, All his letters, however uninteresting, ceremonious, momentary or unmeaning. The Few I find that are not fit to light candles, even from the greatest names, is really incredible.' Nevertheless she continued to persevere with what she regarded as a pious duty and the last literary work of her life was her *Memoirs of Dr Burney*, published in 1832.

In October of the year of General d'Arblay's death, Fanny moved into what she regarded as probably her last dwelling, 11 Bolton Street, Piccadilly. Alexander was at Cambridge but James, who lived no further than Buckingham Gate, helped install her in the new lodgings and paid her morning visits frequently in the desolate months to come. Bolton Street was conveniently near the parks, Green Park, Hyde Park and St James's, and Fanny, who adhered strictly to her regime of exercise and diet, was able to take a walk with her dog, Diane, and very often with Elizabeth Ramsay, daughter of the landlord at Ilfracombe, who had come to live with her and look after her.

It was very convenient too that James and his wife, with whom he was now reconciled, lived so near in Buckingham Gate. James's books had made him one of the great navigators of his age. He had published in the previous year the last volume of his book on the South Seas. Now he was working on his *Chronological History of North-Eastern Voyages of Discovery*. The house in Buckingham Gate was a centre for serious whist players but most of them were literary men such as Lamb, Hood, Southey, Crabb Robinson, and, until he made adverse criticisms of *The Wanderer*, even Hazlitt.

Many years before, when Fanny had gone as Second Keeper of the Robes to the Court of Queen Charlotte, it had been her hope that she could ask favours of the Royal Family, not for herself but for her brothers. James was desperate for a ship of twenty-eight guns and she had hung on at Court, ill and depressed, to ask for it. It had been in vain. But with his books speaking for his abilities it was easy to interest the Duke of Clarence, now an Admiral of the Fleet, in his promotion and by great good fortune Fanny had an opportunity to speak to the Princess Augusta on his behalf. Accordingly James received notice that he had been appointed Rear-Admiral on the retired list. His wife was aware of Fanny's intervention in the matter and grateful to her. The rest of the family were delighted, especially since he had had such an unsuccessful career, considering his abilities. Dr Burney attributed James's lack of promotion to his Whiggish political views and the truculence with which he expressed them. Whatever may have been the reason, his friends had always considered an Admiral's rank to be the only one suited to such a character.

The belief that promotion would rejuvenate James was, alas, not well founded. In 1820, Fanny describes him as 'changed and broken; he is weak and stoops cruelly'. In 1821, after an evening's whist, James sat up to smoke before he went to bed and died suddenly at his own fireside in a manner most suitable and indeed enviable. He had reconciled himself with his father's memory and had resolved the domestic unhappiness of former years. It is much to the credit of the Burney family that their sympathies immediately went out to Sarah Harriet, once James's close friend and now denied the privilege of mourning for him as a wife. She was short of money, frail and without a home of her own, but after the publication of her fourth novel she was offered by Lord Crewe a post at £300 a year to take charge of his grandchildren in a house in Park Street maintained solely for her and them.

Fanny's brother Charles had died at the end of 1817 of apoplexy after coming very near to a bishopric and certainly after he had lived down the early disgrace that attended his university career. He had reason to fear the illness that took him and had written so to Fanny, complaining about the disorders of his 'Noddle' and 'strange, partial, quick pains in the back of his head, very alarming'. Now, in 1819, Charles Rousseau Burney, that unworldly harpsichordist whom Fanny remembered as an awkward boy, was dying of an illness so painful that Hetty confessed to her sisters she had prayed for his relief from it. Except for Marianne Bourdois, prosperously widowed, whose marriage had been of Fanny's making, Hetty's girls were unmarried because they had no dowries. The rewards of music are scanty and though she had been beautiful and talented as a girl, Hetty had had a hard life.

Only four of Dr Burney's children remained, Hetty, Fanny, Charlotte and Sarah Harriet. M. d'Arblay had perceived before he died that Charlotte, though ten years younger than Fanny, had the same sense of the ridiculous and the same lively enjoyment of life. But Charlotte, who had lost two husbands, was now mourning for the death of her youngest son, Ralph Broome, and had years ahead of her nursing the elder of her two sons, Clement Francis, a fellow of Caius College whose declining health was already giving her serious concern. Later she was to prove Fanny's closest companion in her last years.

If Fanny hoped to revive the affectionate relationship between herself and Mrs Piozzi, now that their passions were spent and so much of the interests they had in common still remained, she was to meet with an unyielding front of polite hostility, which may or may not have disguised some remains of friendship. They exchanged formal letters, parading the breadth of their reading and lamenting the change of taste in the arts. Fanny holds out a pathetic hand for comfort and Mrs Piozzi stays implacably at arm's length, talking brightly about Mary Shelley's *Frankenstein* and the reputation of young Lord Byron. Perhaps the tone of the letters is becoming more relaxed by early 1821, a little more gossipy, a little less guarded, but in May Mrs Piozzi died, after a fall on a journey from Penzance to Clifton, in her eighty-second year. The eulogium in Fanny's journal compared her to that other lost friend, Madame de Staël: '. . . neither of them was delicate nor polished, though each was flattering and caressing; but both had a fund inexhaustible of good humour and sportive gaiety that made their intercourse with those they wished to please attractive, instructive and delightful . . .'

With the death of the older generation of Burneys, the younger members of the family, Dr Burney's grandchildren, come into prominence. It is not surprising that so many of them are lovely and talented and that so many of the young men are scholars of some reputation. What is surprising is that they do not live long: Norbury Phillips, Susan's son, whom it is difficult not to like, even over the years and in such reported speech, died at twenty-nine and his brother William at forty-one. Esther's daughter Cecilia died young and Charlotte outlived all three of her children, Ralph Broome her youngest dying at twenty-five and Clement Francis at thirty-seven. The brilliant Marianne, their sister, lived to be forty-two. Alexander d'Arblay, only son of exceptional parents, lived a year longer and died unmarried and unsuccessful at forty-three.

There is little doubt that one of Fanny's chief problems in the second part of her life was the management of her wholly lovable, erratically clever son, brought up by parents whose affection for him was undeniable but nevertheless as odd a character as any of the Burneys produced. He was thin, with dark hair and eyes and a tendency to illness from his earliest years. Something called worm-fever afflicted him regularly and was held to account for his extreme slenderness. Later, when a curious instability began to manifest itself, so that he could not concentrate on anything for long, certainly not a purpose or ambition, it began to seem possible that the two were connected and were symptoms of an illness not even now identified. The total inertia that overcame him at the end of his short life must surely have been linked to these other problems. Fanny exerted all her powers of persuasion, spent every penny that could be spared from the household, and more, and canvassed any friends or relations who could be useful. Extreme unworldliness was probably her diagnosis of the case, but some may wonder whether there was a clinical explanation of his eccentricities.

Alex had, in spite of his disapproval of Cambridge mathematics, graduated as tenth wrangler, to the natural pride of his parents, especially Fanny, whose assiduous control of his vacations was largely responsible for his success. He sat for a scholarship examination and was made a scholar of Christ's College and later a Fellow. His father was, at the time, in an agony of suffering and his mother was endeavouring not to understand what the outcome of his illness would be. When he had taken his degree Alex had still to decide upon his career but after his father's death theology absorbed him to the exclusion of all else. Even an offer from the Duc de Luxembourg to help him to a commission in the French Guards was of no interest now that he had discovered theology. He was ordained as a deacon and then, in April 1819, as a priest of the Church of England.

It was five years before Fanny, using every scrap of influence she could muster, was able to find Alex a living. This was at a new chapel in Camden Town. During that time Fanny did all she could to recommend Alex to the church, even dropping the title he had inherited from his father but which, she feared, would make him seem an oddity in England. In 1820–1 when he had a breakdown of health, attributed by his mother to excessive mental application, she sent him off for a summer's mountain-climbing in Switzerland. He did not return to England until the following spring, having spent the winter in Paris while Fanny's sisters condoled with her on 'the delicacy of that sweet youth's frame and constitution'.

Alex was now twenty-seven. He had been introduced to many distinguished men during his winter in Paris since his father's friends enabled him to meet poets, mathematicians and scientists. Fanny must have been wondering if he would ever settle to a profession and his friends in Paris felt very much the same. They encouraged him to return to England and set about gaining advancement in the Church. He was discovered to be an impressive rhetorical preacher and was twice asked to preach at St Paul's, but the knack of pleasing those who could have given him a benefice still eluded him. A talent for poetic sermons, such as that by which he enraptured the ladies in Ely Cathedral, was becoming his forte, but he still had no parish of his own.

While he was without any future in his chosen profession, Alex fell in

217

love with Caroline Angerstein, granddaughter of Mrs Locke, the friend of his mother and aunts. The Lockes had always been wealthy, and Amelia Locke had married the even wealthier John Angerstein, owner of a town house and a country house and very hospitable to the young people of his circle. Alex begged his mother to intercede for him but she must have known how unlikely it was that the Angersteins would allow their daughter to marry a poor parson. As if to emphasize the poverty of his career he had chosen, Alex at twenty-nine was now offered his first job, as curate in Camden Town at £200 a year with £50 deducted for rent. Fanny knew in her heart that it would be impossible for Alex to perform his routine duties in this post without neglect or omissions, but she was grateful to Archdeacon Cambridge, the same George Cambridge who had given her so much unhappiness so long ago, for his help in placing her son after five fruitless years. He sat beside her in the pew and heard his protégé preach his first sermon as curate of the new chapel of Camden Town. He congratulated Fanny loudly and firmly as soon as he could and the various important clergy all assembled for the occasion, including the Bishop of London, also expressed themselves 'gratified' and even 'highly gratified'. It must have seemed that Alex was launched at last.

Archdeacon Cambridge, who appears to have understood Alex very well, made useful suggestions for keeping the young man in an unaccustomed routine. 'A steady middle-aged man-servant' was suggested, one who could persuade Alex to be punctual. In August Fanny took rooms near her son to settle him into his new position and by November she found that she could leave him with a very suitable couple she had engaged to look after him. A wife would have taken charge, but a wife was not so easily come by on his income. For the rest of his life his mother would worry about his health, his extravagance and even his clothes. 'It is not his capability I doubt,' Fanny wrote to Esther, 'that would be affectation, but it is his absence and his carelessness.' A picture emerges of Alex that brings him before us with devastating clearness:

> He is so unused to Controll, so little in habits of punctuality, so indifferent to the customs of the World and so careless of inferences, opinions and consequences that I cannot but tremble to see him advanced at once . . . without some previous practice as an attendant Curate.

Now that Alexander could be supposed to be established in a profession, Fanny was able to give more time to that laborious duty, the editing of her father's papers, so often urged on her by her father himself and by the

Royal Family. One incident, however, from these uneventful years is worth recording, especially as it emphasizes the astonishing span of her life and of her literary sympathies. *The Diary and Letters of Madame d'Arblay* mentions that she greeted with admiration and pleasure Sir Walter Scott, who was brought to her by Mr Rogers (the poet). Sir Walter, in his diary for 18 November 1826, thus describes the visit:

> I have been introduced to Madame d'Arblay, the celebrated authoress of *Evelina* and *Cecilia* – an elderly lady with no remains of personal beauty, but with a simple and gentle manner and pleasing expression of countenance and apparently quick feelings. She told me she had wished to see two persons – myself, of course, being one, the other George Canning. This was really a compliment to be pleased with – a nice little handsome pat of butter made up by a neat-handed Phillis of a dairy-maid, instead of the grease fit only for cartwheels which one is dosed with by the pound. I trust I shall see this lady again.

In the following years, however, Fanny saw few people outside her immediate family circle. Instead she devoted herself entirely to preparing for publication the long-delayed biography of her father. She began by separating the biographical material from the rest. What remained included a great deal of material that she considered only fit to be destroyed:

> The enormous load of Letters, Memoirs, documents, mss, collections, copies of his own Letters, scraps of authorship, old pocket Books filled with personal and business memorandums, and fragments relative to the History of Musick, are countless, fathomless!

There were also papers that were too personal for the sensitive Fanny to print. At first she felt unwilling to destroy any scrap of paper on which her revered father had written, but after Hetty had read some of the collection and agreed with Fanny on its value, she burned quite ruthlessly anything unsuitable to her purpose.

Even more disappointing were the letters. There were 'Bag after Bag' of them, three years' reading, she estimated, and her eyes had always been weak. When she thought she had selected from the three years' reading 'about 3 quarters of an hour's reading to my Lecturers' she discovered that legislation had been passed while she was living in France giving the copyright of a letter to the writer. Since the most interesting letters in her selection were written to Dr Burney by his friends and acquaintances, this statute thinned her volumes drastically and left her in a state of despair. At the same time she was told that if she did not produce a life of her father, others would. She decided that nobody else could be relied upon to do him justice and set to, relying heavily on her own memories as well as the small amount of collected material she had selected as useful. What this cost her is evident from the pitiful letters she herself wrote after her husband's death, the irregular, loosely-formed writing smudged and blotted, sprawling largely across the small black-edged sheets of folded note-paper. To produce the *Memoirs of Dr Burney* must have used up much of his daughter's remaining sight.

Although Fanny was nearly eighty, the reviewers were savagely critical of the *Memoirs,* which were published in 1832. Her style had been increasing in formality for many years now. Dr Johnson and her experience of Court life had all helped to elevate it. And she had tried to give her father's biography grandeur by her way of writing; a relaxed style would have seemed to her impious, even if she had been able to manage it now. But some critics went further and declared that Fanny had written her father's life in order to write about herself. Even among the Burney family there were objections to the *Memoirs.* Fanny had shown her usual discretion when writing of family affairs, but she had felt no obligation to conceal the truth when it was not altogether palatable. As a result Hetty's son, the Reverend Richard Allen Burney, wrote to Alex asking him to persuade his mother to destroy the *Memoirs.* It seems that in his twenty years of marriage he had never confided in his wife the dread secret of the low origins of his grandmother Esther Sleepe. He had no wish to do so now. Worse still, he had applied for, and obtained, a coat of arms from the College of Heralds giving his great-grandfather's name and occupation as 'James Sleepe, gentleman'. Now the *Memoirs* were about to reveal that he was not only poor but 'wanting in goodness, probity and conduct'. Alexander d'Arblay, child of the Revolution, preached a properly democratic outlook and pointed out the impossibility of concealing embarrassing information. Fanny herself was sympathetic, but she saw the life of her father as 'the progress of a nearly abandoned Child, from a small village of Shropshire, to a Man allowed throughout Europe to have risen to the head of his Profession . . .' She had no intention of minimizing this achievement.

An objection that might have been foreseen came from Stephen Allen, also a clergyman now. He criticized the lack of admiration for his mother shown in the biography and the lack of credit given her for her financial contribution to the household. Fanny must have recalled many unhappy incidents when she received this complaint. Perhaps too she remembered a letter she had written to Susan fifty years before, in the early days of her sister's marriage. She wrote that she was looking forward to staying with the Phillips in Ipswich for a number of reasons, such as bread and butter with her tea and a glowing fire in the grate. Then the letter goes on to mention, and quite bitterly, 'treats' of another kind also unobtainable at home:

> If I find myself in good spirits, I shall not have the fear of wrath before my Eyes because I may happen to simper: if I am grave and have had cause for gravity, I shall not conclude that you will be gayer than usual: if I ask you a common question, I shall not expect a stern look for an answer; if I make you a common reply, I shall not take it for granted you will pervert my words into an affront: if I talk of some favourite friend, I shall not prepare myself for hearing him or her instantly traduced; nor yet if I relate something that has made me happy, shall I know my conversation is the fore-runner of an Head-ache.

Stephen Allen had not formed part of the united family in the days when his mother was at her most difficult and he may have heard only a very partial account of life in St Martin's Street. Nevertheless Fanny wrote to him pleasantly, wishing only that Maria Rishton, now dead, could be called on to verify her mother's portrait. Courteous as her answers are, they are unyielding, substantiating with documentary evidence the views she had expressed in the *Memoirs*.

Mrs Waddington, who had been Mary Ann Port, niece of Mrs Delany, was another who challenged the accuracy of the facts given in the *Memoirs*. It was known that Mrs Delany was something of a pensioner of the Duchess of Portland, who sent hampers loaded with delicacies to St James's Place regularly. For that reason the King, when the Duchess of Portland died, gave Mrs Delany a pension of £300 a year and a house in Windsor. Yet Mrs Waddington objected to any suggestion of dependence and Fanny was compelled to search for evidence authenticating what everybody at Court had been aware of. Mrs Ann Agnew, who had been Mrs Delany's maid and written her correspondence in her increasing blindness was appealed to and her letters filed to corroborate Fanny's story. It mattered a great deal to Fanny that she should remain Dr Burney's 'honest Fan'. Unfriendly reviewers were one thing: imputations of inaccuracy quite another.

While his mother was working on her father's papers, Alexander d'Arblay remained in Camden Town. General d'Arblay had seen no future for his son in the Church of England and certainly he remained a curate for ten years. He had had his sermons published and the sermon on the death of George IV had been very much admired. But Alex, 'unstable as water', continued to alternate between carelessness in dress and an excess of dandyism ('a gold coat'), between social success at parties and sitting up all night versifying the Psalms. He was much too thin and often feverish. His mother had known how to take care of her frail health but Alexander seems never to have regarded such matters. In 1833 his prolonged absences from his parish led to complaints but he continued to attend balls and fêtes and to spend money, borrowing if necessary from his mother. He had friends at Dover and it was there that he met Mary Ann Smith to whom he at once decided to become engaged. Fanny, willing perhaps to relinquish the responsibility for her forty-year-old son, declared in characteristic language that Mary Ann 'had put me in Heaven! so much I like her! – so much that love is the only proper word'.

It was, of course, impossible for a married couple to set up house on Alexander's salary, which had not risen in the ten years he had been employed at Camden. His constant truancy both suggested that the job was unsuitable for him and made it difficult for even his indefatigable mother to find him another. He resigned from his curacy at Camden and to the consternation of Fanny and Mary Ann Smith disappeared. Letters sent to him care of friends were returned and Charlotte Barrett, for one, expressed the suspicion that he had a mistress hidden away. But Alexander's problems were more intractable than that. He had sunk into a profound lethargy, an indifference to those about him which could not be altered even by Mary Ann. 'I have taken to my bed frightfully of late – I find it more and more irksome to leave it,' he writes, and ends, 'O it is a madness – a delusion without a name!'

It was at this point that Archdeacon Cambridge, faithful still to his ambiguous attachment to Fanny, offered her son the newly-opened Ely Chapel in Ely Place, Holborn. Alexander could do no other than accept, though he doubted his own capability for the post, and he dedicated the sermon he preached for the re-opening, as he had his former published sermons, to the Archdeacon in gratitude. But the chapel had been closed for some time and it was damp. Alex preached his first sermon on 27 November and immediately after the Christmas services he found himself ill with influenza. He sent word to his mother that she was not to go to his bedside, and other relatives and friends were also asked not to go near him. On 19 January 1837 he died.

Alexander d'Arblay was buried beside his father in Bath and the family, who had long been anxious about the effect of his behaviour on his mother, must have found it very difficult to utter the appropriate commiserations. Charlotte, writing to Fanny, found an eminently tactful way of expressing what the whole family thought: '. . . this poor darling was no match for the World, it seems a mercy for him to be taken to Heaven.' His mother, when she reflected on the matter, could only agree. And yet he had been an integral part of all her worldly happiness, a son when it seemed she would never have children, a link between her and her *cher ami*.

Fanny was to live three years more, without husband or son but certainly not without those who would care for her. Glimpses of her in her old age are caught here and there, a small figure in black setting out from Half Moon Street, wearing black gloves because no muff was black enough for General d'Arblay's widow, the dog Diane and Elizabeth Ramsay accompanying her. We read of her solemn pact with Charlotte to eat nourishing food: 'wines, recommended by the Faculty, Tops and Bottoms – jellys – Ginger-bread nuts – Bisquit and Currant Jelly – Sponge Bisquits dip'd in light wine.' Charlotte, ten years younger than Fanny and the only surviving relative she had after Hetty died in February 1832, seemed to wish for nothing now but the company of her elder sister, but she had become almost an invalid in Brighton with her daughter, Charlotte Barrett to look after her. Here Fanny spent a recuperative month after her removal to Mount Street, and it was from Brighton eight months later that Charlotte paid her last visit to Fanny and to London.

There was nobody left now of Fanny's generation and she had no child, only Mary Ann Smith who had never become Madame la Comtesse d'Arblay, but who insisted that it was Alexander's wish that she should live with Fanny and care for her like a daughter. The apartment in Half Moon Street had been chosen for Alexander's convenience rather than her own, so to accommodate Miss Smith she moved first to Mount Street and then, for some reason not provided by the letters, to Lower Grosvenor Street. Here, still reading and editing, but this time her son's papers and not her father's, she came to the end of her eyesight, reporting a successful preliminary cataloguing of all Alex's writings, a wretched task that filled her with regret for his wasted talent. She was busy, too, with her will – she was eighty-seven – and had invited Charlotte Barrett to be executor. Charlotte was also to edit her journals and letters for publication after her death.

At the end of 1839 it was clear that Fanny was dying and Charlotte

Barrett stayed with her for six weeks. It is said that she saw phantoms and after so long, so full a life, we can only speculate on which of the remarkable men and women of her time haunted her sickbed. Was it Garrick entertaining a small girl with impersonations, or Dr Johnson in the formidable power of his knock-down arguments, or the old King talking incessantly in the draughty bedrooms of Kew? She was drifting further away from those around her, refusing to admit the Archdeacon, whom she had loved once, when he came to pray for the sick, unwilling to make the effort to talk to anyone at all. And yet she again recovered, long enough at least to see another anniversary of Susan's death on 6 January and to die on it, fully conscious that she was dying, able to give directions to those who would manage her affairs but content to die, trusting in the phrase her husband had used, *à notre réunion*. She was buried with her son and near her husband in Wolcot Churchyard in Bath, having spanned the period from the mid-eighteenth century to the early reign of the young Victoria and lived in the vanguard of history for all those years.

BIBLIOGRAPHY

In writing this book I have relied chiefly on:

The Early Diary of Frances Burney, 1768-78 (2 volumes), Annie Raine Ellis (ed), 1889

The Diary and Letters of Madame d'Arblay, 1778-1840 (7 volumes), Charlotte Frances Barrett (ed), 1842-6

The Journals and Letters of Fanny Burney (7 volumes), Joyce Hemlow (ed), Oxford University Press, 1972-8

The Barrett Collection of Burney Papers in the Manuscript Room of the British Museum

Other books I have found helpful include:

Balderston, K. (ed), *Thraliana,* Oxford University Press, 1942

Burnett, John, *A History of the Cost of Living,* Pelican, 1969

Boswell, James, *Life of Johnson,* Oxford University Press, 1970

Clifford, James, L., *Hester Lynch Piozzi,* Oxford University Press, 1968

Dobson, Austin, *Fanny Burney* (Men of Letters Series), 1903

Fitzmaurice, H. W. E. P., Marquis of Lansdowne (ed), *The Queeney Letters,* 1934

Fletcher, Ronald, *The Parkers at Saltram,* BBC, 1970

Fortescue, S. E. D., *The Story of Two Villages: Great and Little Bookham,* Great Bookham, 1975

Gérin, Winifred, *The Young Fanny Burney,* Thomas Nelson, 1961

Hahn, E., *A Degree of Prudery,* Barker 1951

Hawkins, J., *Life of Johnson,* 1787

Hayward, A., *Autobiography, Letters and Literary Remains of Mrs Piozzi,* 1861

Hemlow, Joyce, *The History of Fanny Burney,* Oxford University Press, 1958

Hill, Constance, *Fanny Burney at the Court,* Lane, 1912

——, *The House in St Martin's Street,* Lane, 1907

——, *Juniper Hall,* Lane, 1904

Hyde, Mary, *The Thrales of Streatham Park,* Harvard University Press, 1977

Johnson, R. Brimley, *Fanny Burney and the Burneys,* Paul, 1926

Kamm, Josephine, *The Story of Fanny Burney,* Methuen, 1966

Kershaw, S. W., *Fanny Burney and Surrey* in Cox, J. C. (ed), *Memorials of Old Surrey,* Allen, 1911

Lamb, Charles, *Essays of Elia,* Macmillan, 1899

Lonsdale, Roger, *Dr Charles Burney: A Literary Biography,* Oxford University Press, 1965

Macalpine, Ida and Hunter, Richard, *Porphyria, A Royal Malady,* British Medical Association, 1968

Macaulay, T. B., *Critical and Historical Essays* (2 volumes), Dent, 1843

Manwaring, G. E., *My Friend the Admiral,* 1931

Masefield, M., *The Story of Fanny Burney*, Cambridge University Press, 1927

Morley, E. J. (ed), *S. H. Burney* (The Letters of Sarah Harriet Burney)

de Nolde, Baroness Elizabeth (ed), *Madame de Staël to Benjamin Constant*, 1907

Scholes, Percy, A., *The Great Dr Burney*, 1948

Seeley, L. B., *Fanny Burney and Her Friends*, Seeley, 1889

Stuart, D. M., *The Daughters of George III*, 1939

Tourtellot, A., *Be Loved No More*, 1938

Trevelyan, G. M., *English Social History*, Penguin, 1970

Turberville, A. S., *Johnson's England*, Oxford University Press, 1933

Vulliamy, C. E., *Mrs Thrale of Streatham*, 1936

Watson, John Steven, *The Reign of George III, 1760–1815*, Oxford University Press, 1960

White, T. H., *The Age of Scandal*, Penguin, 1950

Williams, E. H., *Life in Georgian England*, Batsford, 1962

Woolfe, Virginia, *The Common Reader* (books 1 and 2), Hogarth Press, 1925 and 1932

Wright Roberts, W., 'Charles and Fanny Burney in the Light of the new Thrale Correspondence in the John Rylands Library', reprinted from the *Bulletin of the John Rylands Library*, vol. 16, 1932

INDEX

INDEX

Burney, Charles Parr D.D., nephew of
Fanny Burney, son of above, 182,
184
Burney, Charles Rousseau, cousin of
Fanny Burney, 215
Burney, Charlotte Ann, sister of
Fanny Burney, *see* under Francis or
Broome
Burney, Edward Francesco, artist,
cousin of Fanny Burney, 23
Burney, Elizabeth, formerly Mrs
Stephen Allen, *née* Allen, step-
mother of Fanny Burney, 10, 16,
19, 26, 33, 45, 60, 61, 63, 103,
154, 155, 165
Burney, Esther, *née* Sleepe, mother of
Fanny Burney, 9, 16, 20, 26
Burney, Esther (Hetty) sister of Fanny
Burney, married her cousin Charles
Rousseau Burney, 15, 30, 36, 63,
82, 99, 115, 118, 185, 204, 218
influence on Fanny, 20
talent on harpsichord, 31
courtship by Seaton, 21, 22
marriage, children, 22, 170, 179,
180
attempts at matchmaking for
Fanny, 51-4
husband's death, 215
her death, 223
Burney, Frances (Fanny) *see* d'Arblay
Burney, Frances, Fanny Burney's
niece, daughter of Hetty, 180
Burney, James, brother of Fanny
Burney, 15, 56, 86, 118, 140, 159,
165, 184, 185, 204
birth, disposition, 5, 24, 25
goes to sea, 24
voyages with Captain Cook, 25
friendship with Molesworth
Phillips, 160
gives Fanny in marriage, 156
marriage, children, 180
relationship with half-sister, 48
publications, 181
friendship with Lambs, 181, 182
promotion to Rear-Admiral, 214
death, 215
Burney, Marianne, niece of Fanny
Burney, daughter of Hetty, *see*
Bourdois
Burney, Martin, nephew of Fanny
Burney, son of James, 181
Burney, Rebecca, aunt of Fanny
Burney, 30
Burney, Richard, uncle of Fanny
Burney, 57
Burney, the Rev Richard Allen,

nephew of Fanny Burney, son of
Hetty, 220
Burney, Richard Thomas, half-brother
of Fanny Burney, 27
Burney, Sally, niece of Fanny Burney,
daughter of James, 182
Burney, Sarah *née* Payne, wife of
James (Mrs Battle), 180
Burney, Sarah Harriet, novelist, half-
sister of Fanny Burney, 47, 48,
148, 154, 155, 157, 165, 169, 184,
215
Burney, Susanna Elizabeth, sister of
Fanny Burney, *see* Phillips
Bury St Edmunds, 49
Byron, George Gordon, 197, 216

Cambridge, Charlotte, 118, 140
Cambridge, the Rev George Owen, 94,
99, 100, 103, 104, 105, 106, 111,
112, 119, 218, 222, 224
Cambridge, Richard Owen, 94, 98, 99,
100, 101, 103, 104, 105, 106, 111,
162
Cambridge University, 25, 140, 182,
213
Camilla Cottage or Camilla Lacy, 38,
158, 186, 205
Carter, Elizabeth, 107
Chapone, Hester *née* Mulso, 69, 94,
100, 101, 103, 111
Charlotte, Queen of England, 94, 103,
107, 112, 113, 115, 117, 119, 120,
121, 122, 124, 125, 129, 131, 132,
134, 135, 136, 137, 140, 141, 142,
145, 152, 155, 156, 160, 161, 162,
164, 172, 175, 179, 209, 210, 211,
213, 214
Chateaubriand, François Auguste René,
Vicomte de, 194
Châtre, Marquise de la, 147
Chavagnac, Adrienne de, 173
Cheltenham, 130, 132
Chessington, Surrey, 16, 17, 36, 60,
67, 98, 100, 103, 155, 156
Cholmondeley, Mary, *née* Woffington,
67, 78
Clarence, Duke of, 121, 214
Clifford, Professor James, 71
Coke, Mrs, 45, 47, 147
Condé, Louis-Henri-Joseph de
Bourbon, Prince de, 193
Cook, Captain James, 110
Cooke, Catharine, 37
Crewe, Frances Ann, *née* Greville, 14,
78
Crisp, Samuel, 10, 11, 16, 17, 36, 37,

229